Title and Title Conflicts in respect of Intermediated Securities under English Law

Title and Title Conflicts in respect of Intermediated Securities under English Law

By

Wenwen Liang

CAMBRIDGE SCHOLARS

PUBLISHING

Title and Title Conflicts in respect of Intermediated Securities under English Law,
by Wenwen Liang

This book first published 2013

Cambridge Scholars Publishing

12 Back Chapman Street, Newcastle upon Tyne, NE6 2XX, UK

British Library Cataloguing in Publication Data
A catalogue record for this book is available from the British Library

ISBN (10): 1-4438-4855-7, ISBN (13): 978-1-4438-4855-8

To my parents.

TABLE OF CONTENTS

TABLE OF CASES

A-G for Hong Kong v Reid [1994] 1 AC 324 (PC)
Armitage v Nurse [1998] Ch 241 (CA)
Armory v Delamirie (1772) 1 Strange 505, 93 ER 664
Assaf v Fuwa [1955] AC 215
Australian Guarantee Corp (NZ) Ltd v CFC Commercial Finance Ltd [1995] 1 NZLR 129
Bahia and San Francisco Rly Co, Re (1868) 3 QB 584
Bailey v Barnes [1894] 1 Ch 25 (CA)
Balkis Consolidated Co v Tomkinson [1893] AC 396 (HL)
Bank of England v Culter [1908] 2 KB 208
Bank of Ireland v Evans' Charities Trustees in Ireland (1855) 5 HL Cas 389, 10 ER 950
Barlow Clowes International Ltd (in liq) v Vaughan [1992] 4 All ER 22
Barton v London and North Western Rly Co (1889) 24 QBD 77 (CA)
Bentinck v London Joint Stock Bank [1893] 2 Ch 120
Blackwood v London Charted Bank of Australia (1874) 5 PC 92 (Judicial Committee)
Brace v Duches of Marlborough (1728) 2 P Wms 491, 24 ER 829
Bray v Ford [1896] AC 44 (HL)
Brimnes, The [1973] 1 WLR 386, affd [1975] QB 929
CA Pacific Finance Ltd, Re [2000] 1 BCLC 494
Capell v Winter [1907] 2 Ch 376
Cave v Cave (1880) 15 Ch D 639
Central Newbury Car Auctions Ltd v Unity Finance Ltd [1957] 1 QB 371 (CA)
Chrimes, Re [1917] 1 Ch 30
Claydon v Bradley [1987] 1 All ER 522 (CA)
Colonial Bank v Cady and Williams (1890) 15 App Cas 267 (HL)
Colyer v Finch (1856) 5 HLC 905, 10 ER 1159
Cottam v Eastern Counties Rly Co (1860) 1 J & H 243, (1860) 70 ER 737
Crouch v Crédit Foncier of England (1873) 8 QB 374
Damon Cia Naviera SA v Hapag-Lloyd International SA, The Blankenstein, The Bartenstein, The Birkenstein [1985] 1 All ER 475 (CA)
Davis v Bank of England (1824) 2 Bing 393, 130 ER 357
Dearle v Hall (1828) 3 Russ 1; 38 ER 475; [1824-34] All ER Rep 28

TABLE OF LEGISLATIONS

United Kingdom

Bills of Exchange Act 1882 s 24, s 27(2), s 29
Cheques Act 1957
Companies (Model Articles) Regulations 2008 SI 2008/3229 sch 3 s 63
Companies (Tables A to F) Regulations 1985 SI 1985/805 regs 24-28
Companies Act 2006 s 126, s 127, s 750(1), s 768(1), s 769, s 770(1), s 786 (4)
Companies Clauses Consolidation Act 1845 s 14, s 46
Factors Act 1889
Financial Markets and Insolvency (Settlement Finality) Regulations 1999 SI 1999/ 2979 sch
Financial Markets and Insolvency Regulations 1996 SI 1996/1469
Financial Services and Markets Act 2000 (Carrying on Regulated Activities by Way of Business) Order 2001 SI 2001/1177
Financial Services and Markets Act 2000 (Compensation Scheme: Electing Participants) Regulations 2001 SI 2001/1783
Financial Services and Markets Act 2000 (Regulated Activities) Order 2001 SI 2001/544 art 45, ch viii, ch vix
Financial Services and Markets Act 2000 pt xv, s 242, s 253, s 285, s 286, s 288, s 293
Government Stock Regulations 2004 SI 2004/1611 Pt 3, reg 7(4), reg 8, reg 9(3), reg 9
Hire Purchase Act 1964 pt iii
Law of Property Act 1925 s 53(1)(c), s 136, s 199 1(ii)(b)
Local Authority (Stocks and Bonds) Regulations 1974 SI 1974/519 reg 6
Pensions Act 1995 s 33(1)
Sales of Goods Act 1979 s 20A, s 20B, s 21
Stock Transfer Act 1963 s 1
Trustee Act 1925
Trustee Act 2000
Uncertificated Securities (Amendment) (Eligible Debt Securities) Regulations 2003 SI 2003/1633
Uncertificated Securities Regulations 1995 SI 1995/3272 (now revoked) reg 19, reg 20, reg 23

Uncertificated Securities Regulations 2001 SI 2001/3755 reg 2, reg 3, reg 20, reg 21, reg 22, reg 23, reg 24, reg 31, reg 32, reg 33, reg 35, reg 36, reg 38, pt 2, sch 1 (18), sch 4

Belgium

a Law of 2 January 1991
a Law of 22 July 1991
a Law of 7 April 1995
a Law of 14 December 2005
Royal Decree No 62 of 10 November 1967

Canada

Securities Transfer Act, 2006, SO 2006, c 8, Consolidated Statutes of Ontario
Securities Transfer Act, SA 2006, cs-4.5, Consolidated Statutes of Alberta
Securities Transfer Act, SNS 2010, c 8, Consolidated Statutes of Nova Scotia
Uniform Securities Transfer Act

Germany

Civil Code (Bürgerliches Gesetzbuch-BGB) s 793, ss 854-1296
Stock Corporation Act (Aktiengesetz-AktG) s 10
Law on Investment in Funds (Investmentgesetz) s 33

Luxembourg

Grand-Ducal Decree of 17 February 1971 (as amended in 1994 and 1996)
Securities Act 2001

Switzerland

Code civil Suisse du 10 décembre 1907 (Etat le 1er janvier 2013) art 3, art 933, art 934, art 935, art 973
Federal Intermediated Securities Act art 3, art 37, art 84, art 29(1)

United States

SEC Rules 15c 3-3
Security Investor Protection Act of 1979
Uniform Commercial Code art 8 pt 5, art 8 -105, art 8-303, art 8-502, art 8-503, art 8-504

International Conventions

HCCH Convention of 5 July 2006 on the Law Applicable to Certain Rights in Respect of Securities held with an Intermediary
UNIDROIT Convention on Substantive Rules for Intermediated Securities art 9, art 14, art 21, art 17 (c), art 18

PREFACE

This book examines property issues in respect of intermediated securities under English law, namely title and title conflicts between a true owner and a purchaser. Intangible book entry securities held with an intermediary, often commingled with the holding of other clients of the intermediary, often give rise to uncertainty in property rights in the securities of an investor under most legal systems, for example, whether property rights can be established and how title conflicts are dealt with.

The general property law implications of intermediated securities and responses of national laws and international uniform law are examined. English property law and trusts law are investigated to identify their mechanisms of recognising property rights. Title conflicts in respect of chattels, certificated bearer securities, and certificated registered securities, are examined to identify the underlying policies and mechanisms. Priority rules across legal and equitable property rights are reviewed to explore their application to title conflicts in respect of intermediated securities as legal and equitable title. Solutions to title conflicts of national laws and international uniform law are exposed as a basis for seeking a better solution for English law.

This book identifies the flexible framework of English property law for establishing property rights over commingled intangibles, in particular through trusts; establishes the policy of priority rules as of comparing the merits of rights and preferring a vested right of a true owner over a subsequent purchaser, in particular a vested right under fiduciary relations. The conclusion is that given the general principle of English property law for vested rights and averse to preventive regulation or remedial mandatory insurance schemes, title conflicts may be tilted towards purchasers in a mild rather than a radical way, by introducing a good faith purchaser rule to intermediated securities or leaving it to judicial discretion where estoppel might work in favour of a purchaser.

The book is based on my PhD thesis completed in 2011. The author is indebted to so many people and organisations without their help the book would not have been possible: to the China Scholarship Council and The University of Manchester for awarding the Manchester-China scholarship; to Professor John Birds for his supervision, to Professor Iain MacNeil and Professor Joseph Jaconeli for their examination and comments; to Professor

Yongping Xiao and Professor Thévenoz for comments and help; to UNIDROIT (International Institute for the Unification of Private Law) for allowing me to attend their diplomatic conferences to adopt the Geneva Securities Convention as academic observer, in particular Professor Herbert Kronke and José Angelo Estrella Faria; to UNIDROIT and the UK Foundation for International Uniform Law for sponsoring a research visit at UNIDROIT, in particular Sir Professor Roy Goode and Frédérique Mestre; to the Max Planck Institute for Comparative and International Private Law for sponsoring a rcscarch visit at their Institute; to the Swiss Institute of Comparative Law for allowing use of their library; to Carol Koulikourdi, Amanda Millar, and Emily Surrey of Cambridge Scholar Publishing for devoting their time and work to this book. Lastly but most importantly to my mother Guirong Pan and my father Xinzhen Liang for their support and love; and to Michael Will and Wiltrud Will who give me their support like parents.

INTRODUCTION

Background

Intermediated securities, also known as securities held with an intermediary, indirectly held securities, or book entry securities, have challenged many areas of law developed for the direct holding of certificated securities.

To many, securities, basically a bundle of intangible rights against the issuer, are synonymous with certificates incorporating or merely proving the intangible rights. They are not. With the paper crunch in major securities markets certificated securities are either immobilised or eliminated to facilitate trading based on computer technologies. This is often an electronic securities holding system composed of a pyramid of intermediaries between an issuer and a final investor. At the top a central securities depository or securities registrar maintains securities accounts for direct counterparties, often custodian banks or major securities brokers, and records their holding of securities on their securities accounts which are electronic entries; custodians and major securities intermediaries maintain securities accounts for clients and record their holding on their securities accounts in the same way; this may be repeated for tiers until a final account holder who does not maintain securities accounts for others and holds securities for himself. A final investor may have securities accounts with all tiers of intermediaries and his holding is recorded on all these securities accounts, i.e., a transparent system, or an investor may solely have securities accounts with his immediate intermediary and his holding is solely recorded on these accounts, i.e., a non-transparent system. Securities of the same issue are often fungible. In a non-transparent system, an intermediary commingles the holding of all investors of the same issue of securities with his upper-tier intermediary. Thus in a non-transparent system an investor has securities held with his intermediary, recorded on his securities account with his intermediary, but not identifiable at the level of any upper-tier intermediary or the issuer.[1]

The change is not simply a technical one from certificated securities to immobilised, dematerialised or uncertificated securities, or from direct

[1] See 1.2, 1.3, 4.1, 4.2, and 4.3 for further analysis.

holding to indirect holding (in respect of the issuer-investor relationship). It has major legal implications for property law, corporate law, and conflict of laws. Traditional law on securities transactions is based on the direct holding of physical certificates. It is essentially a physical model. Securities are treated as tangibles and possession of certificates is crucial for holding the rights to securities. It is not surprising that there would be legal uncertainties to apply the physical model to the indirect holding of intangible securities. Legal uncertainties arise where the law does not provide for a predictable and sound solution, does not govern an issue, does not fit the market reality, or complicates transactions by imposing legal requirements designed for the traditional direct holding of certificated securities on the indirect holding of uncertificated securities.[2]

As to property law aspects, it is uncertain whether the right of an investor in intangible securities held with his intermediary is proprietary or personal. Most civil law countries do not recognise property rights over a pool of intangible fungibles held with another under the principle of specificity and segregation, although it is possible to establish property rights over intangibles held with another segregated in some way.[3] Without property rights a client would only have a personal claim against his intermediary for the return of equivalent securities which could not survive the insolvency of the intermediary. Secured transactions in intermediated securities may be invalidated for failure to fulfill formalities based on possession of tangibles.

The indirect holding cutting-off the issuer-investor relationship may cause uncertainty as to whether an investor is recognised by the issuer as an investor and the way an investor enjoys corporate rights attaching to securities. As regards conflict of laws it is difficult to establish the *situs* of intermediated securities under classical rules for tangibles.[4] Legal uncertainty in rights in intermediated securities is a major impediment to the development of intermediated securities in the long run.

Legal uncertainty regarding intermediated securities has been identified and effectively dealt with by national and international legal efforts. The US, Canada and Switzerland, Luxembourg and Belgium have codified legal rules on the property aspects of intermediated securities.[5]

---

[2] UNIDROIT Secretariat, 'Explanatory Notes to the Preliminary Draft UNIDROIT Convention on Harmonised Substantive Rules regarding Securities Held with an Intermediary' [2005] Rev dr unif 36, 44, 46.

[3] RM Goode, 'The Nature and Transfer of Rights in Dematerialised and Immobilised Securities' [1996] JIBFL 167.

[4] See Chapter One for a detailed analysis.

[5] US, Uniform Commercial Code Article 8; Canada, Uniform Securities Transfer

Internationally there are the Hague Securities Convention on the choice of law applicable to the proprietary rights in securities held with an intermediary adopted under the auspices of HCCH and the Geneva Securities Convention regarding substantive rules on the property aspects of intermediated securities recently adopted under the auspices of UNIDROIT.[6] A Securities Law Directive covering property law, corporate law and conflict of laws with regard to intermediated securities is in the drafting process in the EU.[7] There is much literature by academics, governments, practitioners and professional organisations, on legal implications and suggestions regarding general property law issues in respect of intermediated securities.[8]

Under English law there is a statutory framework for the top tier of the securities settlement system on title, title transfer and title conflicts. Other than legal title at the top tier, intermediated securities are subject to general law. There are government reports, academic monographs and articles on general property law and discrete articles on corporate law issues regarding intermediated securities.[9]

Act; Switzerland, Federal Intermediated Securities Act; Belgium, Royal Decree No 62 of 10 November 1967, a Law of 2 January 1991, a Law of 22 July 1991, a Law of 7 April 1995, a Law of 14 December 2005; Luxembourg, Grand-Ducal Decree of 17 February 1971 (as amended in 1994 and 1996).

[6] HCCH Convention of 5 July 2006 on the Law Applicable to Certain Rights in Respect of Securities held with an Intermediary; UNIDROIT Convention on Substantive Rules for Intermediated Securities.

[7] K Löber and P Paech, 'Interconnecting Law of Securities Holding and Transfer—A Chance for Seamless International Improvements' [2007] JIBFL 9; P Paech and K Löber, 'Post Trading of Securities: Shaping the European Response to Legal Barriers' [2009] JIBFL 211; Giovannini Group, 'Cross-Border Clearing and Settlement Arrangements in the European Union (November 2001)'; Giovannini Group, 'Second Report on EU Clearing and Settlement (April 2003)'; see also <http://ec.europa.eu/internal_market/financial-markets/securities-law/indcx_cn.htm> acccsscd 26 January 2013.

[8] RD Guynn and others, 'Modernizing Securities Ownership, Transfer and Pledging Laws (International Bar Association 1996)'; IOSCO/BIS, 'Recommendations for Securities Settlement Systems (November 2001)'; Group of Thirty, 'Global Clearing and Settlement – A Plan of Action (2003)'; CW Mooney, 'Beyond Negotiability: A New Model for Transfer and Pledge of Interests in Securities Controlled by Intermediaries' (1990) 12 Cardozo L Rev 305.

[9] Financial Markets Law Committee, 'The FMLC Report on Property Interests in Indirectly Held Investment Securities: An Analysis of the Need for and Nature of Legislation in the UK' [2005] Rev dr unif 339; Law Commission, 'Law Commission Project on Intermediated Investment Securities First Seminar – Objectives for a Common Legal Framework (22 March 2006)'; Law Commission,

Other than the direct participants in the CREST system, rights of holders of intermediated securities are subject to general law. It is possible under English law to recognise the rights of these holders of intermediated securities as proprietary under trusts. Traditionally the custody of bearer securities has been governed under the law of bailment where an investor retains legal title to securities. Bailment under English law is only applicable to tangibles. It is however allowed under trusts to hold intangibles through another. Thus intermediated securities held by an investor with his intermediary are analysed under trusts law. An investor retains proprietary interests in intermediated securities which are equitable. The trust can accommodate the issue of retaining property in a pool of intangibles held through another. A preliminary question is whether a trust can be established under the requirement of certainty of subject matter, in favour of an investor holding securities commingled with other clients' holding of the same issue of securities, by his intermediary with the upper-tier intermediary. The answer is either by a co-ownership concept that a trust is over the commingled pool of securities and all clients are co-owners in proportion to their holding, or by the argument that intangibles are incapable of segregation and the certainty of subject matter requirement is inapplicable to intangibles.[10]

It is widely acknowledged that an investor other than a direct participant in CREST retains an equitable proprietary interest in intermediated securities. There are still uncertainties. For example, the allocation of

---

'Law Commission Project on Intermediated Investment Securities Second Seminar: Issues affecting Account holders and Intermediaries (23 June 2006)', Law Commission Project on Intermediated Investment Securities Third Seminar: Issues affecting Transferees of Intermediated Securities (27 July 2006)', 'Interim Advice in relation to The EU Legal Certainty Group Advice and the UNIDROIT Convention on Substantive Rules regarding Intermediated Securities' (October 2006), The UNIDROIT Convention on Substantive Rules regarding Intermediated Securities Updated Advice to HM Treasury (May 2007), The UNIDROIT Convention on Substantive Rules regarding Intermediated Securities: Further Updated Advice to HM Treasury (May 2008); RM Goode, The Nature and Transfer of Rights in Dematerialised and Immobilised Securities' [1996] JIBFL 167; J Benjamin, *Interest in Securities: A Proprietary Law Analysis of the International Securities Markets* (Oxford University Press, Oxford 2000); E Micheler, *Property in Securities: A Comparative Study* (Cambridge Studies in Corporate Law, Cambridge University Press, Cambridge 2007); M Yates and G Montagu, *The Law of Global Custody* (3rd rev edn, Tottel Publishing, London 2009); L Gullier and J Payne (eds), *Intermediated Securities: Legal Problems and Practical Issues* (Hart Publishing, Oxford 2010).

[10] See 2.4.2.1 for a detailed analysis.

shortfalls in a commingled account for clients held by an intermediary with his upper tier intermediary is not clearly addressed; perfection and priority of security interests need to be clarified; the adverse impact of exceptions to the no-look-through and upper-tier attachment rule; and the resolution of title conflicts between a prior owner and a good faith purchaser, i.e., the protection of good faith purchasers is unclear.[11]

Regarding title conflicts, i.e., the protection of good faith purchasers against adverse claims of prior owners, purchasers of bearer securities have been protected under negotiability; purchasers of certificated registered securities have been protected under quasi-negotiablity through estoppel. The operation of both negotiability and quasi-negotiability rely on the certificates. Intermediated securities are uncertificated which gives rise to uncertainties whether negotiability and quasi-negotiability are available to purchasers of intermediated securities. An analysis of the policies of negotiability and quasi-negotiability is necessary to see the compatibility of the policies with intermediated securities and the implementation of these policies through detailed legal rules.[12]

Meanwhile the trust analysis introduces equitable title to intermediated securities. The issue of the good faith purchaser can be seen in the perspective of priority rules of general property law. The principal priority rule is the first in time rule subject to statutory exceptions and other modifying factors. There is no general good faith acquisition rule. A good faith purchaser of legal title cannot defeat a prior legal title, although a good faith purchaser of legal title can defeat a prior equitable title. It is a complex system of rules given the diversity of rights under English law, i.e., legal right, equitable right and mere equities. Scenarios of good faith purchasers of intermediated securities can be classified as follows: a purchaser of a legal title to intermediated securities against a prior legal title or a prior equitable title; a purchaser of an equitable title of intermediated securities against a prior legal title, or against a prior equitable title via the CREST system, or against a prior equitable title not via the CREST system. It is possible for the legal title of a direct participant in the CREST system acquired in good faith to defeat any prior title, legal or equitable, under the Uncertificated Securities Regulations 2001 SI 2001/3755. Other than a purchaser of legal title, the position of a purchaser of an equitable title to intermediated securities is subject to general law. The treatment of the good faith purchaser of intermediated

[11] Financial Markets Law Committee, 'The FMLC Report on Property Interests in Indirectly Held Investment Securities: An Analysis of the Need for and Nature of Legislation in the UK' [2005] Rev dr unif 339.
[12] See Chapter Three.

securities is not uniform, depending on what title a purchaser gets and whether the transaction is via the CREST system. There is much support for the view that reform of rules on title conflicts under English law is necessary.[13]

The protection of good faith purchasers is one aspect of the issue of title conflicts. The other side is the protection of prior owners. A balance has to be struck between the protection of good faith purchasers and prior owners. Internationally one approach goes so far in favour of purchasers that it generally limits prior owners' claims to their intermediaries and protects good faith purchasers with a procedural bar, and if exceptionally an action can be commenced against purchasers it protects good faith purchasers against prior owners with a substantive defense. Another approach continues the good faith acquisition model of civil law. The first approach is very preferential to purchasers and leaves prior owners largely at the mercy of their intermediaries. Thus prevention of intermediary insolvency and insurance against intermediary insolvency are necessary to guarantee the rights of prior owners and maintain the reliability of the indirect holding system.

The tendency is to separate the rights of a purchaser from prior owners and treat the rights of a purchaser as a claim against his intermediary. As it is widely believed that an investor's rights in intermediated securities is a personal claim against his intermediary but meanwhile valid against third parties. It is a kind of mixed right. Property rights in intermediated securities highlight once again the issue of the rights *in rem*-rights *in personam* dichotomy. The key lies in treating the boundary between personal and property rights. The difference between personal and property rights is crucial in the insolvency of the obligor. Treating personal rights as property assumes the rarity of failure of obligors. When obligors do fall insolvent the result may be disastrous. Prevention of the failure of obligors is necessary through financial regulation. Compensation schemes are also necessary in case of obligor failure. Otherwise it is doubtful whether it would be proper to treat claims as property.[14]

Research Topic and Methods

Despite much literature on the general legal implications of intermediated securities, research into specific topics is yet to be undertaken. This book examines the property law implications of intermediated securities with a

---

[13] See Chapter Four and Chapter Five.

[14] See Chapter Six.

focus on title conflicts in respect of intermediated securities under English law with reference to codified national laws and international uniform law. It aims to examine, under English property law, whether proprietary interests can be established in intermediated securities, and if so, how title conflicts between a prior holder and a purchaser of intermediated securities, both innocent, caused by the intervention of a third party, are resolved.

The major research methods are the black-letter approach, policy analysis and the comparative law approach. Relevant general principles in statutes and case law in force will be examined to see the applicability and potential results of their application to intermediated securities. The underlying polices of the black-letter law will be sought in order to explore their potential extension to intermediated securities. Comparative law is a useful tool to dig into the rationale and justification of legal rules in response to social reality. This is particularly true in the case of intermediated securities which have bewildered many legal conceptions and legal systems. Reference will be made to codified national laws and international uniform law as a benchmark and inspiration to review current rules and make suggestions under English law.

Structures

Chapter One introduces the practices of intermediated securities and legal uncertainty in property law, i. e., the difficulty in establishing property, or rights *in rem*, in intangible book entry securities held with an intermediary, because of intermediation, the practice of commingling and fungibility, under most legal systems. National and international law responses will be exposed.

Chapter Two explores property law, proprietary rights under trusts law, and the securities holding system in England and on this basis, title to intermediated securities under English law. Firstly, characteristics of English law will be examined, including the relation of property rights to contractual claims, the role of equity, the subject matter of property rights, the recognition of property over intangibles, and the idea of relative title, and property rights as remedies, as well as the impact of general property law principles on title conflicts. Secondly, the contractual and proprietary nature of a beneficiary's right under a trust will be examined to demystify the mixed nature of trusts and its implications for title conflicts. Thirdly, intermediated securities in England will be introduced, the statutory legal framework on legal title to intermediated securities at the top tier, and other than that, how title to intermediated securities is analysed under general property law and trusts law.

Chapter Three explores how title and title conflicts in respect of certificated securities are dealt with as background for exploring title conflicts in respect of uncertificated intermediated securities. Firstly the *nemo dat* principle and its exceptions under common law estoppel and statutes will be introduced. Secondly title and transfer of title to certificated securities of bearer securities and registered securities will be examined. Thirdly title conflicts under negotiability in respect of bearer securities will be analysed, from the perspective of its rationale, evolution and policy, and then the possibility of extension to intermediated securities will be considered. Fourthly title conflicts in respect of registered securities will be analysed, from the perspective of issuer-true owner relationships, issuer-transferee relationships, and true owner-transferee relationships respectively; the central theme is use of common law estoppel to allocate loss between innocent parties caused by strangers; the potential of such estoppel in the context of title conflicts in respect of intermediated securities will be investigated.

Chapter Four introduces the statutory legal framework regarding legal title at the top tier of intermediated holding. The statutory framework on title, transfer of title, and conflicts of legal title to intermediated securities will be introduced. Emphasis will be laid on the statutory estoppel against a prior holder of legal title to claim title against an innocent purchaser, with analysis of its function, its common law origin, its link with negotiability and estoppel in respect of certificated registered securities, and the special statutory compensation and system infrastructure as a way to balance the protection of a true owner and a purchaser.

Chapter Five explores title conflicts in respect of intermediated securities under the priority rules across legal and equitable title under general property law. As a preliminary issue the disposition of intermediated securities will be examined as disposition of equitable interests. Given the resemblance of securities holding systems to payment systems, the nature of credit transfer will be examined. Then the priority system will be analysed: the general rule of first in time and the merits of rights, the priority between legal title and equitable title, and between equitable title and mere equities; the better equity rule and postponement between equitable title; the *Dearle v Hall* rule of notice, will be presented with their policies and the results of their extension to intermediated securities; then a summary analysis will be made of the policies of priority rules and their consistency with intermediated securities.

Chapter Six explores better solutions to title conflicts with regard to intermediated securities. Firstly the factors to be considered and balanced in dealing with title conflicts are examined as well as mainstream arguments. Secondly a comparative law briefing of approaches under national laws and international uniform law will be given. Thirdly the issue under English law will be reviewed, whether the current situation is satisfactory, whether it is necessary to reshuffle the issue of title conflicts, and possible approaches and results thereof will be presented and analysed.

LIST OF ABBREVIATIONS

FISA	Federal Intermediated Securities Act
USR	Uncertificated Securities Regulations

CHAPTER ONE

INTERMEDIATED SECURITIES AND PROPERTY LAW IMPLICATIONS

1.1 Securities

Generally speaking securities are transferable financial assets, or more exactly transferable contractual claims or rights against the issuer in the final analysis.[1] Contractual claims or rights were personal and non-transferable under classical legal doctrines. On the other hand, it is highly desirable that contractual claims are made transferable as a kind of wealth and value alongside land and chattels. A monetary claim is a personal right against an obligor which can only be enforced through a personal or *in personam* action.[2] It is however at the same time an asset with economic value which makes it the object of an ownership right if sufficiently specific. It can then be defended against the whole world. The validity of being enforceable against the whole world of personal claims makes personal claims proprietary. Once proprietary, personal claims can be owned, defended, transferred, or given as security.[3] Before statutory establishment of securities as a special statutory chose in action and the introduction of certificate as the title to securities, assignment and novation were available to achieve the transfer of securities as intangible rights. Assignment and novation achieved qualified facilitation of the transfer of securities due to their strict requirements of formalities.[4] To resolve the difficulty securities certificates were introduced to represent the contractual claims to make them tangible and capable of transfer as

[1] M Smith, *The Law of Assignment: The Creation and Transfer of Choses in Action* (Oxford University Press, Oxford 2007) 59-66.

[2] J Dalhuisen, *Dalhuisen on Transnational Comparative, Commercial, Financial and Trade Law Volume 2: Contract and Movable Property law* (4th edn, Hart Publishing, Oxford 2010) 268.

[3] ibid.

[4] J Benjamin, *Interest in Securities: A Proprietary Law Analysis of the International Securities Markets* (Oxford University Press, Oxford 2000) 64-68.

tangibles. For bearer securities, certificates represent title to securities and the transfer of securities certificates represents transfer of ownership to securities. For registered securities, the issuer register represents title to securities and a change in the issuer register represents the change of title. Securities certificates are introduced to facilitate the transfer of title to securities but certificates are not sufficient to constitute transfer of ownership of securities. Securities certificates entitle a holder to be registered with the issuer.[5] In both cases securities certificates play an important role, which is so important indeed that securities are often considered as tangibles, which may be accurate with bearer securities, but less so with registered securities. Securities certificates facilitate the proof and transfer of ownership to securities by giving a tangible form to intangible rights. And rules on tangibles are ready to apply to certificated securities without the need for devising new rules to intangibles. It is one example of the genius of legal fiction. Indeed it has been so successful that it has brought about the collapse of the system of securities certificates.

1.2 Intermediated Securities

Securities markets based on paper certificates developed to huge scales and centralised stock exchanges were established which in turn precipitated the development of securities trading. In the middle 20th century, developed securities markets were unable to execute certificated transfers in a timely way, i.e., the so-called paper crunch. Delayed delivery of securities certificates after payment was a serious source of risk if securities certificates as proof of ownership or proof of right to claim ownership to securities could not be delivered to buyers in time. In response two approaches were introduced: viz., immobilisation and dematerialisation.[6] Immobilisation operates in this way: all securities certificates or a global note representing the whole issue are deposited in a central securities depositary which maintains securities accounts for direct participants and records their holding on their securities accounts, direct participants then maintain securities accounts for its clients and record their holding, from tier to tier, up to a final investor who holds securities for himself. Ownership or title to securities or interests in securities is the book entry record on the securities accounts with an intermediary. The

[5] See M Yates and G Montagu, *The Law of Global Custody* (3rd rev edn, Tottel Publishing, London 2009) 8.
[6] ibid 14-15.

adoption of tiers of holding may be attributed to cost and efficiency factors. Access to the central securities depositaries is not open to all in the same way that a central bank will not open an account for an individual depositor. Dematerialisation is similar in the tiers of holding of securities represented by book entries on a relevant securities account. The only difference between dematerialisation and immobilisation is that there are no securities certificates or a global note deposited with a central securities depositary. There are no securities certificates at all. The initial issue of securities is by entries in a register in a central system, often a securities settlement system established by statutes, representing the whole issue of securities, akin to an issuer register. Another situation is that securities certificates are eliminated and replaced by a register with a system Operator.[7] They are securities "in dematerialised form, in relation to which ... ownership, as against the rest of the world, consists of a chose in action represented by a credit in ... [an] account (a 'depot') with a clearing house, depository or custodian (collectively 'depositories')."[8]

The essence of immobilisation and dematerialisation is replacing paper certificates as title or proof of title to securities with electronic book entry on securities accounts with intermediaries. It eliminates the paper crunch and facilitates the speedy transfer of securities. It also eliminates the risk of loss of certificates. It however introduces other sources of risk such as operation risk and intermediary risk. For example the computer system may break down or an intermediary is dishonest or falls insolvent. It also enables a great variety of innovative operations which add to the legal uncertainty in the interests in securities of an account holder.

Intermediaries maintain securities accounts for clients. There are two ways intermediaries stand between an issuer and a final investor. Intermediaries either serve as record keepers, only transmitting the holding information of each final investor to the issuer and transmitting rights to securities to investors, or cut off the issuer-investor relationship. As record keeper an intermediary keeps the individual holding of each client on his own books and on his securities accounts with his upper-tier intermediary,

---

[7] RD Guynn and others, 'Modernizing Securities Ownership, Transfer and Pledging Laws (International Bar Association 1996)'; C Bernasconi, R Potok and G Morton, 'General Introduction: Legal Nature of interests in Indirectly Held Securities and Resulting Conflict of Law Analysis' in R Potok (ed), *Cross Border Collateral: Legal Risk and the Conflict of Laws* (Butterworths, London 2002).

[8] *Re Lehman Brothers International (Europe) (in administration); Pearson v Lehman Brothers Finance SA* [2010] EWHC 2914 (Ch) [2] (Briggs J); [2010] All ER (D) 232 (Nov).

through tiers of intermediaries in this way up to the issuer. The issuer knows each final investor. This is known as a transparent system. The major difference between this kind of system and traditional paper-based securities holding system is a change in the proof of title, from paper certificates to electronic entries. Countries adopting the transparent model include Nordic countries, Spain and China, to give a few examples.[9] Where an intermediary cuts off the link of a client with upper-tier intermediaries and the issuer, an intermediary keeps individual holding of investors on his own books but holds the same issue of securities of all clients[10] in one omnibus securities account with his upper-tier intermediary, which makes the clients of one intermediary only known to his intermediary but unknown to any upper-tier intermediary or an issuer in the regular course of transaction. The non-transparent approach undoubtedly eases the administration of accounts, reduces transfers of book entries across all levels of intermediaries, increases opportunities of trading, and creates a huge securities base for profitable exploitation such as securities lending. It is even argued that only the non-transparent system is intermediated holding as interests in securities becomes truly indirect and intermediated by intermediaries.[11] This paper adopts a wide meaning on intermediated holding and treats transparent holding as intermediated holding given that securities are indeed held through intermediaries. The transparent system poses fewer legal issues. For example, which are the subject matter of the right of an investor, the underlying securities or some derivative rights from the underlying securities; and the issue of establishing property rights over fungibles under the specificity principle.

The holding of securities through intermediaries happens in various contexts. Firstly, access to the securities settlement system is limited to qualified participants with the necessary computer infrastructure and financial resources, which most individual and small institutional investors cannot afford. Giant custodian banks can afford to become participants and act as intermediaries for institutional investors. For example investment

---

[9] UNIDROIT, 'Working Paper regarding So Called 'Transparent Systems' (UNIDROIT 2006 Study LXXVIII-Doc 44)'; UNIDROIT, 'Supplementary Working Paper regarding So-Called 'Transparent Systems' (UNIDROIT 2007 Study LXXVIII-Doc 44 Add)'.

[10] Or even hold the same issue of securities of all clients and the intermediary's house holding in one omnibus account with his upper tier intermediary, which is prohibited in most countries to avoid potential abuse by the intermediary.

[11] AO Austen-Peters, *Custody of Investments: Law and Practice* (Oxford University Press, Oxford 2000) 12.

banks provide prime brokerage services to hedge funds including the custody of securities, credit extension, trade execution and clearing.[12] Prime brokers again may deal with institutional brokers or investment vehicles only and small investors have to access small brokers to have access to the system. Secondly, there are legally mandatory arrangements such as the unit trust, where a trust manager has to deposit the trust asset with a trustee for the purpose of segregating the trust asset from the manager's asset,[13] and deposit receipts, a structured vehicle for cross-border investment in overseas securities normally inaccessible to small investors.[14] Thirdly, a major financial institution becomes the registered owner of a foreign security through a local custodian, then issues certificates representing his holding to domestic holders. Holders of deposit receipts have indirect interests in the underlying securities.[15] In most developed securities markets indirect holding has been the dominant model and most investors hold intangible securities through accounts with intermediaries. Though there are indeed theoretical and legal possibilities of holding certificates of securities directly against the issuer, the cost is often too high to afford for small investors.

1.3 Legal Implications

Legal implications will be analysed based on the non-transparent intermediated model as it also covers issues in the transparent model.

1.3.1 Intermediation and Source of Rights

The fact that an investor has book entries on his securities account only with his intermediary not visible to any upper-tier intermediary or the issuer raises doubts as to what the investor actually has: the underlying securities issued by the issuer or some kind of derivative rights from the book entry on the securities accounts but relating to underlying securities. When an investor disposes of his rights through instructions to his

---

[12] *Re Lehman Brothers International (Europe)* [2009] EWCA Civ 1161 [1] (Patten LJ); [2009] All ER (D) 83 (Nov); J Benjamin, *Interest in Securities* (Oxford University Press, Oxford 2000) 223-26.

[13] Financial Services and Markets Act 2000 s 242.

[14] J Benjamin, *Interest in Securities: A Proprietary Law Analysis of the International Securities Markets* (Oxford University Press, Oxford 2000) 251-62.

[15] ibid.

intermediary, receives dividends through his intermediary, and exercises corporate right such as voting through his intermediary, the book entry with the intermediary and the intermediary assume a central role in the enjoyment of the rights by an investor. The fact that an investor is unknown to any upper-tier intermediary or an issuer justifies a rule that an investor can only exercise his rights in the securities (underlying securities or derivative rights) against his intermediary. This is the prohibition of upper-tier attachment much called for in the securities profession. The situation is akin to the repackaged product of deposit receipts where a receipt holder exercises rights to the issuer of the deposit receipt rather than the issuer of the underlying securities. Clarification of the source of an investor's rights in intermediated securities is highly desirable. It has bearings on who can be sued to claim rights, priorities between competing titles, system integrity, exercise of corporate rights, and conflict of laws.[16]

1.3.2 Fungible and Commingling[17]

Fungibles mean interchangeable units with the same qualities for the purpose of delivery or transfer obligations. Whether property is fungible also depends on the nature of the obligation with respect to it. If a depository is not obliged to return the specific asset deposited but to deliver its equivalent, the asset is fungible. Securities of the same issue are usually fungible.[18] An intermediary often commingles all clients' holding of the same issue of securities in an omnibus client account with his intermediary. Commingled holding serves to reduce entries on accounts of all tiers of intermediaries and increase efficiency. For example a transaction between clients of the same intermediary is only recorded on the book of this intermediary with no need for record on the books of upper-tier intermediaries. Commingled holding also provides economies of scale as the bulk of securities tend to enjoy greater liquidity and better price, and there are also opportunities for securities lending by intermediaries subject to the consent of clients.

---

[16] RD Guynn and others, 'Modernizing Securities Ownership, Transfer and Pledging Laws (International Bar Association 1996)'; RM Goode, 'The Nature and Transfer of Rights in Dematerialised and Immobilised Securities' [1996] JIBFL 167.

[17] See PR Wood, *Set-off and Netting, Derivatives, Clearing Systems* (2nd edn,Law and Practice of International Finance Series, Sweet & Maxwell, London 2007) 328.

[18] RM Goode, 'The Nature and Transfer of Rights in Dematerialised and Immobilised Securities' [1996] JIBFL 167; AO Austen-Peters, *Custody of Investments: Law and Practice* (Oxford University Press, Oxford 2000) 14-15.

1.3.3 Specific Legal Issues

The market practice of investors holding securities through an intermediary, represented by book entries on his securities account with his intermediary, does pose challenges to establishing the investor's property right in the securities.

The subject matter, whether the underlying securities, or rights derivative from the underlying securities,[19] is intangible, represented by electronic entries on the securities account and commingled with the same issue of securities of other clients of the same intermediary. Firstly, it is vulnerable compared with tangibles capable of possession and apparent ownership, though the law has means to deal with intangible rights for a long time. Secondly, it is commingled with the interests of others and there is no specifically identifiable security to assert property. The pool of the same issue of securities held by an intermediary is always changing and floating. Though property in a bulk is nothing new as there are bulk of tangibles such as wine or wheat, in legal systems adopting the specificity principle of asserting property right, there are still many theoretical barriers for an investor to assert ownership, due to the lack of specificity in an ever-changing pool of intangible asset. Thirdly, the investor's interests in intangible form can only be represented and exercised through his intermediary, which constitutes another layer of complication for property law purposes.

Rights over intangible interests held through another may not be recognised as property in some legal systems, as it does not fit into the recognised scenarios of property where an owner separates with the subject matter of ownership. When an owner separates with the subject matter of ownership, his ownership can be recognised in law, as in the case of bailment or deposit. Bailment requires physical delivery of tangible assets from the bailor to the bailee. The bailor or depositor remains the legal owner and the bailee acquires a special possessory interest but definitely not absolute ownership. The requirement of tangibles is out of the principle of specificity in order for the bailor to retain property rights. The bailee is obliged to redeliver the same tangibles under bailment. Commingling of fungibles with those of others extinguishes a bailment.[20]

---

[19] J Benjamin, *Interest in Securities: A Proprietary Law Analysis of the International Securities Markets* (Oxford University Press, Oxford 2000) 28-30.

[20] *South Australia Insurance Co Ltd v Randell* (1869) 3 PC 101; *Re Goldcorp Exchange Ltd* [1995] 1 AC 74 (PC); RD Guynn and others, 'Modernizing

It is also possible to establish bailment over intangibles held with another by legal fiction under civil law if a bailor has intangibles allocated to him. The commingling of all clients' holding prevents bailment as there are no specific securities allocated to an investor and no action of revendication of specific securities is possible. Normally a special statutory regime is needed to guarantee the proprietary rights of investors in intermediated securities.[21] It is however possible for an investor to retain ownership in a transparent system where his rights can be traced to specific records maintained by a central securities depositary or an issuer without commingling with others' holding at any tier, through legal fiction such as treating record as possession.

1.4 Responses

There are apparent theoretical barriers in many legal systems to recognising property or ownership in the intangible and fungible securities held with an intermediary under property law based on the direct or indirect control over specific tangibles. Meanwhile it is not practical for the law to recognise an investor's property to specific underlying securities against the issuer in an intermediated system where an investor is known solely to his intermediary. However, property is crucial to an investor in the sense of being insulated against the general creditors of an insolvent intermediary. What is expected by market participants is a kind of property right, modified to some extent and different from the classical property right to land or tangibles with direct (or indirect under bailment) and visible control over a specific tangible object, which should be *pro rata* in the pool of client holding of the same issue of securities held by an intermediary, and separate from the asset of the intermediary. It is weakened ownership or property, which is indirect, and proportional in a floating pool of intangible asset.

In response to the issue of protecting ownership in commingled intangibles held through a third party there are several models adopted for the non-transparent system. Roughly these responses fall into two kinds, i.e., the *sui generis* model and the co-ownership model.

The US Uniform Commercial Code (UCC) Article 8 creates a new

Securities Ownership, Transfer and Pledging Laws (International Bar Association 1996)'.

[21] J Benjamin, *Interest in Securities: A Proprietary Law Analysis of the International Securities Markets* (Oxford University Press, Oxford 2000) 52-53.

kind of rights known as securities entitlements, a *sui generis* package of personal rights and property interests, confers the investor *pro rata* property interests in all interests in the financial asset held by his intermediary. The rights are personal rights against the intermediary to dispose of the securities entitlement and exercise corporate rights attaching to the underlying securities, but meanwhile the financial asset held by his intermediary is not property of the intermediary and not subject to claims of the general creditor of the intermediary.[22] The policy is that unlike certificated securities where investors hold certificates as title and enjoy rights against the issuer, or investors are entered in the issuer register as title and enjoy rights against the issuer, the practices of tiered holding and pooling of securities cut off any relation between an investor and an issuer. The focus should be the investor-intermediary relationship under which an investor enjoys rights in the underlying securities through his intermediary and the tiers of upper-tier intermediaries. The limitation of an investor's rights in the underlying securities to his intermediary requires that his holding is safe in the event of the insolvency of his intermediary. [23]

The Canadian Uniform Securities Transfer Act, based on the US UCC Article 8, adopted by the Uniform Law Conference of Canada in 2004, has been implemented in many states of Canada since 2007.[24]

The Swiss Federal Intermediated Securities Act (FISA) establishes a complete legal framework on the proprietary aspect of holding and disposition of securities through intermediaries. Despite its earliest draft to introduce a modified co-ownership in the traditional property law framework,[25] the final FISA establishes intermediated securities as a new

---

[22] Uniform Commercial Code Art 8 pt 5.

[23] CR Reitz, 'Reflections on the Drafting of the 1994 Revision of Article 8 of the US Uniform Commercial Code' [2005] Rev dr unif 357, 361, 362.

[24] Canadian Securities Administrators' Uniform Securities Transfer Act Task Force, Uniform Securities Transfer Act (Approved at the Uniform Law Conference of Canada Annual Meeting, August 22-26, 2004). For example, Securities Transfer Act, SA 2006, c S-4.5, Consolidated Statutes of Alberta-Alberta; Securities Transfer Act, 2006, SO 2006, c 8, Consolidated Statutes of Ontario-Ontario; Securities Transfer Act, SNS 2010, c 8, Consolidated Statutes of Nova Scotia-Nova Scotia. See also ET Spink and MA Paré, 'The Uniform Securities Transfer Act: Globalized Commercial Law for Canada' (2004) 19 BFLR 321; RM Scavone, 'Stronger Than Fictions: Canada Rethinks the Law of Securities Transfers in the Indirect Holding System' (2007) 45 Can Bus LJ 67.

[25] H Kuhn, B Graham-Siegenthaler and L Thévenoz (eds), *The Federal Intermediated Securities Act (FISA) and the Hague Securities Convention (HSC)* (Stämpfli's Commentary, Stämpfli Publishers Ltd., Berne 2010) 129.

kind of property, i.e., personal or corporate rights of a fungible nature against an issuer which are credited to a securities account, and may be disposed of by the account; effective against the custodian and any third party and beyond the reach of other creditors of the custodian.[26] It is personal or corporate rights against the issuer,[27] depending upon custodians for the holding and disposition of such rights,[28] but meanwhile proprietary in that it is effective against third parties, in particular against creditors of insolvent custodians, and protected as absolute property rights.[29] It is a new kind of mixed right of personal and proprietary nature.[30] The major difference from the US and Canadian definition is that the right is against the issuer while the US and Canadian style of right is solely against the intermediary, though in both systems intermediaries are essential for the exercising of rights in both systems.

Belgian law recognises the investors of one intermediary in the same security as co-owners in the security held by the intermediary, each with a notional portion of the pool of securities and rights for revendication of equivalent securities in the case of intermediary insolvency, superior to the general creditors of the insolvent intermediary.[31] Luxemburg establishes the investors' rights as ownership in a given number of securities in the pool of the same securities by his intermediary for clients which is represented by book entry and not traceable to upper-tier intermediaries, together with a claim of revendication of the quantity of securities, superior to the general creditors of the insolvent intermediary.[32] These regimes adopt the traditional property law concept with modifications catered to intermediated securities by specifying the special consequences of the rights of investors.

The Geneva Securities Convention, with its functional approach, provides that a credit of securities to a securities account confers on the

[26] Swiss FISA art 3.

[27] H Kuhn, B Graham-Siegenthaler and L Thévenoz (eds), *The Federal Intermediated Securities Act (FISA) and the Hague Securities Convention (HSC)* (Stämpfli's Commentary, Stämpfli Publishers Ltd., Berne 2010) 164-66.

[28] ibid 167-69.

[29] ibid 171-73.

[30] ibid 143, 172.

[31] Belgian Royal Decree No 62 of 10 November 1967; a Law of 2 January 1991; a Law of 22 July 1991; a Law of 7 April 1995, Royal Decree of 27 January 2004; a Law of 14 December 2005.

[32] Luxembourg Securities Act 2001 replacing the Grand-Ducal Decree of 17 February 1971 (as amended in 1994 and 1996).

account holder the right to receive and exercise any rights attached to the securities, and the right to effect a disposition or grant an interest.[33] These rights are effective against third parties and against an administrator and creditors in any insolvency proceeding.[34] Though no property interests are expressly mentioned, these provisions in fact establish mixed rights of an account holder in the intermediated securities credited to his account, entitled to rights attaching to securities and to dispose of securities, which are effective against third parties. It merely sets out the results of these rights without delineating the legal nature of such rights, as personal, proprietary, or mixed. However its basic assumption is that the rights are in fact of a mixed proprietary and personal nature.

[33] The Geneva Securities Convention art 9.
[34] The Geneva Securities arts 9, 14, 21.

CHAPTER TWO

PROPERTY IN INTERMEDIATED SECURITIES UNDER ENGLISH LAW

The issue of title to intermediated securities will be examined after an introduction to the dematerialised securities holding system in the UK. Property under general property law and trusts law will be examined. Title to intermediated securities, as well as title conflicts, will be analysed under property law and trusts law principles.

2.1 Intermediated Securities in the UK

Securities under English law and dematerialisation will be introduced. The issue of recognising title under dematerialisation will be investigated.

2.1.1 Securities and Dematerialisation

Securities are choses in action by nature under English law.[1] Company bonds and shares become statutory choses in action subject to special rules designed for liquidity free of common law limits on assignment of choses in action. Most bonds and equities are registered, and money market instruments are bearer securities. For registered securities, securities certificates are *prima facie* evidence of title to securities,[2] subject to the issuer register. Transfer of registered securities takes place through delivery of securities certificates and a change of holder in the issuer register. Transfer of bearer securities, mainly money market instruments, takes place by delivery of securities certificates.

It can be seen that securities certificates do not play a crucial role as conclusive evidence of title under English law where registered securities

---

[1] *Halsbury's Laws of England* (vol 6, 4th edn reissue, LexisNexis, London 2003) [8].

[2] For example, Companies Act 2006 s 768(1); Government Stock Regulations 2004 SI 2004/1611 reg 9(3).

dominate. Holding of certificates is subject to the issuer register, which is also *prima facie* evidence of title.[3] This is different from most civil law countries where securities certificates are considered as reifying the rights to securities and securities *per se* and bearer securities dominate, such as Germany.[4] It may be attributable to the absence of theoretical barriers to recognising intangible rights as subject matter of property rights, unlike the physical model of property law which considers tangibles alone as subject matter of property and has to accommodate intangibles into the framework of property through legal fiction.[5] Choses in action have always been a recognised category of property rights and are capable of assignment under equity and statutes under English law.[6]

This perhaps explains the choice of dematerialisation of securities and the direct holding system as regards the direct participants in the settlement system. The Uncertificated Securities Regulations 2001 SI 2001/3755 (USR 2001) displace the traditional property law requirements on using certificates for the proof and transfer of title in respect of securities. A demateralised system has been established. The USR 2001 "enable title to units of a security to be evidenced otherwise than by a certificate and transferred otherwise than by a written instrument," … and in these Regulations "relevant system" means a computer-based system, and procedures, which enable "title to units of a security to be evidenced and transferred without a written instrument".[7] It is known as the CREST system now operated by the Euroclear UK & Ireland. The system Operator keeps a register for each issue of securities, which is the operator register of each security, as evidence of title to securities, functionally equivalent to the issuer register of certificated registered securities.[8] The system Operator opens securities accounts for participants and records their holding by electronic book entries in a computer system. An operator

[3] Companies Act 2006 s 127; Government Stock Regulations 2004 SI 2004/1611 reg 7(4).

[4] Civil Code (Bürgerliches Gesetzbuch-BGB) s 793; Stock Corporation Act(Aktiengesetz-AktG) s 10; Law on Investment in Funds (Investmentgesetz) s 33.

[5] J Benjamin, *Interest in Securities*: A *Proprietary Law Analysis of the International Securities Markets* (Oxford University Press, Oxford 2000) 312-19.

[6] M Smith, *The Law of Assignment: The Creation and Transfer of Choses in Action* (Oxford University Press, Oxford 2007) 11-34.

[7] USR 2001 reg 2, replacing the Uncertificated Securities Regulations 1995 SI 1995/3272.

[8] USR 2001 reg 3 (1).

register records the name of the participants in the system, thus it is a direct system regarding the direct participants and the issuer.[9] As regards deposit receipts of international securities the system Operator intermediates in the sense that participants holders are not known to a foreign issuer and only the issuer of the deposit receipt is recorded on the register of a foreign issuer. Participants are mainly stock exchanges, central counterparties, financial institutions, settlement banks. Participating securities cover most equities, bonds and money market instruments and funds, as well as international securities.[10] Conversion is allowed between certificated and uncertificated forms.[11]

2.1.2 Title to Dematerialised Securities

2.1.2.1 Legal title at the top tier

The operator register of each issue of securities serves as title to dematerialized securities. Dematerialised securities are by nature registered securities. Bearer securities are transformed into registered securities. The operator registers of securities replace certificates as title to securities. The change from bearer securities to registered securities has implications for the issue of title conflicts between a prior owner and a good faith acquirer, viz. whether negotiability is lost.[12] For certificated registered securities there is no fundamental change in the evidence of title (from an issuer register to an operator register). The issue of title conflicts between a prior owner and a good faith acquirer is affected less radically.[13] In the CREST system title of direct participants in the CREST system are recorded on the Operator registers of the securities which are functionally the same as issuer registers of certificated registered securities. There is no uncertainty in recognising legal title of direct participants whose title is recorded on the operator register and public to all, in the same way as holders of certificated registered securities are recorded on the issuer registers. With statutory displacement of paper certificates as title to

[9] But not necessarily so regarding the clients of the direct participants who may not record the individual holding of each client with the system records.
[10] For background information, see the website of Euroclear UK & Ireland, <https://www.euroclear.com> accessed 26 January 2013.
[11] See 4.2, 4.3.
[12] See 3.3 and 4.5.1.
[13] See 3.4 and 4.5.2.

securities, the operator register of securities serves as title to securities. Direct participants of the CREST system are registered on the operator registers of securities and enjoy legal title, under enabling statutes rather than common law.

2.1.2.2 Title other than legal title at the top tier

Direct participants of the settlement system are major financial institutions and they maintain securities accounts for small financial institutions which maintain securities accounts for small investors such as individual investors, thus providing indirect access to the settlement system. Pooling and commingling are normal and an intermediary often holds all client holding of an issue of security in one client account with his intermediary, but mostly separate from his own house holding, as required by general law and financial regulation.[14] Thus most investors are not registered on the register of the settlement system Operator or the issuer register. There are indeed legal uncertainties as to investors' proprietary interests in securities held through intermediaries under English law, which is however less radical compared with civil law traditions, due to the characteristics of English property law. English property law has no barrier to recognising claims as valid against third parties, or in the case of intermediated securities, investors' claims against their intermediaries in respect of intermediated securities as valid against third parties, for example creditors of an insolvent intermediary. The practical uncertainties for establishing trusts due to the pooling of intangibles securities have been resolved by a co-tenancy analysis.[15]

[14] The general law of trusts and the FSA Client Asset Sourcebook; RM Goode and L Gullifer, *Goode on Legal Problems of Credit and Security* (4th edn, Sweet & Maxwell, London 2008) 244-47.

[15] Such as failure to establish a trust by an investor in pooled securities held by his intermediary for all clients, because of uncertainty of subject matter required for a trusts, this has been tackled by arguing for co-tenancy of all clients over the pool of securities in case law and commentary. "A trust of part of a fungible mass without the appropriation of any specific part of it for the beneficiary does not fail for uncertainty of subject matter, provided that the mass itself is sufficiently identified and provided also that the beneficiary's proportionate share of it is not itself uncertain." *Re Lehman Brothers International (Europe) (in administration); Pearson v Lehman Brothers Finance SA* [2010] EWHC 2914 (Ch) (Transcript) [225] (Briggs J); [2010] All ER (D) 232 (Nov). See also *Hunter v Moss* [1994] 3 All ER 215(CA); *Re Harvard Securities* [1997] 2 BCLC 369 (Ch); *Re CA Pacific Finance Ltd* [2000] 1 BCLC 494; *White v Shortall* [2006] NSW SC 1379; RM

Indeed investors in the UK normally establish themselves as beneficiaries under trusts with their intermediaries as trustees, under a series of sub-trusts and trusts.[16] A preliminary assumption is that under the trusts analysis an investor of intermediated securities has rights to the underlying securities.[17]

It is noteworthy that it is not necessarily the fact that there is always a trust. Parties can establish a trust if they intend so. An account holder may have a contractual claim against his intermediary for redelivery of equivalent securities according to the agreements between the parties. And there is still room for bailment in case of deposit of certificated securities. Trust is a legal mechanism available to the parties to recognise the proprietary interests of an account holder in the intangible and pooled intermediated securities. If the parties intend that an account holder retain property interests in the intermediated securities, it is recognised under the current law of trusts.

An introduction of English property law and trusts will be given as background for further analysis of property in intermediated securities.

2.2 Property under English Law in General

It is necessary to review the basics of English property law before examining whether proprietary interests can be established over intermediated securities held through intermediaries. The issue of *numerus clausus*, will be introduced, with the impact of equity on English property law. The issue of the *in rem-in personam* dichotomy will be scrutinised, as well as principles following from the *in rem-in personam* relationship, i.e., the subject matter of property rights, the recognition of indirect property rights, and the issue of publicity of property rights. Title and relative title will be presented as well as the responsive nature of property rights as remedies. Finally a short introduction to title conflict will be given.

Goode, 'Are Intangible Assets Fungible?' [2003] LMCLQ 379; see 2.4.2.1 for further analysis.

[16] *Re Lehman Brothers International (Europe) (in administration) (No 2)* [2009] EWCA Civ 1161 [4] (Pattern LJ); [2009] All ER (D) 83 (Nov); G Davies, 'Using Intermediated Securities as Collateral: Equitable Interests with Inequitable Results' [2007] JIBFL 70, 70.

[17] See Chapter One.

2.2.1 Principles

Under English law property is a relation between people in respect tangible and intangible things. Things are the subject matter of property rather than property. Property rights must be alienable and exigible against third persons. The effect of binding third parties is particularly important, which makes the crucial distinction between proprietary and personal rights, for example, a holder of property held by another in insolvency is entitled to get the property back while a creditor cannot.[18] Things which can be separated from a particular person and can be transferred can be the subject matter of property rights under the separability and transferability thesis of property rights.[19] Transferability or transmissibility is important in that an interest which is transmissible to the holder's successors is more valuable than one which stops with the holder.[20] Property rights can be directly over tangible things, or intangible rights such as personal rights against other persons in respect of tangible things but valid against third parties. Thus intangibles can be the subject matter of property rights.[21] The point that a personal right in respect of things can be proprietary and valid against third parties is a unique feature of English property law. Civil law only admits property rights, i.e., rights *in rem*, over tangibles; personal rights are not enforceable against third parties.[22] Ownership is considered the supreme and fullest right possible over tangibles. For example under German law, ownership is the absolute dominion of the owner over a specific object which is public to the world.[23]

---

[18] W Swadling, 'The Law of Property' in P Birks (ed) *English Private Law* (Oxford English Law, Oxford University Press, Oxford 2000) 206; M Yates and G Montagu, *The Law of Global Custody* (3rd rev edn, Tottel Publishing, London 2009) 9-10.

[19] JE Penner, *The Idea of Property in Law* (Oxford University Press, Oxford 1997) 111-27.

[20] AM Honoré, 'Ownership' in AG Guest (ed) Oxford Essays in Jurisprudence (Oxford University Press, Oxford 1961).

[21] J Benjamin, *Interest in Securities: A Proprietary Law Analysis of the International Securities Markets* (Oxford University Press, Oxford 2000) 312-13; RM Goode and E McKendrick, *Goode on Commercial Law* (4th edn, LexisNexis, London 2009) 29-30.

[22] JM Milo, 'Property and Real Rights' in JM Smits (ed) *Elgar Encyclopedia of Comparative Law* (Edward Elgar, Chelteham 2006).

[23] N Foster and S Sule, *German Legal Systems and Laws* (4th edn, Oxford University Press, Oxford 2010) 494-94; see also BGB §§ 854-1296.

2.2.1.1 The *numerus clausus* issue

The validity of property rights against third parties without their consent makes it necessary to limit arbitrary creation of property rights by party autonomy for the sake of transaction security. As to the scope of property rights, there are two competing viewpoints. Firstly, under the *numerus clausus* approach,[24] only those recognised explicitly in law are property rights; the list of property rights is closed; and contractual arrangements between parties cannot create property rights binding third parties. This principle is developed by three milestone cases, namely, *Keppel v Bailey*[25], *Hill v Tupper,*[26] and *King v David Allen (Billposting) Ltd*[27]. Secondly, it is held in *National Provincial Bank v Ainsworth*[28] that the list of property rights is not closed but it is difficult for a right to be recognised as property right in law unless three criteria are satisfied: i.e., "definable, identifiable by third parties, capable in its nature of assumption by third parties", and with "some degree of permanence or stability".[29]

Neither is absolute. For the *numerus clausus* principle, the list has been expanded by equity historically.[30] As for the second open approach, actually no new property right has been admitted ever since the decision of *National Provincial Bank v Ainsworth.*[31] What is in common to the two approaches is to restrict the contractual creation of rights over things to bind third parties and to protect the certainty and security in transactions. However, as property rights are designed to maximise the efficiency of the allocation of scarce resources in society,[32] the list of property rights cannot be expected to be satisfactory in all time. The list of property rights has been subject to adjustment from time to time. One feature of English

---

[24] *King v David Allen (Billposting) Ltd* [1916] 2 AC 54 (HL); W Swadling, 'The Law of Property' in P Birks (ed) *English Private Law* (Oxford English Law, Oxford University Press, Oxford 2000) 206.

[25] (1834) 2 My & K 517 (LC), 39 ER 1042.

[26] (1863) 2 H & C 121 (Exch Ct), 159 ER 51.

[27] [1916] 2 AC 54 (HL).

[28] [1965] AC 1175 (HL).

[29] *National Provincial Bank v Ainsworth* [1965] AC 1175 (HL) 1247-48 (Lord Wilberforce); see also AM Honoré, 'Ownership' in AG Guest (ed) *Oxford Essays in Jurisprudence* (Oxford University Press, Oxford 1961).

[30] W Swadling, 'The Law of Property' in P Birks (ed) *English Private Law* (Oxford English Law, Oxford University Press, Oxford 2000) 211.

[31] [1965] AC 1175 (HL).

[32] See RA Posner, *Economic Analysis of Law* (7th edn, Aspen Publishers, Austin 2007) 31.

property law is its definition of property is less formal than that in civil law and it is easier to recognise new property rights. The strict and rigid definition of property under civil law leads to difficulties in recognising new property rights, which can only be governed by property by analogy. In this aspect, equity has played a significant role in expanding the list of property rights which will continue, though less apparently than before.

2.2.1.2 The role of equity

The dualism of common law and equity is a novel aspect of English law. It is a product of specific historic circumstances well preserved by the conservative and tolerant English legal culture. In the beginning, claimants suffering from the rigidity and injustice of the common law resorted to the King for justice who responded with mercy and sympathy in order to establish his authority in competition with common law courts. Then a permanent Chancellor, and Court of Chancery later, as representative of the King, was established to deal with aggrieved claimants in common law courts. Remedies developed from discrete reactions in individual cases to systemic rules based on conscience which gave the system its name equity.

Equity recognised personal rights under common law as property rights by allowing transfer of debts before this was permitted by common law.[33] Equity developed the idea of equitable ownership by granting specific enforcement of personal obligation of the trusted person (trustee) to the person who vested the property in his trustee, which later developed into property rights, transferable and good against the trustee and the creditors of the trustee.[34]

It is widely believed that it has been rare for equity to recognise new property rights for a long time.[35] The flexible approach to property rights and personal rights of equity has contributed to the open and flexible English property law.

---

[33] S Worthington, *Equity* (Clarendon Law Series, 2nd edn, Clarendon Press, Oxford 2006) 59-63.
[34] S Worthington, *Equity* (Clarendon Law Series, 2nd edn, Clarendon Press, Oxford 2006) 59-63.
[35] W Swadling, 'The Law of Property' in P Birks (ed) *English Private Law* (Oxford English Law, Oxford University Press, Oxford 2000) 212.

2.2.1.3 An *in rem-in personam* dichotomy?

Under English law property is simply valid against third party strangers without their consent, greater than personal rights which only bind parties with their consent, because of their different importance as appreciated by society. A personal right against an obligor in respect of things can be enforceable against third parties which makes the personal right proprietary. So strictly rights under English law can be classified into property rights over tangibles in the narrow sense, property rights which are personal rights in respect of tangibles valid against third parties, and pure personal rights.[36] Unlike civil law countries with a strict *in rem-in personam* dichotomy, property is not endowed with vital political significance to citizen freedom. Property has never been proclaimed as the foundation of individual freedom and liberty in Britain as in civil law countries which experienced radical revolutions.[37] The unrestrained individualism attributing fundamental importance to absolute property for individual freedom went through modification and qualifications in later centuries. It is not so in England where the feudal ownership of land by the King is kept intact and no one could claim absolute ownership over a piece of land.

2.2.2 Several Features

Absent the *in rem-in personam* dichotomy there are several noteworthy aspects of English property law.

2.2.2.1 Subject matter

English law has a wide scope of subject matter of property right. While civil law ownership can only be asserted over tangible things, the subject matter of property right under English law can be over both tangibles and intangibles.[38]

---

[36] RM Goode and E McKendrick, *Goode on Commercial Law* (4th edn, LexisNexis, London 2009) 31.

[37] TG Watkin, 'Changing Concepts of Ownership in English Law during the Nineteenth and Twentieth Centuries' in M Dixon and GLLH Griffiths (eds), *Contemporary Perspectives on Property, Equity and Trusts Law* (Oxford University Press, Oxford 2007); J Hackney, 'Usucapio and the Law of Trusts' in J Getzler (ed) *Rationalizing Property, Equity and Trusts: Essays in Honour of Edward Burn* (Lexis-Nexis UK, London 2003).

[38] J Benjamin, *Interest in Securities: A Proprietary Law Analysis of the*

2.2.2.2 Property over intangible rights

Civil law on rights *in rem* traditionally only admits direct rights over tangibles excluding intangibles given the unavailability of direct control. Intangible rights such as intellectual property rights are governed by special statutes or classical law on rights *in rem* by analogy.[39] English property law has no difficulty in recognising property rights over intangibles such as choses in action, i.e., things to be acquired through action. Choses in action are rights *in personam* against specific individuals but acquire property-like qualities.[40] More accurately choses in action are rights in respect of the property of other legal owners which the law allows the holders of such rights to treat as things in their own right.[41] For example choses in action cover bank deposit, company shares, and debts,[42] and most financial assets.[43] As property rights, choses in action are valid against third party strangers and free of third party interference. Choses in action blur the boundary of rights *in personam* and rights *in rem*.

This is a feature of English property law which is flexible to adapt to the evolution of society. The civil law restriction to rights *in rem* over tangibles makes it ill adapted to modern society where intangibles are of great economic value. Civil law has to adopt an economic ownership conception that someone who in a legal sense is not the legal owner has a right to the value of the thing,[44] by either treating intangible rights in a special regime such as intellectual property rights, or recognising the proprietary effects of an intangible right without admitting it into the *numerus claurus* list of property rights, or by customs on commercial and financial markets, i.e., under *lex mercatoria*.[45]

International Securities Markets (Oxford University Press, Oxford 2000) 318.

[39] JM Milo, 'Property and Real Rights' in JM Smits (ed) *Elgar Encyclopedia of Comparative Law* (Edward Elgar, Chelteham 2006).

[40] JE Penner, *The Idea of Property in Law* (Clarendon Press, Oxford 1997) 108.

[41] ibid 130.

[42] J Benjamin, *Financial Law* (Oxford University Press, Oxford 2007) 341-42.

[43] I MacNeil, *An Introduction to the Law on Financial Investments* (Hart Publishing, Oxford 2005) 8-14; J Benjamin, *Financial Law* (Oxford University Press, Oxford 2007) 25, 441-44.

[44] JH Beekhuis, 'Civil Law' in FH Lawson (ed) *Structure Variations in Property Law* (International Encyclopedia of Comparative Law vol VI Property and Trusts, Chapter 2, JCB Mohe (Paul Siebeck), Tubingen).

[45] JM Milo, 'Property and Real Rights' in JM Smits (ed) *Elgar Encyclopedia of Comparative Law* (Edward Elgar, Chelteham 2006).

2.2.2.3 Beneficial ownership under a trust

A beneficiary under a trust has beneficial ownership over the trust assets. A beneficiary has no direct control over the property but has personal rights against the trustee in respect of the property. A beneficiary's claim against the trustee in respect of the trust asset binds third parties except equity's darling. It is the validity against third parties that makes a beneficiary's interest in the trust asset proprietary.[46]

Civil law with a fundamental distinction of rights in *personam* and rights *in rem* would not allow the split of ownership into the trustee and the beneficiary. [47] Ownership in civil law is axiomatic that an owner has all ownership rights: rights of disposition, management and enjoyment.[48] There is only one ownership which cannot be split.

2.2.2.4 Publicity; title conflicts

Civil law only recognises *rights in rem* over tangibles under classical property law. Property aspects over intangibles or personal claims are governed either by special statutes or classic property law by analogy. There is a strict *numerus clauses* principle. [49] Thus civil law countries often have strict procedures on the creation of property rights to prevent hidden proprietary burden for protecting third parties and transaction safety.[50] This policy is also known as reputed ownership and false wealth that an owner of property subject to hidden burden or encumbrance actually does not own the property. The hidden burden or encumbrance means a personal claim against the owner in respect of the property which is intangible and invisible to third parties, unlike direct possession over tangibles, for example. Out of this fear is born the hostility to the trusts

---

[46] See 2.3 for a full analysis of beneficiaries' proprietary rights under trusts.

[47] J Dalhuisen, *Dalhuisen on Transnational Comparative, Commercial, Financial and Trade Law Volume 2: Contract and Movable Property law* (4th edn, Hart Publishing, Oxford 2010) 315.

[48] DJ Hayton, *The Law of Trusts* (Fundamental Principles of Law, 4th edn, Sweet & Maxwell, London 2003) 8.

[49] J Dalhuisen, *Dalhuisen on Transnational Comparative, Commercial, Financial and Trade Law Volume 2: Contract and Movable Property law* (4th edn, Hart Publishing, Oxford 2010) 281.

[50] PR Wood, *Comparative Law of Security Interests and Title Finance* (2nd edn, Law and Practice of International Finance Series, Sweet & Maxwell, London 2007) 41, 48, 147.

mechanism and strict check over the creation of security interests.

This is not so under English law. Because English law recognises intangible rights as the subject matter of property rights, that is a personal right (which is intangible) in respect of tangible property can be enforceable against third parties other than the obligor, it is reasonable to expect that such property rights cannot be as direct and specific as property rights with direct control over tangibles. English law has no such fear for reputed ownership or false wealth as long as transaction safety can be tackled despite hidden encumbrances on property. Under English law, personal claims in respect of specific property can be recognised as valid against third parties and treated by law as tangible things. The principle of specificity and publicity is less strict as it is more pertinent to tangibles but less pertinent to intangible rights. Although publicity has been regarded as the basis that property rights are public to all and as such can be exerted against the whole world, it is more accurate that that those who know of a right in an asset must respect it. It is the knowledge of the interest that counts.[51]

As long as third parties can be effectively protected against secret property rights in appropriate circumstances, there is nothing wrong for one to deal with the property of another, For example, a beneficiary's claim against a trustee in respect of the trust property is recognised as valid against third parties except equity's darling. Indeed the freedom to create hidden proprietary interests does give rise to conflicts between the proprietary rights but conflicts do not arise everyday and can be resolved. For example if a trustee disposes of the trust asset in breach of trust the beneficiary can recover the trust asset from the transferee except a transferee who has acquired the trust asset in good faith for value without notice of the beneficiary's interest.

2.2.3 Possession and Relative title

2.2.3.1 Possession, no ownership

English law considers mere physical possession or right to possession as worthy of legal protection, without resort to a superior ownership, as Roman law and civil law with Rome law heritage. "The English law of ownership and possession, unlike that of Roman law, is not a system of

[51] ibid 263.

identifying absolute entitlement but of priority of entitlement."[52] It is even commented that English property law can be discussed without any reference to ownership.[53] Possession and right to possess, unlike ownership, is not absolute but relative to each other, and the better title wins.[54] It is in fact true to any legal system that property cannot be absolute, since a system of absolute ownership is equally faced with the problem of sorting out conflicts between competing absolute ownership.[55]

Property under English law is not absolute. Ownership, the highest control of property rights, is considered to be redundant under English law according to authority. Possession is considered to be of paramount importance and title, i.e., right to possession, counts in disputes over a thing. It follows that there is no *vindication* under English law that one can claim as the owner. In *Armory v Delamirie*[56], a boy who found a ring and asked a goldsmith to find its value, was held to be entitled to get back the ring from the goldsmith who refused to return it. The basis was not that the boy had ownership but the boy had possession, which, though did not entitle him to absolute ownership against the true owner, entitled him against the goldsmith's taking away. Possession is recognised and protected by law against interference of third party strangers, but subject to someone with a better right to possess.[57] The emphasis on possession by common law is considered to be a preservation of earlier practices when everything was open to access and possession constituted control against third parties.[58]

Relative title and relative property[59] arise out of practical concerns to protect the status quo of possession and peaceful enjoyment of things, against third party strangers without title but subject to those with better

---

[52] *Waverley Borough Council v Fletcher* [1996] QB 334 (CA) 345 (Auld LJ).

[53] ELG Tyler and NE Palmer, *Crossley Vaines' Personal Property* (5th edn, Butterworths, London 1973) 39; J Gordley, *Foundations of Private Law: Property, Tort, Contract, Unjust Enrichment* (Oxford University Press, Oxford 2006) 50-52.

[54] WW Buckland and AD McNair, revised by FH Lawson, *Roman Law and Common Law: A Comparison in Outline* (1965 reprinted, 2nd edition, Cambridge University Press, Cambridge, 1952) 62-88.

[55] FH Lawson, 'Common Law' in FH Lawson (ed) *Structure Variations in Property Law* (International Encyclopedia of Comparative Law vol VI Property and Trusts, Chapter 2, JCB Mohe (Paul Siebeck), Tubingen).

[56] (1772) 1 Strange 505, 93 ER 664.

[57] W Swadling, 'The Law of Property' in P Birks (ed) *English Private Law* (Oxford English Law, Oxford University Press, Oxford 2000) 220.

[58] JE Penner, *The Idea of Property in Law* (Clarendon Press, Oxford 1997) 149.

[59] D Fox, 'Relativity of Title at Law and in Equity' (2006) 65 CLJ 330.

title. This is a rule for preserving the current situation unless there is dispute. Possession is apparent control and deserves the protection of law as such. This is a pragmatic approach. Property rights bind third party strangers. Actually in reality it is only necessary for property to bind third parties who are concerned and interested, such as competing creditors of an insolvent debtor. It is unnecessary to exaggerate the validity of property right as binding the world as most people are simply not interested.

Relative title follows from the approach to rights by ranking their importance and utility and awarding different legal protection, without attaching to a fundamental *in rem-in personam* dichotomy. On the scale there are rights of property and personal rights. From personal rights to property rights there is no disruption but continuous conversion.[60] Relative title and the legislative and judicial ease with sorting out title conflicts, as well as the limited validity of property rights as good against relevant third party strangers rather than the whole world, greatly facilitate the recognition of rights as property rights. With due protection of relevant third party strangers, there are fewer fears of interfering with the security of transaction by allowing creation of property rights by party autonomy. Economically it contributes to the maximisation of use of things or rights. Then as a guarantee of third party rights and interests, there are rules of protection against abuse of property rights. This is a strategy of first granting freedom and then limiting its adverse consequences rather than limiting freedom from the beginning. For example, in the case of trusts, it opens the possibility to a beneficiary of holding beneficial ownership through a trustee of holding legal ownership, for better management of the asset of the beneficiary, then imposes fiduciary duties on the trustee to guard against misuse of the trust asset by the trustee, and provides solutions where things go wrong, for example, where the trustee wrongfully disposes of the trust asset to a third party. Then loss is to be allocated among the three parties, i.e., the beneficiary, the trustee, and the third party, on the basis of fault. The core idea is to respect the party intention of property relations with legal rules ready to intervene to sort out conflicts with third parties when necessary.

---

[60] S Worthington, *Equity* (Clarendon Law Series, 2nd edn, Clarendon Press, Oxford 2006) 62-63.

2.2.4 Property as a Responsive Remedy

Property law is not an isolated branch of law. It evolves in close interaction with other branches of law, such as contract and tort. People live in a collective community and would not survive isolated. Social situations are intertwined and individual legal categories are artificially created to analyse the complex social situation in a rational and simple way. It follows from the complex and organic whole of social situations that legal categories must interact with each other in a similar way rather than isolated and compartmentalised. Indeed it is suggested that the early idea of ownership and possession was a remedy of criminal law of larceny, and the private law of tort on detinue, trespass, conversion.[61] English law has developed rather by the provision of practical remedies than by the assertion of ideal rights.[62]

The English property law is a good illustration of the progressive evolution of legal rights. Property rights evolved from judicial remedies granted to parties in possession against interferences. Possession is protected *per se*, without resort to an abstract concept of ownership, though only relative, against relevant parties, not absolute. There is no necessity for claiming the property right to be absolute against the world. A party in possession is safe in his title, free from interferences, as long as the party with better title does not appear.

The responsive and remedial property law is in contrast with the civil law proclamation of absolute authority of property law. It is interesting that the civil law formula is an absolute right, free of interference, while the English formula is a passive and responsive remedy valid against interference.

This conforms to the evolution of substantive rights from judicial remedies. The case law system of judge-made law illustrates the development of rights as judicial remedies to interferences. It is not a clear-cut issue which precedes, legal right or judicial remedy, at least under a case law system. The responsive paradigm of property law is preserved, without efforts to establish a rigid codified system of rights *in rem* as in civil law countries, together with the openness and flexibility of the system to admit new property rights.

---

[61] FH Lawson, 'Common Law' in FH Lawson (ed) *Structure Variations in Property Law* (International Encyclopedia of Comparative Law vol VI Property and Trusts, Chapter 2, JCB Mohe (Paul Siebeck), Tubingen) 139-43.
[62] ibid.

Property law illustrates the gradual and progressive nature of English law. It shows the path of the evolution of rights as out of practical responses to real life disputes. It is said that a sweeping contrast between English common law in the mediaeval time (and until now to a large extent) is the "product of judges working in the court system"[63], while Roman law (and civil law countries inheriting the Roman tradition) is "the product of jurists working within the court system".[64] Despite the lack of systemic clarity and coherence in the judge-made law,[65] the approach has its merits of the greater flexibility and readiness to accommodate novel phenomena in the evolution of society. It has no theoretical difficulty in incorporating intangibles as capable of being the subject matter of property right as it does not restrict property right to tangibles. Historically common law only recognised property rights over tangibles but this was changed through equity. For example, English law did not need a reification theory of treating the securities certificates as chattel incorporating the rights against the issuer and then subject shares to the rules on chattel. English law recognises property over intangibles and does not need to give intangibles a physical form to establish property over intangibles. Most securities are registered shares, characterised as choses in action against the issuer, or more exactly an intangible right as a claim against the issuer. [66] Transfer of securities takes effect by the transfer of securities certificates and registration of the transfer with the issuer.[67] Thus the elimination of securities certificates has had mild impact in England than in countries relying on securities certificates as incorporating the rights to securities.[68]

2.2.5 Protection of Property right; Title Conflicts

It is imaginable that title conflicts must be present due to the open and relaxed approach to property rights under English law that property rights can be established rather informally over a great variety of subject matter, which can be indirect and with relative validity. Thus English law must be

[63] A Watson, *Roman Law & Comparative Law* (The University of Georgia Press, Athens 1991) 251.
[64] ibid.
[65] ibid 265.
[66] JE Penner, *The Idea of Property in Law* (Clarendon Press, Oxford 1997) 107-08, 110.
[67] E Micheler, *Property in Securities: A Comparative Study* (Cambridge University Press, Cambridge 2007) 21-25.
[68] ibid 73-74, 85-86.

ready to cope with title conflicts. Firstly the principle is protecting the vested title, i.e., the *nemo dat* rule that no one can transfer more than what he has, subject to common law and statutory carve-outs. There is no general *bona fide* purchaser rule which subjects the ownership of a vested owner to a purchaser as in civil law. There is a preference for vested rights over a purchaser. Secondly due to the great variety of property rights with differing contents and effects priority is given to rights with greater merits under the principle of relative title, for example, the good faith purchaser of legal title overriding a prior equitable title, and better equity between conflicts of equitable title. This is a very individualistic approach which avoids generalisation and decides priority of title or title conflicts based on the individual merits of rights.[69]

2.2.6 Conclusion

Under English law property rights are rights in respect of things between parties, valid against relevant third party strangers. Property rights are relatively fixed but the issue of *numerus clausus* is not strict. It is possible to admit new property rights as long as third parties can be effectively protected. The subject matter capable of being subject to property rights can be tangibles or intangibles. Property rights can be over tangibles or personal rights in respect of tangibles both of which are valid against third parties. Formality on the creation of property rights is relaxed, for example, the requirement of the publicity of property rights. Possession and title, i.e., right to possess, are protected as valid against third parties without resort to a superior right of ownership. Title is not absolute but relative and may be subject to better title. Title conflicts are dealt with preference for vested rights of the same quality as a principle, subject to common law and statutory exceptions. Between rights of different qualities, title conflicts are resolved based on better rights or better equity. The open and flexible English property law is closely related to its flexible case law system as a whole.

2.3 Trust

Trust is a typical combination of personal and proprietary rights under English law. A beneficiary has a personal claim in respect of the trust asset

---

[69] See Chapter Five.

against the trustee, which is valid against third parties. A beneficiary enjoys proprietary interests in this way. This part will try to demystify this eccentric feature of English property law, with an introduction to its personal and proprietary nature; its evolution and transformation from personal rights to proprietary rights; the importance of personal obligations of the trustee in realising the proprietary rights and the proprietary effects against third parities; as well as title conflicts in the trusts context.

2.3.1 Introduction

Trust is a complex relation in respect of property. A trustee is the owner of property or right under a trust, obliged under the trust instrument or operation of law to transmit the benefits from the property or right to the beneficiary. This relation in respect of the trust asset is free of third party intervention and enforceable against third parties. If the trust asset (property or right) is misappropriated by a trustee in breach of trust to a third party, a beneficiary is entitled to claim the property or its substitutes against the third party transferee unless the transferee is a good faith purchaser of legal title for value without notice of the trust.

A trust arises by express intention or operation of law. A settlor transfers assets to a trustee to be held for the benefit of a beneficiary, or declares himself trustee of his own property to be held for a beneficiary. This is express trust. A trust may arise where an express trust fails or where a court holds that since it is unfair for someone to hold the legal title absolutely he should hold the asset for the benefit of someone else. This is implied trust. There are two kinds of implied trusts: resulting trusts and constructive trusts. A resulting trust arises where a transferee is required by equity to hold property on trust for the transferor, or for the person who provided the purchaser money.[70] A constructive trust is imposed where it is unconscionable or inequitable for the owner of property to hold it for his own benefit.[71] An express trust depends on the intention of a settlor. An implied trust by operation of law depends on the fairness in specific situations as appreciated by the courts. Both kinds of trusts reveal the inherently flexible nature of trust. A settlor may decide the scope of rights to be reserved for the beneficiary and the obligations of the trustee to

[70] JE Martin, *Modern Equity* (18th edn, Sweet & Maxwell, London 2009) 251.
[71] D Hayton, P Matthews and C Mitchell, *Underhill and Hayton Law of Trusts and Trustees* (17th edn, LexisNexis Butterworths, London 2007) 74.

guarantee the beneficiary's interests.[72] Courts depend on specific factual situations to find whether an implied trust has arisen.

A trust is a bilateral relation with respect to the trust asset between a trustee and a beneficiary and remains so if the trust is in normal function without breach of trust by the trustee. A trustee deals with third parties as absolute owner. But a beneficiary has a personal claim against the trustee who is obliged to hand to a beneficiary benefits from managing the property and properly perform this primary obligation, as provided for in the trust instrument and law. The personal claim of the beneficiary against the trustee is guaranteed by the trustee obligations to guard the trust asset for the benefit of a beneficiary. Generally the trustees' duties are: to hold the trust property and keep separate from their own property; to safeguard the value of the trust; to administer the trust honestly and impartially for all beneficiaries; to keep accounts of management of the trust asset for inspection by the beneficiaries; to avoid conflicts of their self-interests and interests of the beneficiaries; and to exercise reasonable care and skill.[73] The obligation to turn the benefits to a beneficiary does not affect third parties if a trustee acts properly within his powers and consistent with his obligations as trustee. There is no need for the personal claim of the beneficiary against the trustee and the corresponding trustee obligation to be known to third parties, if parties under the trusts do not want to and the beneficiary's claim against the trustee can be satisfied. It is a personal relation between a beneficiary and a trustee in respect of the trust asset. Breach of trust by a trustee may trigger the proprietary aspect of the trust mechanism. That is where there is a conflict between a transferee of the trust asset and a beneficiary's interest in the trust asset, the beneficiary's claim against the trustee binds the transferee except an equity's darling.[74]

A trust may change into a tripartite relation if the personal claim of a beneficiary cannot be satisfied because a trustee violates his trustee obligations and deals with the trust asset for the benefit of himself rather

[72] Beneficiaries' interests depend upon whether a trust is a bare trust, a fixed trust, or a discretionary trust, a beneficiary is an equitable owner of the specific assets under a bare trust; in the latter two a beneficiary has an interest in the trust fund which is ever- changing but no interest in specific assets, see RM Goode and E McKendrick, *Goode on Commercial Law* (4th edn, LexisNexis, London 2009) 42 and J Mowbray and others, *Lewin on Trusts* (18th edn, Thomson Sweet & Maxwell, London 2008) 15-23.

[73] DJ Hayton, *The Law of Trusts* (Fundamental Principles of Law, 4th edn, Sweet & Maxwell, London 2003) 141-42.

[74] D Waters, 'The Trust in a Changed and Yet Changing World' [2008] JTCP 205.

than the beneficiary, in a way inconsistent with the trustee powers and trustee obligations. It is tripartite in that a beneficiary's claim which is in normal course hidden to third parties is entitled to claim against a defaulting trustee and his transferee as a third party to the trust. It is hidden in the sense that the trustee has the best legal title to the trust asset which is public to all parties concerned while the beneficiary really holds the economic benefit of the trust asset through a personal claim against the trustee. The personal claim is intangible and not visible to outsiders unless after inquiry.[75] Beneficiaries may choose personal or proprietary claims against both the trustee and the third party, depending on which is more favourable in specific circumstances. A beneficiary's interests in the proper performance of the trustee obligations is tied to the trust asset and follows the trust asset and its substitutes, even though misappropriated by a trustee to a third party. A beneficiary's claims against the trustee in the trust asset are valid against third party counterparties to the trustee except a good faith acquirer of legal title to the trust asset for value without notice, known as equity's darling.[76] A beneficiary's interest in the trust asset is thus proprietary in that the claim against the trustee is valid against third party strangers without their consent.

Another tripartite situation is trustee insolvency. The trust asset should be separate from the general asset of a trustee and not available to the general creditors of the trustee. The trust asset is separate and segregated from the asset of a trustee. This assumes critical importance if the trustee falls insolvent as beneficiaries can get the trust asset back ahead of general creditors.

With a trustee holding the legal title as absolute owner and a beneficiary enjoying proprietary claims valid against third party strangers, trust is widely believed to create division of ownership and separate the ownership into the legal owner the trustee and the equitable owner the beneficiary. The so-called double ownership is considered as a typical eccentric feature of common law to civil law systems with the maxim of the unity of ownership. The double ownership is not firmly established as believed however, even within the common law as there are disputes over the beneficiary's interests as personal only against the trustee or proprietary against the world. It is in the final analysis the separation of the

[75] PR Wood, *Principles of International Insolvency* (2nd edn, Law and Practice of International Finance Series, Sweet & Maxwell, London 2007) 279, 286.

[76] FW Maitland, *Equity: A Course of Lectures* (Cambridge University Press, Cambridge 1936, 1969 reprint) 139-40.

incidents of ownership rather than ownership itself.[77] Equitable title or beneficial title may still be used for ease of expression.

2.3.2 Evolution

Trust is a mixture of personal and proprietary rights. A beneficiary has a personal claim against the trustee which is valid against third parties. This can be seen more clearly in the evolution of trusts, which developed from purely personal claims to property as valid against third parties.

Trust started with "use" in land.[78] The general idea is that a relative or friend held the title to land under a duty to hand the benefits to the beneficiaries. It served those who were not allowed to hold property, or not able to properly hold or manage property. It also served to evade burdens on transfer of title. A trustee's obligations were personal in nature in the sense that they could only be exercised against the trustee. If the land or asset went into the hands of third parties there were no proprietary remedies to a beneficiary with respect to the trust asset against the third parties. It should be noted that due to the close personal relations between the trustee and beneficiary, the risk of breach of trust was low. Trustees were often gentlemen of high morality and the office of trustee was considered as recognition of personality and honour.[79] The situation of close community in a local society was a natural deterring factor of breach of trust.

With wider use of trusts, breaches of trust did happen from sporadic to frequent. The Chancery Courts were resorted to for remedies when parties were aggrieved at common law courts. At first the Chancery Courts gave personal remedies only against a trustee, later individual proprietary remedies against a dishonest transferee from a trustee who knew the trust, then general remedies against transferees from trustees except those equity's darling, on the basis that the conscience of a trustee, then the conscience of a dishonest transferee, then the conscience of any transferee except those categorised as equity's darling, were such affected that it would be unfair for them to retain the asset and that they should return the

---

[77] JE Martin, *Modern Equity* (18th edn, Sweet & Maxwell, London 2009) 19-21.

[78] FW Maitland, *Equity: A Course of Lectures* (Cambridge University Press, Cambridge 1936, 1969 reprint) 23-42; JE Martin, *Modern Equity* (18th edn, Sweet & Maxwell, London 2009) 8-12.

[79] For a description of the moral character of the trusts mechanism, see G Watt, *Trusts and Equity* (Oxford University Press, Oxford 2010) 15-16.

asset to the beneficiary. Beneficiaries' remedies gradually evolved from personal to proprietary.

The reasons for the transformation may be found in multiple factors: the emphasis on the conscience and the moral obligation of a trustee and third parties in general, the policy of protecting the beneficiary in a weaker position, the judicial readiness to set a general remedy for easy administration of justice, as well as the competition for jurisdiction between the Chancery Courts and the other courts. Many factors were proper to specific social situations in the specific period of Britain and the responses of equity were accidental. However there is one decisive factor that allowed the development of trusts, i.e., the absence of a clear-cut *in rem-in personam* distinction. This, in part, explains the difficulty in rationalising the trust to civil lawyers entrenched in the doctrinal maxims of the unity of ownership and the dichotomy of personal and proprietary rights.

There was apparent preference towards a beneficiary with little regard to third parties. It is related to the origin of trust in a family context as well as the general tendency to prefer vested rights over third parties under common law, i.e., the *nemo dat* rule. Trusts used to serve the elder and young in the holding of family property. It was often not an active trading trust involved in the ordinary course of commerce and for making profit. This causes problems in later centuries when active management of assets is the purpose rather than static holding of property. It is particularly so when the separation of ownership and management and its flexibility in allocating rights and obligations between the trustee and beneficiary are much exploited in commercial and financial transactions.[80]

2.3.3 Trustee Obligation; Fiduciary Obligation

The personal obligations of the trustee will be examined since the claims of a beneficiary against a trustee and a beneficiary's beneficial interests depend upon the proper performance of trustee obligations.[81]

It is apparent that trustee obligations are at the core of the trust upon

---

[80] D Waters, 'Convergence and Divergence: Civil Law and Common Law' in D Hayton (ed) *Extending the Boundaries of Trusts and Similar Ring-Fenced Funds* (Kluwer Law International, The Hague 2002); see also 5.2.6.

[81] See D Hayton, 'The Irreducible Core Content of Trusteeship' in AJ Oakley (ed) *Trends in Contemporary Trust Law* (Clarenden Press, Oxford 1996).

which a beneficiary's interests and the purpose of the trust depend.[82] Trustee obligations are specified in the trust instrument, limited by default fiduciary duties under equity and statutes.[83] The essence of trustee obligations is to serve the beneficiary's exclusive interests in the trust asset. In general a trustee is obliged to segregate the trust asset from his own asset, manage the trust asset with due diligence and prudence, keep accounts of transactions of the trust asset, and transmit the proceeds from the trust asset to the beneficiary.

Segregation is a basic duty of trusteeship failure of which prevents the constitution of a valid trust,[84] which is enhanced in financial regulation in the FSA Client Asset Source Book Chapter 7. The significance of segregation is highlighted by the recent Lehmans cases.[85] Lehman Brothers International Europe (LBIE) was the principal United Kingdom trading subsidiary of Lehman Brothers Holdings Inc. LBIE provided a wide range of investment services to clients and held considerable amounts of money on behalf of its clients. A central theme of cases after LBIE went into insolvency is to identify and return client assets held by LBIE. It is not an easy task given the complex transaction structures exploring the boundary of rights *in rem* and rights *in personsam*. One issue is whether there is a trust in favour of clients. It is general law that the segregation of house assets and client assets satisfies the certainty of subject matter requirement to establish a valid trust. LBIE is meanwhile

---

[82] *Speight v Gaunt* (1883) 9 App Cas 1 (HL); *Armitage v Nurse* [1998] Ch 241 (CA) 253-54 (Millet LJ); JE Martin, *Modern Equity* (18th edn, Sweet & Maxwell, London 2009) 525-27.

[83] Trustee Act 1925, Trustee Act 2000.

[84] "It is fundamental to the existence of a trust that the trustee is bound to keep the trust property separate from his own and apply it exclusively for the benefit of his beneficiary. Any right on the part of the Defendant to mix the money which he received with his own and use it for his own cash-flow would be inconsistent with the existence of a trust." *Paragon Finance v DB Thakerar & Co* [1999] 1 All ER 400 (CA) 416 (Millett LJ). See also A Al-Attar, 'Client Money' [2009] JIBFL 530.

[85] Relevant key judgements are: *Re Lehman Brothers International (Europe) (in administration), Pearson v Lehman Brothers Finance SA* [2010] EWHC 2914 (Ch), [2010] All ER (D) 232 (Nov); *Re Lehman Brothers International (Europe) (in administration)* [2010] EWCA Civ 917, [2010] All ER (D) 15 (Aug); *Re Lehman Brothers International (Europe) (in administration) (No 2)* [2009] EWCA Civ 1161, [2009] All ER (D) 83 (Nov); *Re Lehman Brothers International (Europe) (in administration) (No 2)* [2009] EWHC 2141 (Ch), [2009] All ER (D) 36 (Nov); *RAB Capital plc v Lehman Bros International (Europe)* [2008] EWHC 2335 (Ch), [2008] BCC 915.

subject to Chapter 7 of the Client Asset Sourcebook, which applies to client money obtained by an investment firm from and for clients for the purposes of its investment business, alongside the general trusts law. What is in dispute is at what point a trust arises, on receipt by LBIE or on actual segregation by LBIE. It has been held that client asset is not limited to monies actually segregated by LBIE but extended to monies appropriated by LBIE for the purpose of paying the indebtedness to clients.[86]

Equity and financial regulation impose fiduciary duties upon the trustee which reinforce the trustee obligations and the beneficiary interests.[87] Fiduciary duties are based on the conscience of trustees in the trustee-beneficiary relationship. A trustee is endowed with legal title visible and public to third parties and actual power over the trust asset, while a beneficiary is at the mercy of the trustee. A trustee is obliged to act for the benefit of the beneficiary but is in a much stronger position. A beneficiary is entitled to the economic benefits from the trust asset but is definitely in a vulnerable position. Trusteeship is a position of reliance which is however vulnerable to abuse. A trustee is vested with legal title because of the reliance placed on him by the settlor while the trustee may abuse the reliance and the dominant position to make profits for himself. Thus equity intervenes on the basis of the conscience of a trustee and prohibits any deviation from the loyalty and fidelity duties to the beneficiary. A trustee is prohibited from making profit from his position as a trustee and breach of this makes the profit to be held by the trustee for the beneficiary.[88] A trustee is obliged to avoid or manage conflict of

---

[86] *Re Lehman Brothers International (Europe) (in administration)* [2010] EWCA Civ 917, [2010] All ER (D) 15 (Aug).

[87] S Worthington, *Equity* (Clarendon Law Series, 2nd edn, Clarendon Press, Oxford 2006) 119-31; E Simpson, 'Conflicts' in P Birks and A Pretto (eds), *Breach of Trust* (Hart Publishing, Oxford 2002).

[88] "It is an inflexible rule of a Court of Equity that a person in a fiduciary position, such as the respondent's, is not, unless otherwise expressly provided, entitled to make a profit; he is not allowed to put himself in a position where his interest and duty conflict. It does not appear to me that this rule is, as has been said, founded upon principles of morality. I regard it rather as based on the consideration that, human nature being what it is, there is danger, in such circumstances, of the person holding a fiduciary position being swayed by interest rather than by duty, and thus prejudicing those whom he was bound to protect. It has, therefore, been deemed expedient to lay down this positive rule." *Bray v Ford* [1896] AC 44 (HL) 51-52 (Lord Herschell). Ses also *Attorney-General for Hong Kong v Reid* [1994] 1 AC 324 (PC); JE Martin, *Modern Equity* (18th edn, Sweet & Maxwell, London 2009) 656.

interests between the beneficiary and himself as well as between beneficiaries.[89] The breach of fiduciary duties is subject to the rule of equitable compensation.

> "The equitable rules of compensation for breach of trust have been largely developed in relation to such traditional trusts, where the only way in which all the beneficiaries' rights can be protected is to restore to the trust fund what ought to be there. In such a case the basic rule is that a trustee in breach of trust must restore or pay to the trust estate either the assets which have been lost to the estate by reason of the breach or compensation for such loss. Courts of Equity did not award damages but, acting in personam, ordered the defaulting trustee to restore the trust estate: see *Nocton v. Lord Ashburton* [1914] A.C. 932, 952, 958, *per* Viscount Haldane L.C. If specific restitution of the trust property is not possible, then the liability of the trustee is to pay sufficient compensation to the trust estate to put it back to what it would have been had the breach not been committed: *Caffrey v. Darby* (1801) 6 Ves. 488; *Clough v. Bond* (1838) 3 M. & C. 490. Even if the immediate cause of the loss is the dishonesty or failure of a third party, the trustee is liable to make good that loss to the trust estate if, but for the breach, such loss would not have occurred: see *Underhill and Hayton, Law of Trusts & Trustees* 14th ed. (1987), pp. 734-736; *In re Dawson, decd.*; *Union Fidelity Trustee Co. Ltd. v. Perpetual Trustee Co. Ltd.* [1966] 2 N.S.W.R. 211; *Bartlett v. Barclays Bank Trust Co. Ltd. (Nos. 1 and 2)* [1980] Ch. 515. Thus the common law rules of remoteness of damage and causation do not apply. However there does have to be some causal connection between the breach of trust and the loss to the trust estate for which compensation is recoverable, viz. the fact that the loss would not have occurred but for the breach: see also *In re Miller's Deed Trusts* (1978) 75 L.S.G. 454; *Nestle v. National Westminster Bank Plc.* [1993] 1 W.L.R. 1260."[90]

Some trustee obligations are considered as so critical that they cannot be subtracted in the trust instrument for the purpose of a valid trust and public policies, known as the "irreducible core of obligations"[91],

> "I accept the submission … that there is an irreducible core of obligations owed by the trustees to the beneficiaries and enforceable by them which is fundamental to the concept of a trust. If the beneficiaries have no rights enforceable against the trustees there are no trusts. …The duty of the trustees to perform the trusts honestly and in good faith for the benefit of

---

[89] *Re Thompson* [1930] 1 Ch 203; JE Martin, *Modern Equity* (18th edn, Sweet & Maxwell, London 2009) 642.

[90] *Target Holdings Ltd v Redferns* [1996] AC 421 (HL) 434 (Lord Browne-Wilkinson).

[91] *Armitage v Nurse* [1998] Ch 241 (CA) 254 (Millet LJ).

the beneficiaries is the minimum necessary to give substance to the trusts, but in my opinion it is sufficient."[92]

The effective enforcement of trustee duties is the key to the realisation of a beneficiary's claim against a trustee. Trustee exemption clauses would generally be supported by the courts except clauses exonerating trustees from the core obligations of trustees,[93] or caused by actual fraud.[94] There are statutory limitations on trustee exemptions clauses. Liability for breach of any obligation (under any rule of law) to take care or exercise skill in the performance of any investment functions, where the function is exercisable by a trustee of a pension trust scheme or by a person to whom the function has been delegated, cannot be excluded or restricted by any instrument or agreement.[95] Any provision of a trust deed of an authorised unit trust scheme is void in so far as it would have the effect of exempting the manager or trustee from liability for failure to exercise due care and diligence in the discharge of his functions in respect of the scheme.[96] Any provision is void in so far as it would have the effect of exempting a trustee of the debenture deed from, or indemnifying him against, liability for breach of trust where he fails to show the degree of care and diligence required of him as trustee, having regard to the provisions of the trust deed conferring on him any powers, authorities or discretions.[97]

2.3.4 Proprietary Remedies

The other of the two aspects of trust: the proprietary side of the trusts will be examined.

Trust is a relation of property. It involves an ownership-management of a fund. A trustee must become the legal owner as against the whole world, including the beneficiary. A trustee is obliged to manage the trust fund for the benefit of a beneficiary or for a purpose. A trust fund must be kept separate from the property of a trustee and ring-fenced against the personal creditors of a trustee. It is said to be a separate patrimony or estate. This feature of trust distinguishes trust from other systems of law: contract, bailment, or agency. Contract creates personal obligations while there is a

---

[92] ibid.

[93] *Walker v Stones* [2001] QB 902 (CA).

[94] *Armitage v Nurse* [1998] Ch 241 (CA).

[95] Pensions Act 1995 s 33(1).

[96] Financial Services and Markets Act 2000 s 253.

[97] Companies Act 2006 s 750(1).

proprietary element in a trust relation. Bailment does not confer legal ownership upon the bailee while a trustee is vested with legal ownership.[98] An agent acting for the principal may or may not deal with property while a trustee deals with third parties as principal with regard to the trust fund.[99] A trustee becomes the legal owner of the trust property but is obliged to deal with the property in a particular way, i.e., not for the benefit of himself, but for the benefit of the beneficiary.

As explained above regarding the obligations of the trustee, a beneficiary's interest in the trust asset depends heavily upon a trustee's proper performance of trustee obligations. A trustee is obliged to keep separate the trust asset and refrain from dealing away the trust fund as his own asset. Where there is breach of duty by a trustee, there are favourable remedies available to a beneficiary. A beneficiary may claim compensation against the trustee or restoration of the trust asset. It is natural and normal in all major legal systems that one puts the asset in the hands of another, has a personal claim against the latter for interests in the asset, and has remedies against the later if the later does not perform duties in respect of the asset. But remedies solely against a trustee are helpless where a trustee dissipates the trust fund and becomes insolvent. And it is in the context of insolvency that a proprietary interest counts most. The strong position of a beneficiary is in the proprietary remedies regarding the trust fund available against third party transferees of the trust fund. A beneficiary's personal claim against a trustee and interests in the trust asset bind the trustee and the whole world except a good faith purchaser for value without notice.

It is the proprietary remedies to a beneficiary to trace the trust fund into the hands of third parties that distinguishes the trust from other similar mechanisms in other legal systems. There is nothing special in depositing one's property with another and benefiting from the management expertise of the other through a contractual arrangement. An owner has personal claims against the other for the redelivery of the asset or for proceeds out of the asset. The other is obliged to segregate the asset from his own and refrain from dealing with third parties as his own asset. The party is also obliged to manage the asset properly. It is similar to the trust relationship as between a beneficiary and a trustee. However there is huge difference when it comes to the breach of duty and the competition between the owner and a third party dealing with the party.

---

[98] JE Martin, *Modern Equity* (18th edn, Sweet & Maxwell, London 2009) 120-22, 189-92.

[99] ibid 51.

A trustee who disposes of the trust property in breach of his core duty is liable to restore the trust property *in specie* or to pay a money substitute. The liability of the money substitute is the objective value of the property which the trustee should have had when the beneficiaries called on him to account for his custody of the trust fund. The trust account is thus falsified to delete the unauthorised disposition of the trust asset.[100] A trustee who carries out an authorised transaction but fails to comply with the duties is liable to make good the loss caused by his breach of duty. The liability is the loss which a beneficiary has suffered. The trustee's account is surcharged with the amount of the beneficiary's loss as if the trustee has received the amount.[101] Where a trustee mixes the trust asset with his own asset the beneficiary is entitled to trace the trust asset into the substitute, by asserting beneficial title or a charge.[102] Equitable interests are enforceable against whoever for the time being holds the trust assets other than someone who is a *bona fide* purchaser for value of the legal interest without notice. [103] Third parties may either be found by the court as constructive trustee and thus obliged to the beneficiary in respect of the trust property, or be found liable as interfering with the beneficiary's interests. In summary there are a great variety of personal and proprietary remedies available both against the trustee and third parties.

English law is different from civil law that the beneficiaries' interests bind third parties except equity's darling in trustee insolvency. Under the German trust-like device a beneficiary enjoys beneficiary's interests in the trust assets, explicitly segregated from the trustee's asset and identifiable under the specificity principle of property rights. The trust asset is severely restricted. Tracing is hardly possible as third parties dealing with the trustee are not obliged to enquire whether the trustee is dealing as trustee. The beneficiary is weak in the face of a third party transferee of the trust asset without notice of the trust as the beneficiary's interests is not visible to third parties while visibility is essential to property under German law. In breach of trust by a trustee, a beneficiary is left with a personal claim against the trustee, rather than proprietary interests.[104]

---

[100] D Hayton, P Matthews and C Mitchell, *Underhill and Hayton Law of Trusts and Trustees* (17th edn, LexisNexis Butterworths, London 2007) 1047.
[101] ibid 1049.
[102] ibid.
[103] *Foskett v McKeown* [2001] 1 AC 102 (HL) 109 (Lord Browne-Wilkinson).
[104] H Kötz, 'The Modern Development of Trust Law in Germany' in D Hayton (ed) *Modern International Developments in Trust Law* (Kluwer Law International, The Hague 1999).

It is the sharp dichotomy of rights *in rem* and rights *in personam* and the policy of protecting third parties that constitute great barriers to granting beneficiaries more and stronger remedies against third parties. As a trustee is vested with ownership the beneficiary has a personal claim against him for the delivery of trust assets and benefit, which, not proprietary, does not bind third parties without notice of the trust. The policy of protecting the security of transactions and acquisition of good title by a good faith third party reinforces this position by denying the beneficiary's interests in the trust asset, which is invisible to third parties. There is case law where it is held that for the sake of fairness the settlor should own the trust asset economically, but not legally.[105] The trust like device in Germany is in essence a contractual arrangement under which a beneficiary suffers from lack of effective remedies if a trustee breaches the trust obligations and thereafter becomes insolvent. The fundamental reason lies in the sharp *in rem-in personam* dichotomy under German law.

2.3.5 Misleading Separation of Ownership

The double ownership and separation of ownership under a trust bewilder civil lawyers entrenched in the unity of ownership. The interest of a beneficiary binding a trustee's creditor and indeed anyone except the equity's darling, i.e., a good faith acquirer for value without notice of the beneficiary interest, again challenges the orthodox distinction of the validity of rights *in rem* or *in personam*. It is noteworthy that it is argued that the incidents of ownership are divided, not ownership. The essence of the property relation under a trust is the division of the incidents of ownership between the trustee and the beneficiary.[106] The beneficiary's share is known as equitable ownership as historically it was only recognised in equity. However, the *in rem* interest of a beneficiary is not as safe as legal title, even under English law *per se*. There have been always disputes over the nature of a beneficiary's interest in the trust asset.[107]

---

[105] ibid.

[106] FW Maitland, *Equity: A Course of Lectures* (Cambridge University Press, Cambridge 1936, 1969 reprint) 29-31; G Watt, *Trusts and Equity* (Oxford University Press, Oxford 2010) 26-30.

[107] T Honoré, 'Trusts: The Inessentials' in J Getzler (ed) *Rationalizing Property, Equity and Trusts: Essays in Honour of Edward Burn* (Lexis-Nexis UK, London 2003); T Watkin, 'Changing Concepts of Ownership in English Law during the Nineteenth and Twentieth Centuries' in M Dixon and GH Griffiths (eds), *Contemporary Perspectives on Property, Equity and Trusts Law* (Oxford

What is true is that a beneficial interest is personal but enforceable against third parties, which is only possible under English property law which does not try to draw a clear line between personal rights from proprietary rights. It is generally accepted that a beneficiary's interest is *in rem* in nature, but indirect through enforcement against a trustee and varying in degree depending upon the category of a trust. In general the beneficiary has an equitable claim against a trustee for the benefit of the proper administration of the trust asset. The allocation of trustee obligation and beneficiary interests can be attuned across a scale,[108] which determines the exact nature of a beneficiary's interest under specific trusts.

2.3.6 Title Conflicts

In the fundamental analysis, the proprietary effects of equitable interests are achieved by a priority rule which gives preference to an equitable interest over a transferee who is not equity's darling, i.e., a good faith purchaser of legal title for value without notice of any prior equitable interest. It reveals the preference for the vested right and the recognition of hidden proprietary rights as binding third parties who have notice of it. The security of transaction is thus achieved as long as parties who have no notice can be protected against the hidden proprietary burden.

2.3.7 Conclusion

Trusts can be established over tangible things and intangible rights, beneficiaries' property interests lie in their claims against the trustees for the benefits from the trust assets, and such beneficiaries' claims against trustees are enforceable against the general creditors of insolvent trustees and third party transferees of misappropriated trust assets by defaulting trustees. Creation of trusts is flexible and informal without much formality as long as some basic requirements, such as the three certainties, can be achieved.[109] There are a great variety of equitable interests which are ranked by their comparative merits.[110] The central idea of trusts is the

---

University Press, Oxford 2007).

[108] D Hayton, 'Exploiting the Inherent Flexibility of Trusts' [1999] JTCP 69.

[109] D Hayton, P Matthews and C Mitchell, *Underhill and Hayton Law of Trusts and Trustees* (17th edn, LexisNexis Butterworths, London 2007) 97; J Mowbray and others, *Lewin on Trusts* (18th edn, Thomson Sweet & Maxwell, London 2008) 83.

[110] See 5.2.3.

beneficiary's claim against the trustee with respect to the trusts asset is valid against third parties except the equity's darling. The personal claims of beneficiaries are meanwhile proprietary. The potential conflicts between the equitable title of a beneficiary and the title of a transferee of the trusts asset are resolved with preference for the prior equitable title while taking into account of the issue of transaction safety, subjecting the prior equitable title to the legal title of equity's darling.

2.4 Title to Intermediated Securities

2.4.1 Legal Title and Equitable Title

Under English law, rights are simply graded continuously on a scale in terms of importance and deserve different legal and judicial protection. Those perceived of greater importance and recognised as valid against third party strangers become property rights. Others are perceived to be better valid only between privies or parties themselves. There are fine boundary areas between the two but nothing absolute. In the proprietary section rights are also graded in greater detail, i.e., legal property and equitable property. However there are major differences between legal title and equitable title in many aspects.

Under English law legal title is a common law concept. Equitable title was created by equity and initially only recognised in the Chancery Courts. Legal title is direct in that an owner is in direct control of the subject matter. Equitable title is indirect in that a holder of equitable title has no direct control over the subject matter but depends on the trustee's control over the subject matter and transfer to the beneficiary of the benefits from the subject matter. Legal title is visible to the world and valid against the world. Equitable title is invisible to third party strangers and subject to legal title. Legal title to moveables enables the owner to sue in conversion. Equitable title to moveables does not enable a holder to sue a third party in conversion, which is a common law remedy unavailable to equity interest.[111] A legal owner can sue in his own name. A holder of equitable title is not entitled to sue a third party without joining the legal owner as a party,[112] except where the equitable title is reinforced by a possessory

[111] *MCC Proceeds Inc v Lehman Bros International (Europe)* [1998] 4 All ER 675 (CA).

[112] ibid; *Performing Right Society Ltd v London Theatre of Varieties Ltd* [1924] AC 1 (HL) 14 (Viscount Cave LC).

title.[113] A possessory title enables a person to claim in negligence for loss caused to him by reason of loss of or damage to property, even though unaccompanied by residual ownership or by possession. It is more than only contractual rights in relation to such property.[114] Creation of equitable title is more formal and strict than creation of legal title. Legal title to chattels is under the protection of the *nemo dat* rule defending an owner against an innocent third party purchaser where a non-owner wrongfully disposes of the legal title. Equitable title is overridden where a trustee disposes of the legal title to a good faith purchaser for value without notice.[115]

2.4.2 Legal Title and Equitable Title to Intermediated Securities

Under the CREST system the operator register of each issue of securities serves as title to each issue of securities. Direct participants are recorded on the operator register of securities they hold. Characterising title to intermediated securities of direct participants of the CREST system (which are actually not intermediated) as legal title and title to intermediated securities of non-participants as equitable title is consistent with reality.[116] Title of direct participants in the CREST system is recorded on the operator register of each issue of securities which are not fundamentally different from holders of certificated registered securities recorded on the issuer register. The Operator does not intermediate or hold title to securities. An issuer knows each direct participant as holder of his issue of securities. The CREST system has a sound authentication infrastructure and admission requirements designed to prevent fraud and guarantee the integrity of title.[117]

On the other hand, title of a holder of intermediated securities other than a direct participant is recorded on his immediate intermediary's book only but commingled with other clients of the intermediary at an upper-tier intermediary. The title of such a holder is only known to his intermediary and his rights and interests to intermediaries are enjoyed by claims against

[113] *International Factors Ltd v Rodriguez* [1979] QB 351 (CA).

[114] NE Palmer, 'Possessory Title' in NE Palmer and E McKendrick (eds), *Interests in Goods* (2nd edn, Lloyds of London Press, London 1998).

[115] E Jenks, 'The Legal Estate' (1908) 24 LQR 147.

[116] See 2.1.

[117] See 2.1.1 for an introduction to the CREST system; see 4.1 and 4.2 for a detailed explanation of the CREST system.

his intermediary in respect of the securities. Title of non-participants of the CREST system enjoys fewer guarantees than title of participants in the CREST system and is more vulnerable to fraud given the involvement of more tiers of intermediaries, as well as the different financial regulation and supervision over the direct participants and non-participants in the system. Direct participants are often subject to strict financial regulation and system admission rules.[118] There are mandatory requirements of message authentication arrangements between direct participants of the CREST system and the Operator in order to guarantee the integrity of title and title transfer.[119] Participants are required to satisfy the standards on participation.[120] The statutory arrangement to guarantee the integrity of title and title transfer is only applicable to the top tier of the CREST system.

A holder of intermediated securities other than a direct participant of the CREST system is believed to enjoy equitable title under a trust. It is different from a holder of certificated securities who deposit the certificates with a custodian. Custody of bearer securities is governed by the law of bailment. Bailment under English law is only applicable to tangibles. Intermediated securities are intangible and incapable of possession which precludes bailment.[121] Trusts allow a trustee to hold intangibles for another. A beneficiary has a personal claim against the trustee in respect of the asset which is valid against third parties.

The position of a beneficiary in the trust asset conforms to the expectations of proprietary interests of investors in intermediated securities. An investor holds through an intermediary securities represented by book entries on securities accounts with the intermediary. An investor depends upon his intermediary to enjoy rights and interests from the underlying securities. Normally an investor only deals with his intermediary without resort to any upper-tier intermediary or the issuer. An investor's title is safe as trust assets against the creditor of his intermediary if his intermediary goes insolvent. An investor may have to deal with an upper-tier intermediary or the issuer if his intermediary is insolvent or misappropriates his securities or does not perform his obligations. This is

---

[118] PR Wood, *Set-off and Netting, Derivatives, Clearing Systems* (2nd edn, Law and Practice of International Finance Series, Sweet & Maxwell, London 2007) 321.

[119] USR 2001 sch 1 and Financial Markets and Insolvency (Settlement Finality) Regulations 1999 SI 1999/ 2979 sch.

[120] For example CREST Terms and Conditions (September 2009) 6.

[121] J Benjamin, *Interest in Securities: A Proprietary Law Analysis of the International Securities Markets* (Oxford University Press, Oxford 2000) 40.

the position of a beneficiary under a trust. Thus an investor has an equitable title in the intermediated securities.

2.4.2.1 Commingling and specificity; co-tenancy

A special feature of the trusts mechanism is its recognition of proprietary rights in a pool of property held by another, or more exactly, of an investor in intermediated securities held by his intermediary for all clients holding the same issue of securities with his upper-tier intermediary, as proprietary rights.[122] The absence of specific securities allocated to an investor on the book of the upper-tier intermediary of his intermediary does not prevent the proprietary rights of the investor, despite that the proprietary rights are equitable and not legal, and as equitable co-tenancy with other clients of his intermediary.[123] The loss of specificity does result in reduced proprietary rights in the sense of co-tenancy subject to the proprietary rights of co-tenants but does not prevent it from being proprietary, which is again only possible under English law which recognises proprietary rights other than absolute property.[124] In case of tiers of intermediaries a final investor has equitable interests under a series of sub-trusts in the underlying securities.[125]

Most legal systems allow an owner to retain ownership in property held by another, for example under a bailment, but the property must be tangible, specific and identifiable in the hands of the bailee. By legal fiction intangibles can be bailed but intangibles must be allocated to a bailor rather than commingled with other bailors. Commingling precludes a bailor's proprietary rights since the bailor has no specific assets to recover.[126] This is the situation in intangible book entry securities held by an intermediary in a commingled account with his upper-tier intermediary

[122] *Re Lehman Brothers International Ltd (2009)* [2009] EWHC 2545 (Ch) [45] (Briggs J); [2009] All ER (D) 313 (Oct).
[123] S Shivji, 'Financial Collateral: Trust Issues in the Administration of Lehman Brothers' [2010] JIBFL 11.
[124] *Re Lehman Brothers International Ltd (2009)* [2009] EWHC 2545 (Ch) [54] (Briggs J); [2009] All ER (D) 313 (Oct).
[125] G Davies, 'Using Intermediated Securities as Collateral: Equitable Interests with Inequitable Results' [2007] JIBFL 70, 72.
[126] D Hayton, 'The Development of the Trust Concept in Civil Law Jurisdictions' [2000] JTCP 159; J Dalhuisen, *Dalhuisen on Transnational Comparative, Commercial, Financial and Trade Law Volume 2: Contract and Movable Property law* (4th edn, Hart Publishing, Oxford 2010) 291-92.

for all clients holding the same issue of securities. An investor can only be a creditor with personal claims against his intermediary for the return of equivalent securities, not valid against the creditor of his intermediary in case of intermediary insolvency or against a transferee in case of intermediary misappropriation of client assets. Thus in legal systems with absolute ownership or property, legislative intervention is necessary to assert that investors have co-ownership in intermediated securities held in commingled accounts, which are not absolute ownership as ownership over tangibles, but a special kind of ownership subject to the rights of co-owners and dependent upon the intermediary.[127]

Under legal systems with the specificity requirement of property right, an investor holding securities through an intermediary who holds the same issue of securities of all clients in one securities account loses property because of the loss of specificity of subject matter and is reduced to a general creditor against the intermediary. It is rare in advanced financial markets that an intermediary holds specific securities for one client in individual accounts in his own book and his upper-tier intermediary without commingling the same issue of securities of all clients in one omnibus account with his upper-tier intermediary. In this way the property of an investor to securities is safe but no advantage can be taken of the fungible nature of book entries and the economy of scale.[128] The problem of civil law with recognising the property in intermediated securities held with an intermediary is the guiding principle of property law of specificity and visibility to third parties over tangibles only, for the sake of third party protection and security of transaction. Often the subject matter must be ascertainable and specific and present, capable of identification and appropriation, to avoid disputes over what are subject to property rights, as it is often vital in critical circumstances such as insolvency. The principle of visibility and publicity follows from and in turn reinforces the principle of specificity by dictating that property must be visible and public to third parties. Hidden proprietary interests such as equitable title are hardly recognised under such a principle. An intermediary holds the securities accounts and appears as owner to third parties, which is an apparent fact which cannot be denied.

It is the absolute supremacy of property that prevents any weakened ownership and makes it hard to accommodate intermediated securities.

---

[127] Such as Belgium and Luxembourg, see 1.4.

[128] Such as convenience of operation for the intermediaries, greater opportunities of dealing with large number of securities and resulting price advantages.

Property or ownership is absolute and must be specific and direct, i.e., over specific securities and exercisable by the owner rather than through an intermediary appearing to be the owner to strangers. On the other hand the property in intermediated securities is not expected to be of such absolute nature due to operational and economic realty. It is fine that all clients with one intermediary holding the same issue of securities enjoy co-ownership in the pool of securities held by the intermediary for all clients. Clients enjoy interests not in specific securities but in proportion to their contribution. And most critically the client assets are not part of the asset of an intermediary and should be insulated from the general creditors of the intermediary if the intermediary becomes insolvent.

Civil law strives to recognise property rights in intangibles held with another by legal fiction but cannot recognise property rights in unallocated intangibles held with another. No co-ownership is available in this context except by statutory intervention. English law is ready to recognise property rights in intangibles held with another under trusts. Trusts always recognise several beneficiaries' property interests in the trust asset in the hands of their trustee under a non-bare trust, which is a co-ownership in the pool of the changing asset, which is not an interest *in specie* in any fixed asset.[129] This is voluntary co-ownership where beneficiaries agree to be co-owners. There is some uncertainty in the case of investors in intermediated securities. An investor has intermediated securities commingled by the intermediary with other clients holding the same issue of securities. An investor cannot have property interest in specific securities since one cannot have property interests in a specific part of a pool of assets without specific allocation to him.[130] There are arguments for implied consent to co-ownership over the intangible intermediated securities, akin to tangibles which are dealt with under statutes and case law. The Sales of Goods Act 1979 ss 20A and 20B establish that a prepaying buyer of part of a bulk of goods is a co-owner in the bulk together with other buyers. In *Re Stapylton Fletcher Ltd*[131], customers paid wine dealers for delivery of wine, wine dealers segregated the wine for delivery from house stock but did not allocate the wine to individual customers, the customer were held to be co-owners over the wine

[129] RM Goode, 'The Nature and Transfer of Rights in Dematerialised and Immobilised Securities' [1996] JIBFL 167.

[130] *Re London Wine Co (Shippers) Ltd* [1986] PCC 121, 137 (Oliver J).

[131] *Re Stapylton Fletcher Ltd (in administrative receivership); Re Ellis Son & Vidler Ltd (in administrative receivership)* [1994] 1 WLR 1181 (Ch).

segregated. There is support for extending the co-tenancy analysis on tangibles to intangibles.[132] The courts have adopted a different approach by distinguishing tangibles and intangibles holding that segregation is inapplicable to intangibles. In *Hunter v Moss*[133], the settlor declared an oral trust over 50 shares in a company in which the settlor owned 950 of the 1,000 issued shares. It was held that the requirement of certainty of subject matter was satisfied.

> "However, since all the shares were of one class in one company and were of such a nature as to be indistinguishable from one another they were all equally capable of satisfying the trust. The owner of shares in a company could declare himself trustee of a specified number of shares in the company, which would be effective to give a beneficial proprietary interest to the beneficiary under the trust and no question of a blended fund would thereafter arise."[134]

This analysis has been followed in *Re Harvard Securities*[135] and *Re CA Pacific Finance Ltd*[136]. It is current law but not without criticism.[137] A challenge from the practical perspective is the failure of the court to address the possibility that the settlor could have proceeded to dispose of 50 shares despite the oral declaration. There was no way to decide whether the 50 shares disposed of belonged to the trust or the settlor.[138] But this approach is current law.

A third approach proposed by Professor Goode is that all holders of securities of the same issue are co-owners as securities of one issue is an indivisible bulk.[139]

---

[132] Law Commission, 'The UNIDROIT Convention on Substantive Rules regarding Intermediated Securities: Further Updated Advice to HM Treasury (May 2008)' [2.63]-[2.65].

[133] [1994] 3 All ER 215 (CA).

[134] ibid 215 (Dillon, Mann and Hirst LJJ).

[135] [1997] 2 BCLC 369 (Ch).

[136] [2000] 1 BCLC 494.

[137] Law Commission, 'The UNIDROIT Convention on Substantive Rules regarding Intermediated Securities: Further Updated Advice to HM Treasury (May 2008)' [2.66]-[2.67].

[138] K Gordon, 'The Certainties of Trust' [2006] TM 218.

[139] R Goode, 'Are intangible assets fungible' [2003] LMCLQ 379.

2.4.2.2 Intermediated securities as equitable title under trusts

It is surprising to find that the trust mechanism conforms to these expectations of proprietary interests in intermediated securities in an amazing way. It admits all kinds of interest, legal or equitable, tangible or intangible, as subject matter under a trust.[140] The trust asset, or more accurate the trust fund, consisting of the original trust assets and from time to time added to the trust asset and substitutes, is an ever changing pool of assets.[141] So a trust can be established over a changing pool of intermediated securities held by an intermediary for all clients. Investors enjoy beneficial or equitable interests in proportion to intermediated securities held by their intermediary in a commingled account, rather than in specific intermediated securities in the pool of trust fund.[142] The intermediated securities held for clients by an intermediary are a trust fund, which is a separate asset from the asset of the intermediary and immune from the general creditors of the intermediary. This is crucial when the trustee is insolvent.[143]

It is well established that the indirect holding model has taken root and proprietary interests are inevitably affected in apparent ways. Trust is a ready and effective mechanism for recognising the proprietary interests in intermediated securities. Thus investors' interests in intermediated securities are normally characterised as beneficial interests under trusts under English law.

> "There is nothing unusual or surprising in the creation of a structure of trusts and sub-trusts between the legal owner and ultimate beneficial owner in relation to intermediated securities. As Mr Moss submitted it is the very basis upon which the modern system for the intermediation of securities works. Thus, ignoring Rascals and the NNA for the moment, where LBIE settled into its depot account a security acquired for the book of an affiliate, with the intent that the affiliate should have a proprietary interest in it, there necessarily existed a structure of trust and sub-trust, pursuant to which LBIE has a proprietary interest as against its depository (which holds the legal rights) and the affiliate has a proprietary interest as against LBIE. Under that structure the depository recognises LBIE as its beneficiary and in turn LBIE recognises the affiliate as its beneficiary."[144]

---

140 J Mowbray and others, *Lewin on Trusts* (18th edn, Thomson Sweet & Maxwell, London 2008) 36, 39-41.

141 J Benjamin, *Financial Law* (Oxford University Press, Oxford 2007) 490-91.

142 M Yates and G Montagu, *The Law of Global Custody* (3rd rev edn, Tottel Publishing, London 2009) 34.

143 V Tyrell, 'Client Monies: The CASS Rules under Scrutiny' [2010] JIBFL 520.

144 *Re Lehman Brothers International (Europe) (in administration); Pearson v*

As a beneficiary an investor is guaranteed proportional proprietary interests in the securities pool held by the intermediary for all clients and the client holding is not the asset of the intermediary even if the intermediary goes insolvent. Admittedly it is equitable proprietary interests, in many ways weakened compared with holders of certificated securities. Holders of certificated bearer securities have title to specific securities represented by certificates, visible to the world. Holders of certificated registered securities have legal title over specific securities represented by the issuer register, visible to all the world, directly exercisable against the issuer. Holders of intermediated securities have proportional title as co-tenants to securities held by their intermediaries in commingled accounts with the upper-tier intermediaries of their intermediaries. Most investors have to use an intermediary despite the possibility of holding securities certificates under English law[145] due to cost and efficiency. A natural consequence is to accept the proprietary interests in a somewhat weakened way. In normal course the interests are personal claims against the intermediary for the benefits of the securities, not against the issuer or any upper-tier intermediary, and its proprictary aspect of the personal claims revive to be enforceable against the general creditors as proprietary when the intermediary goes into insolvency. And indeed the beneficial interests are consistent with market practices that an investor's proprietary interests are modified or weakened, in that they are proportional, normally only enforceable against their intermediary.[146]

While the US, Canada and Switzerland create a new concept of security right combining personal and proprietary interests of an investor against his intermediary and Belgium and Luxembourg adopt special

Lehman Brothers Finance SA [2010] EWHC 2914 (Ch) [397] (Briggs J); [2010] All ER (D) 232 (Nov).

[145] USR 2001 sch 1rule 18.

[146] However there are different views in favour of legal title achieved under bailment through legal fiction by which an investor at any tier of the holding chain enjoy legal title to securities, see A Beaves, 'Global Custody-A Tentative Analysis of Property and Contract' in N Palmer and E McKendrick (eds), *Interests in Goods* (2nd edn, Lloyds of London Press, London 1998); MF Khimji, 'Intermediary Credit Risk-a Comparative Law Analysis of Property Rights in Indirectly Held Securities' [2005] JBL 287, 323; under English law, bailment is limited to tangibles while trust has no such limitation on the subject matter; a bailor retains legal title under bailment; a beneficiary has only equitable title, for the difference between title under bailment and trust, see D Hayton, P Matthews and C Mitchell, *Underhill and Hayton Law of Trusts and Trustees* (17th edn, LexisNexis Butterworths, London 2007) 67.

statues to create statutory co-ownership over intermediated securities,[147] there has been up to now no legislative intervention as to the property issues in respect of intermediated securities, except as regards the top tier of title of electronic holding system. English law has had a trusts mechanism generally competent to cope with the property issue in respect of intermediated securities.[148] The US and Canada adopt the new security entitlement concept. Switzerland describes an investor's rights in intermediated securities as a new kind of property, i.e., personal or corporate rights against an issuer which are credited to a securities account, and may be disposed of by the account; effective against the custodian and any third party and beyond the reach of other creditors of the custodian.[149] These are statutory confirmation of an investor's rights in intermediated securities by describing the personal and proprietary aspects of an investor's rights. Belgium and Luxembourg modify traditional legal concepts to accommodate an investor's rights in intermediated securities. The similarity between all these approaches and English law is the aim to meet investors' expectations of property interests in intermediated securities in a changed market from the direct holding of certificated securities to the indirect holding of uncertificated securities. US, Canada and Switzerland adopt a single code on intermediated securities for clarity and simplicity, as well as for avoiding inconsistency between current law and the market expectations. Belgium and Luxembourg try to incorporate intermediated securities into the current legal framework. English law also seeks to incorporate intermediated securities into the current legal framework which is generally satisfactory despite uncertainty on details.[150]

2.4.3 Title Conflicts

One issue is title conflicts between holders of intermediated securities. Intermediated securities held by intermediaries are vulnerable to intermediary misappropriation despite financial regulation and other deterrents. It is not a new problem and has been present in trusts mechanisms when a trustee

---

[147] See 1.4 for an analysis of these national law reforms.

[148] This is even recognised internationally, for example see L Thévenoz, 'New Legal Concepts regarding the Holding of Investment Securities for a Civil Law Jurisdiction – The Swiss Draft Act' [2005] Rev dr unif 301, 305.

[149] Swiss FISA art 3.

[150] Financial Markets Law Committee, 'The FMLC Report on Property Interests in Indirectly Held Investment Securities: An Analysis of the Need for and Nature of Legislation in the UK' [2005] Rev dr unif 339.

defaults and misappropriates the trust asset. Thus conflicts arise between a prior hidden equitable title and a legal or an equitable title of a transferee of the trust asset. Equity has a general favour for a prior equitable title over a subsequent equitable title, the same as common law, and only subjects a prior equitable title to a subsequent legal title of a good faith acquirer without notice of the equitable title due to the commercial needs of transaction safety. Once characterised as equitable title, title conflicts with regard to intermediated securities are subject to the priority rules on equitable interests. Meanwhile since intermediated securities held by direct participants in the CREST system are characterised as legal title, title conflicts with regard to intermediated securities involves the complexity of priority rules between legal title, between legal title and equitable title, and between equitable title. Resolution of title conflicts under English law is in principle in favour of the vested right and more particularly of equitable interests, as a result of the origin of trusts as a benevolent mechanism for caring the weak and the fiduciary nature of the trustee-beneficiary relation. This tendency is not consistent with market demands of a high degree of transaction security and finality in intermediated securities. The issue of title conflicts will be dealt with in the following Chapters.

2.5 Conclusion

English law has no theoretical barrier to recognising proprietary rights of an investor in intermediated securities, represented by intangible book-entries on books of his intermediary, in a commingled account with the upper-tier intermediary of his intermediary. The trusts law has always recognised the equitable title of a beneficiary against the trustee under a trust with respect to trust assets, tangible and intangible. Analysis of property issues in the context of intermediated securities under English property law and trusts law is generally satisfactory despite uncertainty in specific issues. One issue is title conflicts in respect of intermediated securities, which will be the theme of the rest of this Book.

CHAPTER THREE

TITLE AND TITLE CONFLICTS IN RESPECT OF CERTIFICATED SECURITIES

Conflicts of title to certificated securities will be given as background to the discussion on uncertificated securities. Title to certificated securities is legal title. Firstly the general law on conflicts between legal title to chattels is introduced: the *nemo dat* principle and the common law estoppel, and statutory carve-outs will be briefly introduced. Secondly the transfer of bearer and registered securities will be analysed. Thirdly negotiability of bearer securities will be analysed from its evolution, policy, requirement, to the influence of common law estoppel and commercial customs. Fourthly, title conflicts in respect of registered securities will be presented, from the perspective of true owner-issuer relation, issuer-transferee, and true owner-transferee relation, and the major role of estoppel.

3.1 Conflicting Legal Title to Chattel

The principle of *nemo dat* on title to chattel will be introduced, with common law estoppel as an exception to the *nemo dat* maxim, as well as statutory carve-outs of the *nemo dat* maxim. It is a frequent occurrence that a non-owner transfers the property against the intention of a true owner to an innocent transferee. Title conflicts are between claims to full legal title. It is an issue of who wins at the loss of another,[1] basically an issue of priority.[2]

---

[1] AP Bell, *Modern Law of Personal Property in England and Ireland* (Butterworths, London 1989) 459.

[2] RM Goode and E McKendrick, *Goode on Commercial Law* (4th edn, LexisNexis, London 2009) 61.

3.1.1 *Nemo Dat Quod Non Habet*

Conflicts for title arise between a true owner and a purchaser who gets title from a fraudulent third party. The safety of title and safety of transaction can only be compromised in one way or another, i.e., favouring either a true owner or a subsequent purchaser.[3] English law has always chosen to favour a true owner. The *nemo dat quod non habet* maxim always remains the rule, namely no one can transfer a better title than he himself has. It presupposes something to be owned or ownership. It is thus generally applicable to chattels or chose in possession subject to limited common law and statutory exceptions. A prior issue is the mechanism of transfer of title, and the relation between a contract of transfer and the transfer of title, though it is not a decisive factor in the resolution of title conflicts.

Under English law, when a contract of sale of chose in possession is made, transfer of title may be constituted, even before delivery happens. A defective contract affects the transfer and may reverse the title to the seller even where the goods have been sold to another by the buyer. This is the consensual and causal approach on the transfer of tangibles, i.e., an agreement to transfer title and the transfer of title depends on the contract of transfer for validity, in opposition to the tradition and abstract approach, i.e., transfer of title is constituted on delivery of chattel and transfer of title is independent of the contract to transfer as regards validity.[4] It is not settled whether a transferee derives title from the true owner, or the transferor, or a fresh title distinct from previous title.[5] However, whether a transferee gets a derivative title or a fresh title does not determine whether a transferee gets good title or not.

The *nemo dat* rule grows out of the effect of property rights of binding third party strangers without their consent. The solemnity of property rights and the policy of protecting vested property rights are entrenched in English law. Meanwhile with the development of commerce, case law and

---

[3] This is so in the classical thinking on tangibles though it is different in the case of claims such as registered securities, where there are three parties to allocate the loss, the issuer, the true owner and the purchaser, see 3.4; there are also suggestions that successive purchasers of goods may be involved in loss allocation.

[4] RM Goode and E McKendrick, *Goode on Commercial Law* (4th edn, LexisNexis, London 2009) 216-20; Lv Vliet, 'The Transfer of Moveables in Scotland and England' (2008) 12 Edin L Rev 173, 173.

[5] RM Goode and E McKendrick, *Goode on Commercial Law* (4th edn, LexisNexis, London 2009) 62.

statutes have established exceptions to the *nemo dat* rule out of concerns of protecting the security of transaction. The exceptions to the *nemo dat* rule are generally based on estoppel under which a true owner is estopped by his own act from asserting his title against an innocent purchaser. The position is that *nemo dat* is the rule, and protection of good faith third party purchasers is exceptional. It is the opposite position in civil law countries such as France and Germany where protection of third party purchasers in good faith is the rule (the *bona fide* purchaser rule) and only exceptionally legal tile of the true owner prevails.[6] This is an interesting point that legal title which is conceptually less solemn enjoys a higher degree of protection under English law while legal ownership which is conceptually solemn and supreme enjoys less protection under civil law systems.

3.1.2 Common Law Exceptions to *Nemo Dat*; Estoppel

"'Estoppel' has been described as a principle of justice and of equity which prevents a person who has led another to believe in a particular state of affairs from going back on the words or conduct which led to that belief when it would be unjust or inequitable (unconscionable) for him to do so. The person making the statement, promise or assurance is said to be estopped from denying or going back on it; 'estopped' means 'stopped'."[7] It is considered as one of the most flexible and useful doctrines of the law.[8]

The exceptions are based on the thinking that an owner of legal title who contributes to a false impression to a third party that someone else is the legal owner or has the authority to dispose of the legal title must be subject to the title of the third party purchaser. This is known as the principle of apparent authority or apparent ownership. It is argued the latter is an enhanced one of the former while there is no fundamental difference.[9] It is based on the principle of estoppel that a true owner is prevented from

---

[6] E McKendrick, 'Sale of Goods' in P Birks (ed) *English Private Law* (Oxford University Press, Oxford 2000) 236.

[7] W Blair, 'Negotiability and Estoppel' (1988) 3 JIBL 8; *Halsbury's Laws of England* (vol 16, 4th edn reissue, LexisNexis, London 2003) [951]; P Feltham, D Hochberg and T Leech, *Spencer Bower The Law Relating to Estoppel by Representation* (4th edn, LexisNexis, London 2004) 3.

[8] *Halsbury's Laws of England* (vol 16, 4th edn reissue, LexisNexis, London 2003) [951]; E Cooke, *The Modern Law of Estoppel* (Oxford University Press, Oxford 2000) 1-2.

[9] RM Goode and E McKendrick, *Goode on Commercial Law* (4th edn, LexisNexis, London 2009) 457.

denying the title of a good faith purchaser by his representation or conduct to the purchaser that the seller is the owner. For chattels possession is *prima facie* evidence of title. Therefore an owner parting with possession may be subject to scrutiny whether his act creates a false impression to a third party purchaser that someone else in possession of chattel is the owner or has the authority to dispose of the chattel. However a court is cautious about finding apparent authority on merely leaving possession in another and something more than parting with possession must be shown.[10] The persuasive argument that "whenever one of two innocent persons must suffer by the acts of a third, he who has enabled such third person to occasion the loss must sustain it,"[11] has never found favour in English law which does not impose on owners a duty to safeguard their property rights in this way. Furthermore, it has been held that negligence is not sufficient and a true owner must have done something which misleads others into the belief that someone other than the true owner has the authority.

An owner who colludes with another to allege the other to appear as owner cannot deny the title of the latter to a good faith third party. This is estoppel by representation which is rarely relevant in the case of an innocent owner. An owner may be blamed for negligence and estoppel may arise by conduct, which is however difficult to establish. Negligence of a principal which creates opportunities for an agent to misappropriate the property is not sufficient to create estoppel against the principal. The principal must have done some act which actually misleads a party to believe that another is the owner.[12] Simply leaving the chattel in the possession of another does not impose an estoppel on the true owner. Giving documents equivalent to or representing title plus possession normally enhances the argument for establishing an estoppel against a true owner.[13]

---

[10] *Central Newbury Car Auctions Ltd v Unity Finance Ltd* [1957] 1 QB 371 (CA); F Reynolds, 'Agency and Representation' in P Birks (ed) *English Private Law* (Oxford University Press, Oxford 2000) 186-88; E McKendrick, 'Sale of Goods' in P Birks (ed) *English Private Law* (Oxford University Press, Oxford 2000) 236-37; J Ulph, 'Conflicts of Title and the Obligations of the Seller' in E McKendrick (ed) *Sale of Goods* (LLP, London 2000) 285; KR Handley, *Estoppel by Conduct and Election* (Sweet & Maxwell, London 2006) 61-63.

[11] Dictum of Ashurst J in *Lickbarrow v Mason* (1787) 2 Term Rep 63, 70; 100 ER 35, 40.

[12] *Bank of Ireland v Evans' Charities Trustees in Ireland* (1855) 5 HL Cas 389, 10 ER 950.

[13] RM Goode and E McKendrick, *Goode on Commercial Law* (4th edn,

3.1.3 Statutory Exceptions

In response to the common law caution on establishing estoppel against the true owner and preference for the true owner which hinders commerce, statutes have intervened to provide greater protection and legal certainty to parties in commerce where commercial agents dealing with others' property are regularly in possession of the property of others, transaction is frequent, and safety of transaction is crucial. The difficulty of establishing estoppel against the true owner under common law has been relieved to some extent by the Factors Act 1889, Hire Purchase Act 1964, and Sales of Goods Act 1979.[14] These statutes cover typical persons regularly in possession of the property of others, i.e., mercantile agents, purchasers in hire purchase, sellers in possession after title passes to buyers, and buyers in possession with title retained by sellers. The rationale is that a non-owner in possession with the consent of the owner can transfer good title to a good faith purchaser for value without notice. These statutes are statutory confirmation of title by estoppel under common law where estoppel arises against an owner who holds out another as with authority to deal with property or as owner of property and confers title upon a purchaser.

Statutory intervention is piecemeal and fragmented and the courts remain reluctant to extend the protection for a purchaser outside the statutory sphere.[15] The tradition of preferring the true owner continues to dominate.

Resolution of title conflicts is by nature an issue of priority of deciding which title prevails, the true owner or a purchaser, both innocent, as victims of third party fraud. The principle is the *nemo dat* maxim in favour of the true owner. The policy of third party protection and transaction safety is achieved by estoppel in common law, which is limited and difficult to establish. Statutory exceptions in favour of a purchaser over a true owner are mainly in commercial contexts, based on estoppel in response to commercial needs of transaction safety.

LexisNexis, London 2009) 451-58.

[14] Factors Act 1889; Hire Purchase Act 1964 pt iii; Sales of Goods Act 1979 s 21.

[15] J Ulph, 'Conflicts of Title and the Obligations of the Seller' in E McKendrick (ed) *Sale of Goods* (LLP, London 2000) 173; J Ulph, M Tugendhat and J Glister, *Commercial Fraud, Civil Liability, Human Rights and Money Laundering* (Contract Law Library, Oxford University Press, Oxford 2006) 655-56.

3.2 Title, Title Transfer, and Title Conflicts in Respect of Certificated Securities

Title and the title transfer mechanism of certificated bearer securities and registered securities and their legal characterisation will be examined, plus some general remarks on title conflicts in respect of certificated securities.

3.2.1 Title and Transfer of Title to Securities

Bearer securities are documentary intangibles title to which is the certificate. In the case of registered securities, a duly issued certificate is *prima facie* evidence of title to the security, and the issuer is subject to estoppel rules as against anyone believing the statement to be true and has acted upon the belief to his detriment.[16] However certificates are only *prima facie* title to securities and the *prima facie* title conferred by certificates is liable to be defeated by better title.[17] Entry on the issuer register is the best title available to registered securities under English law,[18] notwithstanding also referred to as *prima facie* title. It should be remembered that under English property law there is no such thing as absolute ownership as the civil law tradition and the English property law only knows relative title.[19] This is akin to chose in possession where possession confers title which is relative and may be subject to the prior possessor or someone with a better title.[20]

The position that a certificate is *prima facie* title to registered securities, and entry on the issuer register is further *prima facie* title is true with all registered securities, despite minor differences in the validity of certificate or register.[21] For example, an entry on a register of government securities

[16] Companies Act 2006 ss 768, 769, 770; BM Hannigan, *Companies* (LexisNexis UK, London 2004) 379.
[17] *Longman v Bath Electric Tramways Ltd* [1905] 1 Ch 646 (CA) 667(Lord Stirling LJ).
[18] *Société Générale de Paris v Walker* (1884) 14 QBD 424; Company Act 2006 s 768.
[19] D Fox, 'Relativity of Title at Law and in Equity' (2006) 65 CLJ 330, 331.
[20] See Chapter One on property.
[21] Local Authority (Stocks and Bonds) Regulations 1974 SI 1974/519 reg 6; Government Stock Regulations 2004 SI 2004/1611 regs 8, 9; Companies Act 2006 s 769.

kept by the Bank of England confers more than merely *prima facie* title,[22] but closer to conclusive title, while an entry on a company register of debentures is more of a *prima facie* nature. This is rooted in the effect of public notice of the issuer. It is the same with the evidential effect of certificates. A certificate of debenture issued by a company is more informal and the *prima facie* title it represents is easier to be rebutted.[23] Discussion on registered securities in this chapter is mainly based on the law regarding shares which are the most common registered securities. They are generally applicable to other registered securities.

3.2.2 Legal Nature of Title Transfer; Assignment or Novation; Transfer of Equitable title

As mentioned above, securities are by nature choses in action, i.e., a bundle of rights against the issuer. Choses in action were not assignable in common law but were assignable in equity or under the law merchant. Bearer securities were made transferable under the law merchant. Bearer securities are transferred by the delivery of certificates. The form of transfer of registered securities is laid down in statutes,[24] however the nature of transferring registered securities has never been clarified in law. Available analysis is assignment or novation. Most commentators support the novation analysis.[25]

Assignment is a unilateral transfer of a debt by an assignor to an assignee without the involvement of a debtor. A debt is considered to be the same in the hands of an assignor and an assignee. The common law had prohibited assignment in order to prevent trafficking in claims and protect debtors until statutory intervention which required the form in writing and giving notice to the debtor.[26] This is known as legal

[22] *Davis v Bank of England* (1824) 2 Bing 393, 130 ER 357; *Bank of England v Culter* [1908] 2 KB 208.

[23] Companies Act 2006 s 769.

[24] For example, Companies Clauses Consolidation Act 1845 ss 14, 46; Stock Transfer Act 1963; Local Authority (Stocks and Bonds) Regulations 1974 SI 1974/519; and Government Stock Regulations 2004 SI 2004/1611 Pt 3.

[25] J Benjamin, *Interest in Securities: A Proprietary Law Analysis of the International Securities Markets* (Oxford University Press, Oxford 2000) 70; E Micheler, 'Farewell Quasi-Negotiability? Legal Title and Transfer of Shares in a Paperless World' [2002] JBL 358, 360.

[26] Law of Property Act 1925 s 136.

assignment.[27] Before legal assignment was available, assignment of legal claims was available in equity. An assignee is subject to equities against the assignor.[28] This is the same with the civil law principle of *assignatus utitur jure auctoris* under which an assignee is subject to the equities and defences available to the debtor against the assignor. The policy is to keep the position of the debtor unchanged.[29]

Novation is another way for transferring contractual claims. A contract between a creditor and a debtor is replaced by a contract between a new creditor and the debtor on identical terms. Novation was an alternative for transferring choses in action when legal assignment was not available. Its advantage is that a transferee actually gets a new claim independent of the claim of a transferor, which is theoretically conducive to cutting off prior equities against the prior creditor. Novation requires the participation of an obligor, which is not a hurdle in the case of registered securities, as registration can be seen as consent of an issuer.[30]

Assignment and novation are designed to facilitate the transferability of claims but in limited ways. The personal creditor-debtor relationship cannot be totally ignored and claims cannot be treated in exactly the same way as chattels.[31] The debtor is involved in an assignment as he has to perform to another party and he may have an extra burden for such change in performance.[32] Thus due consideration has to be taken into account of the debtor which prevents the full transferability of claims as chattels. Novation is more favourable if the issue of debtor consent can be tackled. Securities are a special kind of choses in action since the value of securities lies in their ready transferability and liquidity while the debtor-

---

[27] J Benjamin, *Interest In Securities: A Proprietary Law Analysis of the International Securities Markets* (Oxford University Press, Oxford 2000) 65-66.
[28] ibid 66.
[29] B Lurger, 'Assignment' in JM Smits (ed) *Elgar Encyclopedia of Comparative Law* (Edward Elgar, Cheltcham 2006); J Dalhuisen, *Dalhuisen on Transnational Comparative, Commercial, Financial and Trade Law Volume 2: Contract and Movable Property law* (4th edn, Hart Publishing, Oxford 2010) 399-400.
[30] *Damon Cia Naviera SA v Hapag-Lloyd International SA, The Blankenstein, The Bartenstein, The Birkenstein* [1985] 1 All ER 475 (CA); J Benjamin, *Interest in Securities: A Proprietary Law Analysis of the International Securities Markets* (Oxford University Press, Oxford 2000) 64; HG Beale and others (eds), *Chitty on Contracts* (The Common Law Library, 2004) 1201.
[31] J Dalhuisen, *Dalhuisen on Transnational Comparative, Commercial, Financial and Trade Law Volume 2: Contract and Movable Property law* (4th edn, Hart Publishing, Oxford 2010) 386, 405.
[32] ibid 399.

credit privity is of less importance. Thus the law merchant developed the practice of transferring negotiable instruments as chattels which was later extended to other securities. Possession of certificates confers title to bearer securities and delivery of certificates transfers the title. This is known as negotiability.[33] Legal assignment was not available until statutory intervention in the Victorian era.[34] The formalities of novation were perceived inconvenient for the transfer of debt securities. Thus negotiation developed as a modified form of assignment. Under negotiability the debt is not an intangible but a physical certificate.[35] Negotiability achieves the same absolute assignment as legal assignment but is free of the limitation that an assignee is subject to the equities and defences available to the debtor against the assignor.

Statutory intervention establishes the transfer of registered securities. Registered securities may be transferred by an instrument, executed by a transferor and specifying the full name and address of the transferee, to be submitted by a transferee to the issuer together with the certificates for registration on the issuer register.[36] The issue of certificates of registered securities, for example shares, is to give holders the "opportunity of more easily dealing with their share in the market and to afford facilities to them of selling their shares by at once showing a marketable title, and the effect of this facility is to make the shares of greater value."[37] However, delivery of securities certificates only confers equitable title, while full legal tile has to be obtained by registration on the issuer register by the issuer on production of a transfer form and certificates by a transferee. The need for transferability and the desire of an issuer to know the holder are compromised through the combination of delivery of certificates and registration on the issuer register.

Equitable title may pass prior to the transfer of legal title. The transfer of equitable title will be discussed in the case of sales and gift.

A sale of registered securities normally goes through three stages: conclusion of the sale agreement; delivery of the executed transfer form and certificate by the seller to the buyer, as well as payment by the buyer

---

[33] See 3.3.1.

[34] Supreme Court of Judicature Act 1873 s 25 (6) (repealed).

[35] J Benjamin, *Interest in Securities: A Proprietary Law Analysis of the International Securities Markets* (Oxford University Press, Oxford 2000) 69.

[36] Stock Transfer Act 1963 s 1; Companies (Model Articles) Regulations 2008 SI 2008/3229 sch 3, s 63; Companies (Tables A to F) Regulations 1985 SI 1985/805 regs 23-28.

[37] *Re Bahia and San Francisco Rly Co* (1868) 3 QB 584, 594-95 (Cockburn CJ).

to the seller; and registration of the buyer's name on the register. Equitable title normally passes on the delivery of the transfer form and certificate and payment. Equitable title may exceptionally pass on the conclusion of a sale agreement if the agreement is found specifically enforceable by a court.[38]

In the case of gift, the current law is that the equitable title in shares passes where the donor has done all that it is necessary to be done to complete the gift, short of registration. The *Milroy v Lord*[39] rule that equity will not perfect an imperfect gift was distinguished in *Re Rose (decd), Midland Bank Executor and Trustee Co Ltd v Rose*[40] that the rule is only relevant when a donor has not done everything they can to divest themselves of title in the shares.[41] In *Milroy v Lord*[42], a donor executed a deed purporting to a transfer of shares which were only transferable by entry in the books of the issuer. It was held that there was no valid transfer. In *Re Fry, Chase National Executors and Trustees Corp Ltd v Fry*[43] a settlor executed a transfer of shares but failed to obtain the consent of the Treasury which was essential to the transfer of shares. The transferees argued that settlor had done everything he could to divest himself of the legal and equitable interest in the shares in favour of the transferee. At least his equitable interest in the shares had passed to the transferee. The gift was held incomplete.

Where a donor has delivered the executed transfer form and certificates to the transferee, he has done all he has to do to divest himself of his interests in the shares and the equitable title passes to the donee.[44] In *Re Rose (decd), Rose v IRC*[45], the decreased delivered the executed transfer form and the relevant certificates to the transferee. The decreased died before registration was obtained. It was held that the equitable title had passed to the transferee.

In *Pennington v Waine*[46] the court went further by holding that for an equitable assignment of shares by way of gift, delivery of the shares

[38] PL Davies and others, *Gower and Davies' Principles of Modern Company Law* (8th edn, Sweet & Maxwell, London 2008) 945.
[39] (1862) 4 De GF & J 264, 45 ER 1185.
[40] [1949] Ch 78.
[41] ibid 89 (Jenkins J).
[42] (1862) 4 De GF & J 264, 45 ER 1185.
[43] [1946] Ch 312.
[44] ibid.
[45] [1952] Ch 499 (CA).
[46] [2002] 2 BCLC 448 (CA).

transfer form could be dispensed with if there is a clear intention of the donor to make an immediate gift. The donor gave the executed transfer form to the company and expressed to the donee of the transfer of her equitable interest in the shares. The company also expressed to the donee of the transfer and saying there is nothing for the donee to do. The execution of a stock transfer form can have effect as an equitable assignment without the necessity of a transfer or delivery of the form or the share certificates either to the transferee or to the company.[47]

3.2.3 Title Conflicts between a True Owner and a Good Faith Purchaser

In case of transfer of securities by a non-owner, a *bona fide* purchaser of bearer securities gets an overriding title under the principle of negotiability; a good faith purchaser of registered securities can never get title but may get damages from an issuer on the basis of estoppel, or may be liable to damages to an issuer.

3.2.4 Summary

> "There are only two ways in which according to the law of England a good title can be acquired under such circumstances. If the instruments of title be negotiable instruments, a person taking them for value without notice of any infirmity in the title would have a right to hold them, even as against a prior owner who had never intended to part with the property in them. Or, again, such an owner may have so acted as to be estopped from setting up a claim as against a person who has *bona fide* and for value taken the instruments by way of sale or pledge."[48]

An owner can hardly be held as estopped unless there is fraud on his part, which is outside the discussion on the title conflict between an innocent owner and an innocent transferee.

3.3 Bearer Securities and Negotiability

Negotiability of bearer securities will be examined, from its rationale,

---

[47] ibid 469 (Clarke LJ).

[48] *Colonial Bank v Cady and Williams* (1890) 15 App Cas 267 (HL) 282-83 (Lord Herschell).

its evolution, its requirement, the impact of estoppel, to commercial need.

Delivery of certificates confers title to bearer securities. There is one important feature of bearer securities, i.e., negotiability. One aspect of negotiability is that a purchaser of bearer securities gets good title even against a true owner if he qualifies as holder in due course. A defective intention to transfer, i.e., unauthorised transfer against the intention of a true owner, does not deprive a transferee of the legal title who is otherwise entitled to the legal title and insulate the transferee from the claim of the true owner. This is the only area where the *bona fide* purchaser rule in the civil law sense has a role to play in English law. The *bona fide* purchaser rule in civil law countries means a good faith purchaser for value without notice of any prior title gets good title against the prior title. The title here is legal title. The *bona* fide purchaser rule that a purchaser of legal title defeats a prior equitable title under English law is not a *bona fide* purchaser rule in the narrow sense as it is based on the merits of the legal title.

> "The general rule of law is, that where a person has obtained the property of another from one who is dealing with it without the authority of the true owner, no title is acquired as against that owner, even though full value be given, and the property be taken in the belief that an unquestionable title thereto is being obtained, unless the person taking it can show that the true owner has so acted as to mislead him into the belief that the person dealing with the property has authority to do so. If this can be shown, a good title is acquired by personal estoppel against the true owner. There is an exception to the general rule, however, in the case of negotiable instruments. Any person in possession of these may convey a good title to them even when he is acting in fraud of the true owner, and although such owner has done nothing tending to mislead the person taking them."[49]

3.3.1 Negotiability

Negotiability started with negotiable instruments which were promises of payment. Negotiable instruments have three characteristics: they are transferable; they are enforceable by the holder; and a transferee acquires a better title than a transferor, free of any defence and defect in the prior title.[50] That a transferee acquires a better title than a transferor is most

---

[49] *London Joint Stock Bank v Simmons* [1892] AC 201 (HL) 205 (Lord Herschell).

[50] Bills of Exchange Act 1882 s 29; Cheques Act 1957; EP Ellinger, *Negotiable Instruments* (International Encyclopedia of Comparative Law, Volume IX: Commercial Transactions and Institutions, J.C.B Mohr (Paul Siebeck); Martinus

relevant to bearer securities.

A *bona fide* purchaser of negotiable instruments is often referred to as a holder in due course. English law recognises a holder, a holder for value and a holder in due course. The mind of the holder is evaluated and judged. But a transferee in a forged transfer cannot get title better than a transferor if the transferor forged the endorsement in the transfer of negotiable instrument.[51] This is relevant for establishing good faith whether there is omission to investigate suspicious circumstances of possible defective title which may prevent a holder from being in good faith.

For a bill of exchange, a holder of a bill can transfer a bill, can sue in his own name, and is a *prima facie* holder in due course, but subject to the claim of a holder for value and a holder in due course.[52] It is similar to possession of a chattel where possession confers *prima facie* title. A holder for value is in a better position than a holder but inferior to a holder in due course. He can defeat a plea of want of consideration but cannot get better title than a transferor.[53] A holder in due course gets title to the bill free of equities and defects in the title of the transferor. A holder in due course is similar to a *bona fide* purchaser, who has to acquire the bill for value in good faith without notice of any equity or defect in the title to get a good title. Civil law makes no such distinction and a holder who acquires a negotiable instrument through a series of endorsements regular on their face in good faith without notice of any defect gets good title.[54] English law is more reserved on establishing the status of a holder in due course.[55] A holder in due course is free of claim against a transferor and any predecessor, as well as any lack of authority of a transferor to transfer. The limitation is that a holder in due course cannot claim against parties prior to a forged signature.[56]

In addition to statutory confirmation,[57] an instrument can be accorded

---

Nijhoff Publishers, 2000) 5.

[51] EP Ellinger (ibid).

[52] RM Goode and E McKendrick, *Goode on Commercial Law* (4th edn, LexisNexis, London 2009) 531.

[53] ibid 532.

[54] EP Ellinger, *Negotiable Instruments* (International Encyclopedia of Comparative Law, Volume IX: Commercial Transactions and Institutions, J.C.B Mohr (Paul Siebeck); Martinus Nijhoff Publishers, 2000) 5.

[55] *Sheffield v The London Joint Stock Bank* (1888) 13 App Cas 333 (HL).

[56] Bills of Exchange Act 1882 s 24; RM Goode and E McKendrick, *Goode on Commercial Law* (4th edn, LexisNexis, London 2009) 533.

[57] Bills of Exchange Act 1882; Cheques Act 1957.

negotiability by the law merchant as customs. There are however some basic requirements to be met. An instrument must be capable of being sued by the holder in his own name, capable of transferable by delivery or endorsement.[58] It is in fact ambulatory definition. The essential point is the physical form, such as a certificate, capable of easy transfer, which is illustrated in the debate over whether global bonds are negotiable.[59]

3.3.2 Rationale of Negotiability; Quasi-Currency

Estoppel in respect of negotiable instruments, unavailable with other property, is supported by the special nature of negotiable instruments. Negotiable instruments are quasi-currency like money. Money is fungible and fully negotiable. A *bona fide* purchaser without notice of any defect in the title of money of the transferor gets good title to money which may be stolen or otherwise defective.[60] An instrument is a document of title to money.[61] As a documentary intangible, an instrument is the physical embodiment of the payment obligation, and its possession (with any necessary endorsement) is the best evidence of entitlement of the money it represents.[62] It is treated as chattel but not in the full sense as chattel as the German reification. The reification theory argues that the certificate reifies the intangibles right and is the right *per se*. English law does not need this theory to incorporate intangible rights into the realm of property law. Negotiable instruments are choses in action but their transfer is treated in the same way as chattel. "The status of a holder in due course of a negotiable instrument is essentially that of a *bona fide* purchaser acquiring an overriding title."[63]

Negotiable instruments began with commercial need for creditors of payment obligations to transfer their claims. Promissory notes, bills of exchange, and cheques came into being to suit this need. They evolved to

[58] *Crouch v Crédit Foncier of England* (1873) 8 QB 374, 381 (Blackburn J); *Claydon v Bradley* [1987] 1 All ER 522 (CA) 526 (Dillon LJ).
[59] See 3.3.4.
[60] RM Goode and E McKendrick, *Goode on Commercial Law* (4th edn, LexisNexis, London 2009) 486-87.
[61] Indeed it was argued by one party that "a negotiable instrument must represent money, and a negotiable character cannot be conferred on anything that is not a security for money." *Rumball v The Metropolitan Bank* (1877) 2 QBD 194, 194.
[62] RM Goode and E McKendrick, *Goode on Commercial Law* (4th edn, LexisNexis, London 2009) 513.
[63] ibid 514.

have some nature of money, the most important of which is that a transferee for value without notice of any defect in the title gets a better title than the transferor.[64] The idea of negotiability developed with negotiable instruments has been extended to other securities, known as bearer securities, such as bearer bonds, bearer debentures, bearer scrip and share warrants.[65]

3.3.3 Evolution of Negotiability

3.3.3.1 Estoppel by negligence; only in case of negotiable instruments

It is argued that negotiability is based on estoppel.[66] A good faith purchaser for value gets title to the negotiable instruments because a true owner is estopped as against a good faith purchaser from denying that a possessor of the negotiable instrument has title. However such estoppel can only operate in respect of negotiable instruments. Estoppel is established because of the nature of negotiable instruments and commercial need.

Estoppel will never deprive an innocent owner of registered securities short of fraud on his part. Negligence does not establish estoppel. In *Swan v The North British Australasian Company (Limited)*[67], registered shares were transferable by deeds executed by a transferor and a transferee. A shareholder executed deeds and handed to his broker who wrongfully transferred the shares against the will of the shareholder. It was held that there was no such negligence on the part of the shareholder which estopped him from insisting that title to the shares were not transferred, since negligence must be the proximate cause of the loss to the transferee to operate as estoppel and the estoppel by negligence in respect of negotiable instruments are confined to negotiable instruments excluding deeds. The justification for estoppel by negligence or conduct in respect of negotiable instruments is enhanced by the need of the mercantile community and mercantile law, which would normally fail under common law.

[64] ibid 515-17.
[65] W Blair, 'Negotiability and Estoppel' (1988) 3 JIBL 8, 8.
[66] JS Ewart, 'Negotiability and Estoppel' (1900) 16 LQR 159; E Micheler, 'Farewell quasi-negotiability? Legal Title and Transfer of Shares in a Paperless World' [2002] JBL 358.
[67] (1863) 2 H & C 175, 159 ER 73.

"The arguments drawn from negotiable instruments appear altogether inapplicable (to registered securities). The object of the law merchant, as to bills and notes made or become payable to bearer, is to secure their circulation as money; therefore honest acquisition confers title. To this despotic but necessary principle the ordinary rules of the common law are made to bend. ... The negligence of the holder, on the other hand, makes no difference in his title. However gross the holder's negligence, if it stop short of fraud he has a title. ... The truth is that in the case of a bill of exchange or promissory note, as well as in the case of a deed, the law respects the nature and uses of the instrument more than its own ordinary rules."[68]

The focus of negotiability is not the negligence of a true owner of a negotiable instrument but the innocence of a purchaser who can get title unless he is fraudulent. It is the special nature of the negotiable instrument akin to cash that has been recognised as an exception of common law. Such estoppel against a true owner can only be recognised in respect of negotiable instruments.

"It is surely of the very essence of a negotiable instrument that you may treat the person in possession of it as having authority to deal with it, be he agent or otherwise, unless you know to the contrary, and are not compelled, in order to secure a good title to yourself; to inquire into the nature of his title, or the extent of his authority. The Factors Act (6 Geo. 4, c. 94), which gives validity to sales and pledges by persons entrusted with the documents of title to goods, contained a proviso, 'that the purchaser or pledge had not notice by the documents, or otherwise, that the seller or pledgor was not the actual and bonâ fide owner of the goods sold or pledged-a proviso which, especially after the decision in Fletcher v. Heath, rendered it unsafe to make advances on goods or documents to persons known to have possession thereof as agents only' (per Blackburn J. in Cole v. North-Western Bank). Accordingly the legislature intervened, and altered the law by the 5 & 6 Vict. c. 39. The recital is noteworthy, that 'advances on the security of goods and merchandise have become an usual and ordinary course of business, and it is expedient and necessary that reasonable and safe facilities should be afforded thereto.' ... It was truly said that it was due to the Act of the legislature that documents of title to goods may safely be taken by way of pledge from an agent, and that there had been no such legislation in relation to negotiable instruments. But why not? The answer, to my mind, is plain-because it never was supposed to be necessary in order to give validity to such a transaction in the case of negotiable instruments. It is admitted that, in the case of a sale, legislation was not requisite; that the fact that the instruments were negotiable sufficed; ... The

[68] *Swan v The North British Australasian Company (Limited)* (1863) 2 H & C 175, 184-85 (Byles J); 159 ER 73, 78.

> truth is, in my opinion, that what the Factors Acts have done is to attach some of the elements of negotiability to documents of title to goods, to render the mere possession of them evidence of authority to deal with them in the ordinary course of business, and to preclude the necessity of any further inquiry."[69]

It is the nature of negotiable instruments that possession of the instruments signifies authority to dispose of the instruments precluding the necessity of any inquiry. The position that possession is title can only be established with respect to bearer securities and property under statutory intervention, such as the Factors Act.

3.3.3.2 By statutes and the law merchant

Negotiable instruments are established by statutes[70] and the law merchant. In addition to instruments established by statutes, the law merchant from time to time admits new kinds of negotiable instruments. The evolution of law merchant is a process of judicial recognition of commercial customs.

> "It is no doubt true that negotiability can only be attached to a contract by the law merchant or by a statute; and it is also true that, in determining whether a usage has become so well established as to be binding on the Courts of law, the length of time during which the usage has existed is an important circumstance to take into consideration; but it is to be remembered that in these days usage is established much more quickly than it was in days gone by; more depends on the number of the transactions which help to create it than on the time over which the transactions are spread; and it is probably no exaggeration to say that nowadays there are more business transactions in an hour than there were in a week a century ago. Therefore the comparatively recent origin of this class of securities in my view creates no difficulty in the way of holding that they are negotiable by virtue of the law merchant; they are dealt in as negotiable instruments in every minute of a working day, and to the extent of many thousands of pounds. It is also to be remembered that the law merchant is not fixed and stereotyped; it has not yet been arrested in its growth by being moulded into a code; it is, to use the words of Cockburn C.J. in Goodwin v. Robarts, capable of being expanded and enlarged so as to meet the wants and requirements of trade in the varying circumstances of commerce, the effect of which is that it approves and adopts from time

[69] *London Joint Stock Bank v Simmons* [1892] AC 201 (HL) 217-18 (Lord Herschell).

[70] Bills of Exchange Act 1882; Cheques Act 1957.

> to time those usages of merchants which are found necessary for the convenience of trade; our common law, of which the law merchant is but a branch, has in the hands of the judges the same facility for adapting itself to the changing needs of the general public; principles do not alter, but old rules of applying them change, and new rules spring into existence. Thus it has been found convenient to treat securities like those in question in this action as negotiable, and the Courts of law, recognising the wisdom of the usage, have incorporated it in what is called the law merchant, and have made it part of the common law of the country."[71]

Whether a usage is in use for so long, or whether a usage is so often employed in transactions as to bind the courts and be accepted as the law merchant, is an issue of judicial discretion. Most bearer securities under English law have been accorded negotiability through customs, such as bearer bonds, bearer debentures, bearer scrip and share warrants. There is one limitation that an instrument has to be capable of physical possession and delivery, which can be seen in the example of global bonds.

3.3.4 Negotiability of Global Bond

Normally a global note or global representing the whole issue of bond is issued by entries in the operator register or issuer register in a bond registration and clearing system. Title to bonds are entries on accounts of account holders. Transfer of title to bonds are by debits and credits on relevant accounts of account holders. A global bond is structured to be both registered and bearer bond to benefit from the advantages of both. On one hand, the global note is designed to satisfy the requirement of negotiability of physical certificates, despite that the transfer is by entries between bonds accounts while the global note never moves. On the other hand, global bonds are designed as registered bond to avoid the US law on heavier tax on bearer securities. Bond holders who prefer physical certificates can demand the issue of definitive certificates of the global.[72]

> "It is a strange state of affairs in which entitlements in respect of an instrument which is not negotiable-since global bonds never change hands in practice and can only be transferred to another common depositary, they can hardly be negotiable-are actively traded as if they were negotiable

[71] *Edelstein v Schuler & Co* [1902] 2 KB 144, 154-55 (Bigham J).

[72] PR Wood, *International Loans, Bonds, Gurarntees, Legal Opinions* (Law and Practice of International Finance Series, 2nd edn, Sweet & Maxwell, London 2007) 215-16; J Benjamin, 'Computerisation and Negotiability Part 1' [1995] JIBFL 253.

instruments, which they are not, if only because there is no instrument which is delivered to effect the transfer."[73]

It is not established that they are negotiable since a transaction in global bonds takes place by credits and debits in a securities clearing and settlement system rather than by delivery of physical certificates. Recognition of new negotiable instruments by commercial usage and customs has its limit that an instrument has to be documentary intangibles capable of physical possession and delivery.[74] It is open to argument whether physical certificates are essential for negotiability.

3.3.5 Conclusion

Negotiability is the only area where a *bona fide* purchaser gets good title in priority to a true owner. It is attributed to the nature of negotiable instruments, or rather commercial needs of these instruments. Fundamentally speaking it is based on estoppel against a true owner for negligently leaving the certificate in the hands of another and thus holding out the person as owner to the world, but such estoppel never exists in respect of registered securities or chattel except statutory carve-outs. Thus it is a result of estoppel, the rationale for which is reinforced by commercial needs. To be negotiable an instrument must be capable of physical delivery which is treated as equal to title. Most negotiable instruments gain the status through the law merchant which is in constant evolution. In England negotiable instruments are mainly money market instruments and bearer bonds; most shares are registered. The transformation of negotiable instruments into intangible form prevents these instruments from delivery and thus negotiability. In fact the evolution of negotiability suggests the essence of negotiability as a way of title resolution with preference for the purchaser as demanded by commercial needs, achieved by common law estoppel, and buttressed by commercial customs and case law. Physical certificates and capability of possession and delivery are rather apparent aspects of market practices at a time when physical certificates are treated as a form of indicia of title. The essence is estoppel as required by commercial needs. This may prove

---

[73] M Hughes, 'Bond Issues A Banking Lawyer's Perspective' [2000] JIBFL 263.

[74] A McKnight, *The Law of International Finance* (Oxford University Press, Oxford 2008) 500; M Yates and G Montagu, *The Law of Global Custody* (3rd rev edn, Tottel Publishing, London 2009) 17, 201.

inspiring for the resolution of title conflicts in respect of uncertificated intermediated securities.

3.4 Title Conflicts in respect of Registered Securities

The law on title conflicts between a true owner and a good faith purchaser in the context of registered securities is not referred as the *nemo dat* rule, which assumes something capable of delivery like chattel and which is a loss-allocation between a seller and a buyer. Registered securities are choses in action and a transfer involves an issuer. Thus there is another party to allocate the potential loss.[75] But the result is the same that a prior owner wins. Under the consensualist approach and the preference for vested right, a contract to transfer certificated securities constitutes transfer of equitable title while legal title transfers on registration with the issuer, and a defective intention of the transferor does not confer title. The title of a securities holder whose securities have been misappropriated prevails over a subsequent purchaser where both are innocent. The idea is that an agent without authority or a fraudster cannot confer title. It is the same underlying tenet as the *nemo dat* principle. It has been held if a non-holder wrongfully transfers the securities to an innocent purchaser, an owner of registered securities is entitled to be registered on the issuer register which confers title. An issuer is under a duty to a shareholder to keep the register in the way it has been unless the shareholder otherwise directs the issuer. An issuer is not obliged to register a forged transfer. On the other hand an issuer benefits from the issue of certificates and the circulation of securities in this way it is otherwise unfair to a good faith purchaser for an issuer to disregard his right. Thus an issuer is estopped as to the authenticity of the register and certificate against a good faith purchaser relying on the certificate. The issuer is obliged to pay damages for the loss of title to a good faith purchaser based on estoppel, known as quasi-negotiability.[76] The estoppel against an issuer is not available to a good faith purchaser in a forged transfer as there is no valid certificate to rely on. Rather a transferee in a forged transfer is estopped from denying that the transfer he submits for registration is genuine and obliged to indemnify an issuer against loss resulting from registering a forged transfer. Most discussion is based on cases regarding

---

[75] E Micheler, 'Farewell Quasi-Negotiability? Legal Title and Transfer of Shares in a Paperless World'[2002] JBL 358, 366, 371.
[76] ibid.

shares which are the most common registered securities. It remains true regarding other registered securities, such as debentures.[77]

3.4.1 A True Owner versus an Issuer

The relation between a true owner and an issuer will be examined first from the perspective of duties of each party.

3.4.1.1 A true owner's right against an issuer

Holders of registered securities cannot be divested of title unless with their consent. For example, "transferable shares of the stock of any company cannot be divested out of the proprietors by any act of the company without the authority of the stockholders."[78] Assent of the owner is essential. A holder of registered securities is entitled to claim against an issuer that the issuer is legally bound to keep his name in the register, unless the holder has himself transferred the securities. An issuer is bound to reinstate the holder if the name of a holder is removed as a result of a forged transfer.[79] It is legal right for a shareholder to be reinstated, rather than an equitable relief in circumstances of estoppel.[80]

3.4.1.2 Negligence of the holder

In a forged transfer there is apparently no assent of an owner and a forged transfer does not bind an owner. An owner has no duty to the world to safeguard his rights. Failure to reply to enquiry by a company as to the transfer is not able to estop a shareholder from denying the validity of the transfer.[81] The underlying idea is that a shareholder is under no duty to answer enquiries from a company and guarantees to the world the authenticity of the title.

---

[77] *Cottam v Eastern Counties Rly Co* (1860) 1 J & H 243, (1860) 70 ER 737; *Welch v The Bank of England* [1955] 1 Ch 508.

[78] RR Pennington, *The Law of the Investment Markets* (Blackwell Law, Oxford 1990) 402.

[79] J Birds and others (eds), *Boyle & Birds' Company Law* (7th edn, Jordan, Bristol 2009) 295.

[80] *Sloman v Bank of England* (1845) 14 Sim 475, 60 ER 442.

[81] *Barton v London and North Western Rly Co* (1889) 24 QBD 77 (CA).

3.4.1.3 Issuer duty to the holder

The issuer has a duty to keep intact the title of the holder.

> "The duty of the company is not to accept a forged transfer, and no duty to make inquiries exists towards the person bringing the transfer. It is merely an obligation upon the company to take care that they do not get into difficulties in consequence of their accepting a forged transfer, and it may be said to be an obligation towards the stockholder not to take the stock out of his name unless he has executed a transfer; but it is only a duty in this sense, that unless the company act upon a genuine transfer they may be liable to the real stockholder."[82]

A shareholder's title is guaranteed by the obligation of a company to keep the register intact in a responsible way without the authority of the shareholder. Legal title, of which certificates are *prima facie* evidence, is secure as certificates do not confer title without registration; the registration process serves as a check by the issuer over the authenticity of the transfer, such as authenticity of the certificate (forged certificates may thus be discovered and registration refused) or authenticity of the transfer (enquiry by an issuer to a registered holder as to the transfer); and even if registration is procured based on forged certificates or unauthorised transfer because of issuer failure to identify any suspicious circumstance, a true owner does not cease to be the owner as he can claim to be reinstated on the register. Negligence on the part of a holder of registered securities does not estop him in respect of his title, unless his negligence is the proximate cause of registration.[83]

3.4.2 A Transferee versus an Issuer

3.4.2.1 Estoppel against the issuer

Issuer duty in respect of register and certificate

A certificate issued by a company estops the company from denying to an innocent purchaser that the person stated as shareholder on the certificate is the shareholder.[84] To rely on the estoppel against a company

[82] *Simm v Anglo-American Telegraph Co* (1879) 5 QBD 188 (CA) 214 (Cotton LJ).

[83] *Mayor, Constables & Co of Merchants of the Staple of England v Governor & Co of Bank of England* (1887) 21 QBD 160 (CA) 173 (Lord Esher MR).

[84] P Feltham, D Hochberg and T Leech, *Spencer Bower The Law Relating to*

in respect of a share certificate, a transferee must have relied on the certificate issued by the company, and have changed his position on such reliance. An innocent purchaser is only entitled to claim damages against the company but not to be registered as shareholder. Estoppel does not confer title upon a transferee as it does not change the truth that a transferor has no title.[85] Reliance upon a forged certificate does not estop a company while a transferee of a forged certificate is estopped from denying that the certificate is authenticate and liable to the company for damages suffered by the company to a subsequent transferee, if the transferee submits a forged certificate for registration, registration is made, a certificate is duly issued by the company, and a subsequent transferee of the duly issued certificate submits to the company for registration.

Certificate inconsistent with register

The register of an issuer is open to public inspection. But it is not normal that a transferee inspects the register to check the regularity of a transaction. It is the duty of an issuer to insure that a certificate is consistent with the register.[86]

A certificate issued to a purchaser other than a registered shareholder estops the issuer company from denying the title of the purchaser to the shares, although the purchaser is only entitled to damages rather than being registered as shareholder.[87]

Certificate issued on the registration of a forged transfer; estoppel

In *Balkis Consolidated Co v Tomkinson*[88], a forged transfer was registered by an issuer and a certificate was issued thereupon. The forgery was found after a certificate was issued. The issuer refused to register a subsequent transfer on the basis of the forgery. The issuer was estopped against the transferee in the subsequent transfer from denying that the

---

Estoppel by Representation (4th edn, LexisNexis, London 2004) 70, 250; KR Handley, *Estoppel by Conduct and Election* (Sweet & Maxwell, London 2006) 155-58.

[85] *Balkis Consolidated Co v Tomkinson* [1893] AC 396 (HL); *Dixon v Kennaway & Co* [1900] 1 Ch 833; P Feltham, D Hochberg and T Leech, *Spencer Bower The Law Relating to Estoppel by Representation* (4th edn, LexisNexis, London 2004) 70, 250; KR Handley, *Estoppel by Conduct and Election* (Sweet & Maxwell, London 2006) 155-58.

[86] *Dixon v Kennaway & Co* [1900] 1 Ch 833, 840-41 (Farewell J).

[87] ibid.

[88] [1893] AC 396 (HL).

transferor was the shareholder. The transferee was entitled to damages from the issuer.

A company is under a duty to keep a shareholder register and issue certificates certifying that a shareholder stated in a certificate is a registered member of the company. The issuance of certificates facilitates the dealing in the shares and benefits the company. It is a declaration of the company to the world that the person stated as shareholder in the certificate is a shareholder, entitled to transfer the share. In a forged transfer a *bona fide* purchaser relies on a certificate and pays for the purchase price to a transferor who should not have been registered as shareholder, thus the company is estopped from denying the fact the transferor is a shareholder. The transferee is entitled to damages for his loss of the title to securities at the market price of the shares.[89]

A company is obliged to keep a register of members and alter the register whenever there is a transfer of shares. A company must check the validity of a tender of change but may still be deceived to register as genuine a forged transfer. The company then makes a change in the register and issue certificates thereupon. A certificate is the *prima facie* title of the person stated in a certificate on which buyers rely. This is a representation of the company.[90] A certificate means not only that a company has done their best to ascertain that a registered transfer is an authentic one short of guarantee that it is an authentic one, but constitutes a representation to be relied on by any transferee that a registered transfer is an authentic one and the registered shareholder is the true shareholder.[91]

Duplicate certificate issued through issuer negligence

In *Longman v Bath Electric Tramways Ltd*[92], a company got a share certificate from a transferee for certification of a transfer, later sent the certificate by mistake to the transferor. The transferor forged another transfer with the certificate to a second transferee. The second transferee was held to bear the loss.

The rationale is that the company was under a duty only to the transferee who applied for certification but not to the public. A share certificate was *prima facie* evidence of the title of registered share. The company did enable the transferor to deceive the second transferee by

89 *Re Bahia and San Francisco Rly Co* (1868) 3 QB 584, 594 (Cockburn CJ).
90 ibid 596 (Blackburn J).
91 ibid 598 (Mellor J).
92 [1905] 1 Ch 646 (CA).

sending him the certificate. But the company was under no duty to the public at large of keeping the certificate safe. Negligence on the part of a company was not the proximate cause of the loss of the second transferee, which was the dishonest behaviour of the transferor. There was no estoppel against the company.[93]

No estoppel against a company to a transferee of forged certificates or forged authority

A company has a duty to keep a true register of members which is only a duty to keep current shareholders in the register without their disposition, but not a duty to the public to ensure the authenticity of each transfer it has registered. An onerous duty on companies to take care of the authenticity of the transfer owed to both shareholders and transferees and corresponding allocation of the loss of forgery to companies have never been recognised in English courts.[94]

> "The duty of the company is not to accept a forged transfer, and no duty to make inquiries exists towards the person bringing the transfer. It is merely an obligation upon the company to take care that they do not get into difficulties in consequence of their accepting a forged transfer, and it may be said to be an obligation towards the stockholder not to take the stock out of his name unless he has executed a transfer; but it is only a duty in this sense, that unless the company act upon a genuine transfer, they may be liable to the real stockholder."[95]

Analogy to a forged cheque; banker liability to pay double

The allocation of the loss of a forged transfer of registered shares in analogy to the allocation of loss of a forged cheque to the bank is not accepted either

> "It appears to me that the case is analogous to the case of a forged cheque, and as a banker paying a forged cheque to an innocent holder for value cannot recover back its amount and is compelled to pay it twice over, so here the company must pay the amount of the stock twice over. The duty being cast upon the company to look after the register and the transfers, it appears to me that between two innocent parties the company are not entitled to claim compensation from Burge & Co. nor to resist at Burge & Co.'s expense the recognition of that title, which they themselves have

---

[93] ibid; Companies Act 2006 s 775.

[94] *Simm v Anglo-American Telegraph Co* (1879) 5 QBD 188 (CA) 195 (Lindley J).

[95] ibid 214 (Cotton LJ).

created by their own act."[96]

A duplicate certificate obtained by fraud of someone other than the registered holder

A certificate names the true owner but does not imply that the person in possession is the true owner. In a transfer by someone other than a registered holder, what is relied on by a purchaser is the misrepresentation by the person in possession that he is the true owner, rather than the certificate. There is thus no estoppel.[97]

> "A share certificate under the seal of the company specifying any shares held by a member is prima facie evidence of his title to the shares (see the Companies Act 1985, s 186). But the certificate is not a negotiable instrument or a warranty of title by the company. It makes no representation that the person in possession of it has title to it."[98]

A rogue, by alleging that the true owner had lost certificates and changed address, obtained a duplicate certificate which he then transferred. There was no representation on the part of the company that the person in possession of the certificate was the true owner. The transferee relied on the misrepresentation of the rogue. The proximate cause of loss to the transferee was the misrepresentation of the rogue rather than the issuing of a duplicate certificate.[99]

Estoppel and damages

Estoppel does not create title but establishes damages between a claimant and a person estopped.[100] A certificate issued by a company after registering a forged transfer estops the company from denying to any subsequent transferee that the registered transferor is a shareholder. However the truth is that the registered transferor is not a shareholder and thus the transferee is not entitled to being registered as shareholder in place of the true shareholder but is merely entitled to damages from the company.

> "The doctrine of estoppel was recognised in the Courts of Common Law

[96] ibid 196 (Lindley J, Bramwell, Brett and Cotton LJJ).
[97] *Royal Bank of Scotland plc v Sandstone Properties Ltd and others* [1998] 2 BCLC 429 (QB) 430 (Tuckey J).
[98] ibid 432 (Tuckey J).
[99] ibid 434 (Tuckey J).
[100] *Simm v Anglo-American Telegraph Co* (1879) 5 QBD 188 (CA) 207 (Brett LJ).

> just as much as it was in the Courts of Equity, and it seems to me that an estoppel gives no title to that which is the subject-matter of estoppel. The estoppel assumes that the reality is contrary to that which the person is estopped from denying, and the estoppel has no effect at all upon the reality of the circumstances."[101]

To rely upon estoppel against a company, a transferee must rely upon a duly issued certificate by the company without any intervening event, that is the certificate is not forged, is not in the hands of someone other than the holder registered on the certificate, even if the certificate is issued upon a registration of a forged transaction against the title of the true owner. Thus a transferee must be in a normal and honest transaction to claim damages, rather than title, based upon estoppel against a company.

3.4.2.2 Estoppel against a transferee in a forged transfer

The estoppel against a company in respect of register or certificate cannot be availed to a transferee in a forged transfer as what the transferee relies on is either a forged certificate or a forged power of disposition, rather than anything on the part of the company. Furthermore, such a transferee is estopped from denying the authenticity of the transfer he submits to the company for registration. In submitting for registration, a transferee is obliged to indemnify the company of any loss resulting from registering the transfer. A transferee is obliged to check the regularity and authenticity of a transaction in which he is a direct party. A company is under no duty to check the authenticity of a transfer submitted to it for registration. A transferee of a forged share certificate is in a better situation to check the authenticity of the certificate than an issuer company. An issuer company is under no duty to check the authenticity of share certificates submitted for registration and has no means to check.[102]

Warranty; indemnity

A transferee submitting certificates to an issuer for registration makes a representation to the issuer that the transfer to be registered is genuine, which is a warranty.[103] By registering a forged transfer at the request of the transferee, the registrar breaches its duty to the true holder of registered

---

101 ibid 206 (Brett LJ).

102 *Sheffield Corpn v Barclay* [1905] AC 392 (HL) 396-97 (Earl of Halsbury LC).

103 *Starkey v Governor and Company of The Bank of England* [1903] AC 114 (HL) 118 (Earl of Halsbury LC).

securities and is liable to reinstate the name of the true holder. It is a statutory duty of the registrar to register a transfer. The person making the request to the registrar is obliged by the operation of law to indemnify the registrar against the liability resulting from the exercise of the statutory duty. It does not matter whether the person making the request is innocent or there is no negligence on his part.[104] There is an implied contract of indemnity between a transferee and a company.[105]

> "That independently of the contract implied between the bank and the brokers, the bank owed no duty of care to the brokers and were not liable to them in negligence ... The circumstances of the brokers' request were such that it imported a warranty by them of the genuineness of the documents submitted for where, as in the present case, a stockbroker himself requests, albeit upon the instructions and for the benefit of another, the registration of a share transfer which the company is under a ministerial duty to effect if the documents forwarded by the stockbroker are genuine documents, the sound and expeditious conduct of business requires that the company should be entitled to rely on the documents submitted in support of his request ..."[106]

A transferee who is considered to be in a better position to check the regularity of the transfer is under a duty to do so and warrants to the issuer that the transfer is genuine, otherwise the transferee is liable to the issuer which may be liable to onward transferees, whether the transferee is innocent or not. Such an unfortunate transferee is allocated the loss of fraud by law for the sake of transaction safety on a macro basis.

3.4.2.3 A transferee in a forged transfer disposed the share, then got it back

A transferee in a forged transfer got the transfer registered. The transferee disposed of the shares by way of security and then got the share back. Afterwards the forgery was found. It was held that there was no estoppel against the company in favour of the transferee. There was indeed estoppel between the company and the secured creditor in respect of the

---

[104] *Sheffield Corpn v Barclay* [1905] AC 392 (HL) 399 (Lord Davey).

[105] *Yeung Kai Yun v Hong Kong and Shanghai Banking Corpn* [1981] AC 787 (PC) 788 (Viscount Dilhorne, Lord Salmon, Lord Elwyn-Jones, Lord Scarman and Lord Lane).

[106] ibid 788-89 (Viscount Dilhorne, Lord Salmon, Lord Elwyn-Jones, Lord Scarman and Lord Lane).

certificate. However once the security interest was extinguished the estoppel ceased as estoppel was personal.[107] This shows the difference between estoppel against a company and against a transferee.

3.4.3 A Transferee versus a True Owner; Estoppel against a True Owner

3.4.3.1 Blank transfer

A shareholder who signs a blank transfer to enable his broker to transfer specific shares is estopped from insisting that the transfer is void in law if the broker carries out his mandate;[108] but the shareholder is not estopped if his broker forges a transfer, unless the act of the shareholder is the proximate cause of loss. An innocent shareholder will hardly be held to be estopped in this way.[109]

A shareholder will be deprived of his title to shares by estoppel for his act of enabling another to appear as shareholder to a transferee. It is not based on fault or negligence on the part of a shareholder. It is more an issue of finding suitable and equitable criteria for attributing responsibility for the loss as a result of the act of a third party to one of two innocent parties.[110]

3.4.3.2 Estoppel

A holder of registered securities giving a blank transfer form together with certificates to a broker will not be estopped if the broker transfers the securities against the will of the holder.

"The mere delivery of them with the endorsed blank transfer and power of

[107] *Simm v Anglo-American Telegraph Co* (1879) 5 QBD 188 (CA) 188 (Lindley J, Bramwell, Brett and Cotton LJJ).
[108] *Hibblewhite v M'Morine* (1840) 6 M & W 200, 151 ER 380; *France v Clark* (1884) 26 Ch D 257 (CA).
[109] *Swan v The North British Australasian Company (Limited)* (1863) 2 H & C 175, 159 ER 73; RR Pennington, *The Law of the Investment Markets* (Blackwell Law, Oxford 1990) 400; P Feltham, D Hochberg and T Leech, *Spencer Bower The Law Relating to Estoppel by Representation* (4th edn, LexisNexis, London 2004) 251-53.
[110] FR Malan, 'Share Certificates, Money and Negotiability' (1977) 94 The South African LJ 245.

> attorney signed, irrespective of any act or intent on the part of the owner of the shares, is not of itself sufficient to pass the title to them. If delivered by or with the authority of the owner with intent to transfer them, such delivery will suffice for the purpose. But if there has been no intent on the part of the owner to transfer them, a good title can only be obtained as against him if he has so acted as to preclude himself from setting up a claim to them. If the owner of a chose in action clothes a third party with the apparent ownership and right of disposition of it, he is estopped from asserting his title as against a person to whom such third party has disposed of it, and who received it in good faith and for value."[111]

Fuller v Glyn, Mills, Currie & Co[112] is a rare case where a shareholder, who executed a transfer form and put it with the certificates in the hands of his broker, was found to cloth the broker with full authority to deal with it. A detail in this case was the shareholder allowed the brokers to be registered on the issuer register as shareholder.

A securities broker lent money to a client to buy registered and negotiable securities and procured security interest over the securities thus acquired for his advances to the client, i.e., the so-called contango practice. The broker pledged the securities to a bank to secure his loan from the bank. The bank got legal title to registered securities and took possession certificates of negotiable securities. When the broker became bankrupt the client claimed to be entitled to redeem the securities.[113]

> "As a general rule, no one can found a title upon a forgery, but in certain cases … the law merchant validates, in the interest of commerce, a transaction which the common law would declare void for want of title or authority; and transactions within its operation are as absolutely valid and effectual as if made with title or authority …. There are also cases in which, 'where a man has wilfully made a false assertion calculated to lead others to act upon it, and they have done so to their prejudice, he is forbidden as against them to deny that assertion … But not … 'that if a man has led others into a belief of a certain state of facts by conduct of culpable neglect calculated to have that result, and they have acted on that belief to their prejudice, he shall not be heard afterwards, as against such persons, to shew that that state of facts did not exist.' … they extend to transactions in which a deed is required to transfer an interest or a right; not by validating a void deed, as was supposed on the argument, but by holding that parties shall not be permitted to aver, against equity and good faith, the invalidity of a deed which either by words or conduct they have asserted to be valid,

[111] *Colonial Bank v Cady and Williams* (1890) 15 App Cas 267 (HL) 285 (Lord Herschell).
[112] [1914] 2 KB 168, 177 (Pickford J).
[113] *Bentinck v London Joint Stock Bank* [1893] 2 Ch 120.

and upon which the others have acted."[114]

In this case the client was held to be estopped because the client got advance from his broker to deal in securities secured for the advance, and gave his broker to pledge the secured securities to the creditor of his broker for loans incurred by the broker to his creditor. Furthermore it was market customs for securities brokers to rehypothecate client securities over which brokers had security interest with the authority of clients. There was no fraud on the part of the broker. The client was estopped because he gave full legal title to his broker. This is actually not in the issue of competing title between a true owner and a transferee, both innocent.

3.4.3.3 No estoppel as blank transfer does not transform registered securities into negotiable securities

An owner of registered shares gave a blank transfer form and the share certificate to his creditor who created a legal pledge for his own creditor in excess of the debt by the true owner. It was held that the true owner was not estopped by the blank transfer. The argument that the owner had, by the blank transfer and certificate, enabled another to represent himself as the true owner of the shares, or as having power to deal with the shares as owner, was not supported. The documents themselves showed that the other person was not the owner. Nor was there any evidence of any mercantile usage that holders of such documents were treated as having the right to transfer shares, as if such holders were owners of such shares. There was no evidence that, blank transfers, accompanied by certificates of shares registered in the names of transferors, passed from hand to hand like negotiable instruments.[115]

3.4.3.4 Proximate cause of loss

A shareholder executed a blank transfer deed, his broker fraudulent filled the deed and transferred shares against the will of the shareholder. There was a misrepresentation as to the title to the shares to the transferee. The misrepresentation was made by the broker, not by the shareholder.

---

[114] *Swan v The North British Australasian Company (Limited)* (1863) 2 H & C 175, 176 (Mellor J); 159 ER 73, 75.
[115] *France v Clark* (1884) 26 Ch D 257 (CA) 264 (Earl of Selborne, LC).

The proximate cause of loss to the transferee was the misrepresentation and the fraud of the broker, not the negligence of the shareholder.[116]

An owner does not lose title for negligence unless he is fraudulent. Such negligence as estops an owner and confers title upon a transferee in a forged transfer in respect of negotiable instruments is not a rule in general law.

3.4.4 Status of a Good Faith Purchaser

The superior position of a prior holder of registered securities may be explained by the *nemo dat* principle, reinforced by the holder-issuer relationship as kind of participation akin to partnership. Against an innocent true owner, a good faith purchaser of registered securities can never get title to securities in a forged transfer.[117] Though a good faith purchaser relying on a duly issued certificate can get damages from the issuer on the basis of estoppel after a forgery is registered under the principle of quasi-negotiability, a good faith purchaser in a forged a transfer can not avail himself of the estoppel against the issuer, but is estopped as against the issuer from denying the authenticity of the transfer and is thus under a duty to indemnify the issuer against the loss as a result of registering the forged transfer. Estoppel against the true owner can rarely be established absent fraud on the part of the true owner.

The resort to estoppel to allocate loss of third party fraud and achieve proprietary effect in respect of registered securities indicates the flexibility and versatility of estoppel to achieve the policies pursued by law, for example, the loss allocation to the party in the best place to investigate and authenticate title, in the case of registered securities. The law on title conflicts between a true owner and a transferee, both the victim of fraud, is basically an issue of loss allocation. In the case of registered securities as choses in action, an issuer is also a party to be considered. The underlying rationale of the law is protecting the security of title, akin to the *nemo dat* rule in respect of chattel. On the other hand the security of transaction has to be taken into consideration, especially regarding securities in regular transaction. The approach is to impose the duty to ascertain the authenticity of title in a transaction upon the party who is in the best

[116] *Swan v The North British Australasian Company (Limited)* (1863) 2 H & C 175, 176 (Mellor J); 159 ER 73, 75.

[117] There has never been negotiability in registered securities, see also M Yates and G Montagu, *The Law of Global Custody* (3rd rev edn, Tottel Publishing, London 2009) 20.

position to do so and then allocate the loss to such a party, if there is an omission of duty. A transferee in a forged transfer is in the best position to investigate the title of the counterparty and identify the loss any unusual circumstance. Thus a transferee in a forged transfer is to sustain the loss. If a forged transfer is registered and certificates are duly issued by an issuer, a transferee has no way to identify any suspicious circumstance of fraud or forgery and it is the issuer to sustain the loss. An issuer sustaining loss in this way can turn to the transferee who submits a forged transfer for registration for indemnity. The idea is to insulate the defective title at the most proximate chain in the transaction and prevent its transmission. An innocent transferee in a forged transfer suffers the misfortune of fraud. Although such a transferee can resort to a fraudster for damages it is precarious that his claim can realistically succeed. But it is real life that someone has to bear the misfortune.

Estoppel in respect of registered securities has its peculiarity due to the dual proof of title of certificates and register. However, the policy of loss allocation as a result of third party fraud underlying the estoppel has much wider application. The need of loss allocation is equally present in the markets of intermediated securities of uncertificated registered securities, though without certificates, with similar needs for protection of vested holders and transaction security. The essence of estoppel in respect of registered securities of allocating loss to the party in the best position to prevent loss of third party fraud deserves consideration in the design on sorting out title conflicts regarding intermediated securities.[118]

3.5 Conclusion

The principle for title conflicts under English law is the *nemo dat* maxim. Estoppel is a common law tool to evade the *nemo dat* maxim to cater for the commercial needs of protecting innocent purchasers and transaction safety. Estoppel is the basis of statutory exceptions to the *nemo dat* maxim on chattels. Estoppel is the basis of negotiability of bearer securities. Estoppel is also the mechanism to allocate loss between parties in fraudulent transactions in registered securities. Estoppel is a useful tool to avoid the *nemo dat* principle to achieve liquidity and finality in commerce and financial markets. Despite the elimination of certificates there may still be a role for estoppel in the context of title conflicts with regards to intermediated securities.

[118] See 4.4 and 6.3.4.

CHAPTER FOUR

TITLE AND TITLE CONFLICTS AT THE TOP TIER

4.1 Overview

The current UK securities settlement system is the CREST system, mainly governed by the Uncertificated Securities Regulations 2001 SI 2001/3755 (USR 2001), and operated by Euroclear UK & Ireland. The CREST system is an electronic system in which securities are evidenced and transferred in a dematerialised way without certificates. The Operator keeps an operator register for each issue of participating securities which is the *prima facie* evidence of title to securities, and keeps securities accounts for each system member to record their holding. Transfer of securities is made by electronic instructions communicated between relevant members and the Operator, i.e., changes made on the securities accounts of relevant members by the Operator based on instructions of relevant members. Registration of transfer of securities is made by the Operator on the operator register of each issue of participating securities. The system has links with issuers or their agents to provide the holding information to issuers. The system has payment arrangements with settlement banks of members and the Bank of England, which achieves DVP (delivery against payment).[1] Upon title transfer of securities a transferee's payment obligation becomes irrevocable. CREST adopts the second model of the three models of DVP proposed by the Bank of International Settlement.[2] On the basis of electronic evidencing and

[1] M Evans, 'The Sun Sets on Daylight Exposure: A UK Perspective on Securities Settlement' [2001] JIBFL 515; M Yates and G Montagu, *The Law of Global Custody* (3rd rev edn, Tottel Publishing, London 2009) 216.

2 "Model 1: systems that settle transfer instructions for both securities and funds on a trade-by-trade (gross) basis, with final (unconditional) transfer of securities from the seller to the buyer (delivery) occurring at the same time as final transfer of funds from the buyer to the seller (payment); Model 2: systems that settle

transfer of title the CREST system enables transactions in securities to be executed in dematerialised form, such as title transfer, creation of security interest over securities, as well as the processing of corporate action.[3] The system has clear-cut rules on the authenticity of dematerialised instructions and the validity thereof, which are the very foundation of the system. The system enjoys statutory protection of its rules on the finality of instructions in the system, aimed at reducing the risk of insolvency of members.

The CREST system is established under the USR 2001, which, replacing the Uncertificated Securities Regulations 1995 SI 1995/3272 (USR 1995), set out the basic legal framework of a system to enable title to units of a security to be evidenced otherwise than by a certificate and transferred otherwise than by a written instrument.[4] The USR 2001 cover the following key aspects: approval, compliance and supervision in respect of the Operator of a system, participation of securities, keeping of operator registers of securities and operator records of securities, keeping of issuer-records of securities, conversion between certificated and uncertificated securities, validity of dematerialised instructions and liability for forged dematerialised securities. The USR 2001 displace inconsistent rules requiring that securities be in the certificated form or transferred in the written form.[5]

Relevant rules are revised and new rules are introduced to enhance the arrangements in the CREST system. The Financial Markets and Insolvency

---

securities transfer instructions on a gross basis with final transfer of securities from the seller to the buyer (delivery) occurring throughout the processing cycle, but settle funds transfer instructions on a net basis, with final transfer of funds from the buyer to the seller (payment) occurring at the end of the processing cycle; Model 3: systems that settle transfer instructions for both securities and funds on a net basis, with final transfers of both securities and funds occurring at the end of the processing cycle." Bank for International Settlements, 'Delivery Versus Payment in Securities Settlement Systems Report (September 1992)'.

[3] "Corporate actions means all kinds of action triggered by the issuer or by the terms of a security and affecting the security (equity or debt). Processing of corporate actions: functions which are necessary in the chain of account providers, in order to ensure that the investor participates in corporate actions", 'Second Advice of the Legal Certainty Group: Solutions to Legal Barriers related to Post-Trading within the EU (August 2008)' Recommendation 12; see also M Yates and G Montagu, *The Law of Global Custody* (3rd rev edn, Tottel Publishing, London 2009) 121-22.

[4] USR 2001 reg 2.

[5] USR 2001 reg 38.

(Settlement Finality) Regulations 1999 SI 1999/2979 are adopted to enhance the finality of a payment or transfer of title to securities in recognised payment systems and securities settlement systems to mitigate system risk, which require that a relevant system formulate rules on the time of entry of a payment order and a transfer order and the time of irrevocability of such an order, which will not be displaced by relevant insolvency rules provided that such an order enters into the system before the commencement of an insolvency proceeding against a system participant, even if an insolvency proceeding opens on the same day as the transfer order enters the system. Default arrangements of a relevant system in respect of insolvency of a participant from insolvency displacement rules are also exempted. The Financial Markets and Insolvency Regulations 1996 SI 1996/1469 grant gracious periods to the enforcement of system-charges over participating securities in the CREST system established by members of the system and for securing payment obligations to settlement banks for the purpose of procuring participating securities, to reduce the impact of insolvency of members on the system.

The CREST rules are binding on all participants and recognised by law.[6] It is a noteworthy feature of the legal framework of the securities settlement system that statutes lay out the basic framework and leave details and practices to system rules and contractual arrangements between the Operator and participants which are recognised and supported by law.

Use of the CREST system is optional to an issuer, though full dematerialisation is the trend and may well become compulsory.[7] It is open to all kinds of securities, i.e., shares, stock, debentures, debenture stock, loan stock, bonds, units of a collective investment scheme, rights under a depositary receipt, other securities of any description, interests in a security,[8] and eligible debt securities.[9]

4.2 Title; Operator Register; Registered Securities

The CREST system settles securities issued by issuers of UK, Guernsey, Ireland, the Isle of Man, and Jersey, governed by the law of each

[6] See https://www.euroclear.com, accessed 30 March 2013.

[7] Companies Act 2006 s 786 (4) enables regulations which may prohibit the issue of any certificate by a company in respect of the issue or transfer of securities.

[8] USR 2001 reg 3.

[9] Uncertificated Securities (Amendment) (Eligible Debt Securities) Regulations 2003 SI 2003/1633.

jurisdiction respectively. The discussion is only on securities issued by issuers in the UK excluding issuers in Scotland.

All securities in the CREST system are uncertificated registered securities in the sense that they are represented not by certificates as certificated securities, but by electronic records in the system. The system records of securities constitute the operator register of member or register of securities and confer title to securities. The operator register of members or of securities is established as *prima facie* evidence of title,[10] which is akin to the status of issuer registers of certificated registered securities and is the best title[11] available under English law. It follows from the definition of registered securities that title to securities are entries on the issuer registers. Thus certificated bearer securities, on entry into the CREST system, are transformed into registered securities. Negotiability is thus lost, though it is argued that the finality of transactions in such securities achieved at the top tier of the system is stronger than negotiability.[12]

The operator keeps an operator register for each issue of securities which serves as title to securities. There is no issuer register. The operator register of each issue of securities is established as title to securities.[13] An issuer may be required to keep an updated record based on the operator register of its securities depending on the nature of the securities. The record is not register. Each issuer of shares shall keep an updated record of the entries made in its operator register of members maintained by the operator,[14] the registrar of each issuer of public sector securities shall keep an updated record of the entries made in the operator register of securities maintained by the operator,[15] each issuer of other securities required to maintain a register of securities if not participating in the system shall keep an updated record of the entries made in the operator register of securities maintained by the operator,[16] and each issuer of securities not required to

---

[10] Companies Act 2006 s 127, USR 2001 reg 24, displacing Law of Property Act 1925 s 53 (1) (c), s 136.
[11] Euroclear, 'The Domestic Legal Framework (March 2002)'.
[12] See 4.5.1 for further analysis.
[13] USR 2001 regs 2, 3, 24.
[14] USR 2001 reg 20, sch 4 para 5; Euroclear, 'CREST Rules (April 2012)' r 14 (b) (3).
[15] USR 2001 reg 21, sch 4 para 12, sch 4 para 13; Euroclear, 'CREST Rules (April 2012)' r 14 (b) (4).
[16] USR 2001 reg 22, sch 4 para 14, sch 4 para 15; Euroclear, 'CREST Rules (April 2012)' r 14 (b) (4).

keep a register of members or securities (eligible debt securities) if not participating in the system is not required to keep an record of entries made in the operator register.[17] The difference between certificated bearer securities and registered securities is retained in some way. Issuers of bearer securities have no interest in knowing the holders of the securities and have no need for an issuer record while issuers of registered securities have the interest in knowing the holders and the need for an issuer record.

The USR 2001 establish the operator register of securities as *prima facie* title to securities and achieve delivery against payment and transfer of legal title upon settlement. Its predecessor the USR 1995 were adopted to enable title to units of a security to be evidenced otherwise than by a certificate and transferred otherwise than by a written instrument, i.e., through a computer-based system. In the 1995 framework issuers continued to keep issuer registers but were under a duty to register transfers on Operator instructions.[18] The issuer registers continued to be *prima facie* title to securities[19] and there was no operator register. A transferee acquired an equitable property right in uncertificated units on the generation of an operator instruction to the issuer to register a transfer and acquired legal property in the uncertificated units on registration on the issuer register.[20] Only corporate registered securities were admissible excluding government securities and bearer securities. There was a lag of transfer of legal title behind the transfer of equitable title, which was obviously not the best practice, but was a compromise as a result of the failure of the TAURUS project to replace issuer registers by a central system register.[21]

The issue remains in the 2001 framework in respect of a transfer across registers of the same issue of securities, i.e., from a transferor of certificated securities to a transferee who chooses to hold uncertificated securities or a transferor of uncertificated securities to a transferee who chooses to hold certificated securities, there is a period, though very short, between deletion and entry on the operator register and the issuer register, after the transferor's title is deleted on one register and the entry of the transferee's title on the other register, the transferor retains legal title and

[17] USR 2001 reg 22; Euroclear, 'CREST Rules (April 2012)' r 14 (b) (5).
[18] USR 1995 (now revoked) reg 19.
[19] ibid reg 20.
[20] ibid reg 23; M Kirby, 'Crest and Securities Law Reform' [2000] JIBFL 3.
[21] R Barham, 'CREST: The Phoenix from the Ashes of Taurus' (1993) 8 JIBL 426; E Micheler, *Property in Securities: A Comparative Study* (Cambridge Studies in Corporate Law, Cambridge University Press, Cambridge 2007) 64-67, 74.

the transferee acquires equitable title after deletion from one register.[22]

4.3 Transfer

The transfer can be illustrated by the most common form of transactions, i.e., the delivery of securities against payment of the purchase price.[23] In such a transaction the CREST Operator receives an input of disposition of securities and tries to match it with an input of purchaser of identical securities, then locks the inputs together which is irrevocable unless with the consent of both parties. After pre-settlement check on the sufficiency of stock account of the transferor, the sufficiency of the cash account of the transferee, and the sufficiency of credit of the settlement bank of the transferee with the Bank of England, the CREST Operator executes settlement, i.e., delivery of securities and payment of purchaser price, which involves the simultaneous occurrence of debiting the stock account of the transferor, crediting the stock account of the transferee, crediting the cash account of the transferor, and debiting the cash account of the transferee. Debiting the transferor's securities account and crediting the transferee's securities account constitute the registration on the operator register, thus transfer of title.[24]

The point of final settlement occurs on the point that relevant stock postings data is first received by the local record.[25] In respect of transfer of uncertificated securities in the CREST system not involving conversion between certificated and uncertificated securities the local record is equivalent to the operator register,[26] as the operator register is updated

[22] USR 2001 regs 31-33.

[23] Other transactions include "the dematerialisation of securities in to CREST (with or without a transfer of title); the rematerialisation of securities out of CREST (with or without a transfer of title); deliveries of securities from one CREST member to another with or without a corresponding payment; stock borrowing and lending, repo and collateral movements; certain corporate actions; and international deliveries to or from a counterparty in another CSD," CREST, 'The Domestic Legal Framework (March 2002)' 7.

[24] Euroclear, 'The Domestic Legal Framework (March 2002)' 7-9.

[25] Euroclear, 'CREST Rules (April 2012)' r 5 (2), r 14 (a); local record: those parts of the CREST system which are kept in the United Kingdom the principal purpose of which is to record title to (or other interests in) securities held and transferred by means of the CREST system and details of the CREST members by whom such title (or other interest) is held, Euroclear, 'CREST Rules (April 2012)' r 14 (c).

[26] Euroclear, 'CREST Rules (April 2012)' r 14 (a).

simultaneously to reflect the change in the local record.

An operator register of securities is composed of the "stock accounts of all Members to which are credited units of the relevant participating security; corporate action data; the names and addresses of all members; the CSD (central securities depositories)[27] List; the stock postings held on the local record; the list maintained by EUI (Euroclear UK & Ireland, the system Operator) of participants admitted as CREST IPAs (issuing and paying agents); and parts of the local record for the period of 20 years from the date on which a relevant member ceased to hold the relevant participating security."[28]

Transfer of title is registration on the operator register of an issue of securities simultaneously as a transferor's stock account is debited and a transferee's stock is credited. It is a set of procedures but all executed at the same moment. Thus the transfer of title is a point instead of a period. This simplified transfer of title to uncertificated securities in the system is akin to bearer securities title of which is transferred on delivery of certificates. On the other hand, uncertificated securities are registered securities and their transfer is by nature novation. The transfer is different from certificated registered securities in that transfer of uncertificated securities is by the simultaneous debit of the transferor's account, credit of the transferee's account, and registration on the operator register, while transfer of certificated registered securities is a two-step process of delivery of certificates from transferor to transferee and registration on the issuer register, which are not simultaneous. It can be seen that uncertificated securities are registered securities but transferred in a mechanism more similar to bearer securities. This special feature of uncertificated securities has implications for the law on title conflicts.

The instant transfer of legal title is true only of transfer of securities in the system in a purely dematerialised way. In a transfer involving conversion of uncertificated securities into certificated securities of the same issue or vice versa, registration on the issuer register is based on an operator instruction generated on a registration on the operator register or vice versa. Registrations on the two registers are not simultaneous although the time lag is short.

---

[27] Overseas CSDs are relevant where international deliveries to or from a counterparty in another CSD of securities are involved, or transactions in deposit receipts are involved, Euroclear, 'The Domestic Legal Framework (March 2002)' 7, 32.

[28] Euroclear, 'CREST Rules (April 2012)' r 14 (b) (2).

4.4 Title Conflicts

The issue of fraud and title conflicts persists in the CREST system despite the message authentication system. It is possible that the operator register is amended based on an instruction sent by fraud or other act, which, against the will of the true owner, divests the true owner of title. Title conflicts between an innocent true owner and a good faith transferee persist.

4.4.1 The Scenario

Fraud still persists. An instruction may be forged by strangers in the name of a system-participant. A participant may send an instruction to dispose the securities of his client against the will of his client. A forged dematerialised instruction is an instruction "not sent from the computers of a system-participant or the computers comprising an Operator-system; or not sent from the computers of the system-participant or the computers comprising an Operator-system (as the case may be) from which it is expressed to have been sent."[29] A causative act, is an act which "unlawfully causes the Operator to make, delete or amend an entry on an operator register of securities," excluding "a dematerialised instruction or an act which causes a dematerialised instruction to be sent from the computer of a system-participant."[30] An induced amendment is "an entry on, deletion from, or amendment to an Operator register of securities which results from a forged dematerialised instruction or a causative act."[31] Title conflicts arise from an induced amendment of an operator register against the will of the true owner.

4.4.2 Estoppel against a True Owner

A true owner is estopped from denying authenticity of title in a fraudulent transaction which is apparently normal to third parties according to statutes and system rules.

---

[29] USR 2001 reg 36 (1) (a).
[30] ibid reg 36 (1) (b).
[31] ibid reg 36 (1) (c).

4.4.2.1 Statutory estoppel against a true owner

Transfer of title to uncertificated securities in the system depends on a communication network of properly authenticated instructions. The reliability of the network system is guaranteed by approved network providers of technologies and financial regulation over all sponsors and participants who have direct access to the system.[32] "A properly authenticated dematerialised instruction is expressed to have been sent by a person or on behalf of a person if it is attributable to that person."[33] With the buttress of the reliability of the network, a properly authenticated instruction is established by the USR 2001 as being able to estop a relevant participant from denying that an instruction is not properly authenticated. More specifically a properly authenticated dematerialised instruction expressed to have been sent on behalf of a person by a sponsoring system-participant or the Operator estops the person on whose behalf the instruction is expressed to have been sent from denying to the addressee that that the properly authenticated dematerialised instruction is sent with his authority; or that the information contained in the properly authenticated dematerialised instruction is correct; furthermore such instruction estops the sponsoring system-participant or the Operator from denying to the addressee that he has authority to send the properly authenticated dematerialised instruction; or that he has sent the properly authenticated dematerialised instruction.[34] A properly authenticated dematerialised instruction expressed to have been sent by a person, and not on behalf of another person, estops the person from denying to the addressee that the information contained in the properly authenticated dematerialised instruction is correct; or that he has sent the properly authenticated dematerialised instruction.[35]

Thus a properly authenticated instruction estops a sponsored participant who participates in the system through an agent from denying that his agent has authority and the information is correct, as well as an agent from denying that he has authority and he has sent it. A properly

---

[32] As to the system Operator, see Financial Services and Markets Act 2000 ss 285, 286, 288, 293; URS 2001 pt 2; Financial Markets and Insolvency (Settlement Finality) Regulations 1999 SI 1999/2979 sch. As to intermediaries as custodians or sponsors, see Financial Services and Markets Act 2000 (Regulated Activities) Order 2001 SI 2001/544 chs viii, vix.

[33] USR 2001 reg 35 (10) (a).

[34] ibid reg 35 (2).

[35] ibid reg 35 (3).

authenticated instruction estops a participant who participates in the system as principal from denying that the information is correct and he himself sent the instruction. The dispute on the authority of an agent is excluded. Thus a true owner is estopped from asserting his title in case of interference of title caused by fraud either by his intermediary if he is not a system-participant or by a stranger if he is a system-participant.

The statutory estoppel originates from the common law estoppel with respect to bearer securities and registered securities, as analysed in Chapter Three. It continues the tradition of departing from the contract perspective that a participant is bound to admit that something is true and cannot deny the truth to a third party who relies on the representation, without using property law terminologies, despite its proprietary result: under estoppel, in the case of certificated bearer securities a purchaser gets title overriding that of the true owner under the principle of negotiability; in the case of certificated registered securities, a purchaser other than a transferee in a fraudulent transfer gets damages from the issuer despite that no overriding title can be claimed against the true owner. In one aspect the statutory estoppel is the same as estoppel with respect to certificated bearer securities in that it divests the true owner of title and confers title upon a purchaser. The policy is the paramount importance of system integrity for a purchaser to be confident in the title he acquires through the system. This is the same with certificated bearer securities that commercial needs require a special and strong estoppel which is not otherwise recognised in common law, for example no such estoppel in the case of certificated registered securities. The statutory estoppel in fact replicates negotiability, even to a greater extent with less onerous duty of investigation upon a purchaser.[36] On the other hand the true owner is protected through the authentication arrangements of the system to minimise the occurrence of fraud or unauthorised instruction, as well as statutory damages against the system Operator.

4.4.2.2 Contractual estoppel against a true owner

The statutory estoppel against a true owner is reinforced by system rules of the CREST which binds any participant in the CREST system. By participating in the system a participant agrees to be bound by the system rules on estoppel. A true owner as member of the system agrees that the Operator "shall be entitled without further enquiry to act upon any written

[36] Compare 3.3.

instructions or information or purported instructions or information relating to the Member received in accordance with the CREST Manual or the CREST Rules whether from the Member, the Parent, the Sponsor, or any person reasonably believed by EUI (Euroclear UK & Ireland) to be a person who is legally able to act on behalf of the Member or to be a person notified to it by the Member as having authority to act on the Member's behalf notwithstanding that it may afterwards be discovered that any such instruction or information was not genuine or was not correct or was unauthorised",[37] provided that "EUI has no actual notice that it was not genuine; or any information was incorrect; or it was not sent with the authority of the person on whose behalf it was expressed to have been sent; or it was not initiated by the person entitled to give it; or it was not initiated through the systems, gateway, workstation and associated equipment (as the case may be) operated by the person entitled to give it and at the time it received the actual notice it was practicable for EUI to halt the processing of the instruction or information or purported instruction or information".[38] A true owner thus warrants to the Operator that any instruction from the true owner duly received by the Operator as genuine in an apparent way is genuine as such provided the Operator has no actual notice of anything to the contrary, i.e., a true owner is bound by any instruction purported to be from him as long as it is confirmed by the authentication system. A true owner agrees to warrant the authenticity of instructions and sustain the risk of fraud in the system on becoming a member of the system.

4.4.2.3 Warranty of title

An owner as system member undertakes to the Operator that it has full legal title to the securities he intends to transfer free from any proprietary, equitable or other right of any person (including a person for whom the true owner acts as nominee or agent);[39] and an owner will procure that no person for whom it holds securities as nominee or agent will assert any such interest to prevent a transfer of title to the relevant securities.[40] Thus an owner is estopped from denying that a transfer is executed without his authority or he has no title or has defective title. This precludes the clients

[37] Euroclear, 'CREST Terms and Conditions (September 2009)' 7.3.
[38] ibid 7.4.
[39] ibid 10.1.
[40] Ibid 10.1.

of a system-participant from asserting title if the system-participant acts against the will of clients. A good faith transferee thus gets good legal title.

4.4.3 No Actual Notice of a Purchaser

A purchaser who has no actual notice of any inconsistent situation as stated in the properly authenticated dematerialised instruction is entitled to rely on the information as stated in the properly authenticated dematerialised instruction.[41] Thus the requirement in the statutory arrangement is that a purchaser gets good title if he has no actual notice of any adverse title. It is a clear-cut and simplified approach to the qualification for good title, abandoning the complex case law on the standards of holder in due course under negotiability and the good faith purchaser rule in equity.

4.4.4 Operator Compensation

A true owner of uncertificated securities is at loss in this paradigm of resolution of title conflicts between innocent parties. A true owner divested of title can apply to the courts to order compensation by the Operator for his loss resulting from an induced amendment to an operator register of securities.[42] The liability of the Operator for making an induced amendment shall not be enforceable more than 10 years after the date on which the entry was made or deleted or, in the case of a failure, the failure first occurred.[43] A defrauded true owner will not be awarded by the court

---

[41] An addressee may not accept any of the matters … if at the time he received the properly authenticated dematerialised instruction or at any time thereafter-(a) he was a person other than a participating issuer or a sponsoring system-participant receiving properly authenticated dematerialised instructions on behalf of a participating issuer, and he had actual notice-(i) that any information contained in it was incorrect; (ii) that the system-participant or the Operator (as the case may be) expressed to have sent the instruction did not send the instruction; or (iii) where relevant, that the person on whose behalf it was expressed to have been sent had not given to the Operator or the sponsoring system-participant (as the case may be), identified in the properly authenticated dematerialised instruction as having sent it, his authority to send the properly authenticated dematerialised instruction on his behalf, USR 2001 reg 35 (5); see also Bank of England, 'The Future of Money Market Instruments: A Consultation (November 1999)'.

[42] USR 2001 reg 36 (2).

[43] ibid reg 23 (2).

more than £50,000 for each such induced amendment to an operator register of securities.[44] The court shall award compensation of such amount of compensation as it appears to it to be just and equitable in all the circumstances having regard to the loss sustained by the true owner as a result of the induced amendment to the Operator register of securities. The loss will be ascertained by the same rules on the duty of a person to mitigate his loss as applicable to damages recoverable under common law. The amount of compensation may be reduced if the loss was caused by or contributed to any act or omission of the true owner.[45] A true owner will not get an award of compensation from a court if the Operator identifies a person as being responsible for an induced amendment to an Operator register notwithstanding that it is impossible for the true owner to obtain satisfactory compensation from that person.[46] It follows that the full title of the true owner is lost and compensation is subject to many factors.

4.4.4.1 No other liability

The Operator is not responsible for any other liability than those expressly provided by in the USR 2001 except such as may arise from fraud or other wilful default, or negligence, on the part of the Operator.[47] Except the statutory liability for compensation there is no general liability of the Operator in maintaining any register of securities.[48] The limitation of operator liability is consistent with the practice in respect of certificated registered securities, where there is no general duty of an issuer to the public in general except a duty to the current shareholders to insure they rights are intact. The duty of the Operator to keep Operator registers of participating securities is a statutory duty. The Operator is only liable to pay compensation to a true owner by court orders. There is a cap on the Operator compensation and the Operator is exempted if the party responsible for the loss can be identified, while an issuer of certificated securities is liable to a transferee who relies on certificates issued by the issuer against his total loss regardless whether the party responsible for the loss can be identified. The underlying policy of limited Operator liability

---

[44] ibid reg 36 (6).
[45] ibid reg 36 (7).
[46] ibid reg 36 (4).
[47] ibid reg 36 (9).
[48] USR 2001 reg 23 (1) (a); Euroclear, 'CREST Terms and Conditions (September 2009)' [17.13]; M Yates and G Montagu, *The Law of Global Custody* (3rd rev edn, Tottel Publishing, London 2009) 252-53.

may be that the potential liability of the Operator would be enormous for maintaining the registers of all participating securities.

4.4.4.2 Issuer liability

A true owner can hardly turn to an issuer for damages. The title to securities are entries on the relevant operator register and a transfer of title does not directly involve an issuer. An issuer with a duty to keep a record of securities is under a duty to update the record upon the operator register of its securities. An issuer is only liable where the Operator makes an amendment of the Operator register on instructions of the participating issuer,[49] which is not relevant to title conflicts in a transfer between a true owner and a transferee in the system. Furthermore, when joining the CREST system, a member agrees to take no action against an issuer of participating securities for any liability arising out of any amendment of the relevant Operator register.[50] Issuers are sheltered by the Operator.

4.4.4.3 No effect on general law

Apparently a defrauded true owner, being estopped from denying that title has been transferred, loses property rights to securities and is left with a statutory claim for compensation from the Operator. Apparently a wronged true owner has no property right to be reinstated on the Operator register and no property right against a transferee. Thus the paradigm on resolving title conflicts between an innocent true owner and a good faith transferee has undertaken a fundamental change, from in favour of a true owner by leaving a true owner intact and allocating loss to an issuer or a transferee to in favour of a transferee by allocating loss to a true owner with potential compensation from the Operator or a third person.

A true owner's right against a fraudster who causes an inducement or sends a forged dematerialised instruction which divests the true owner of title, or any other person, is not affected by the USR 2001.[51] The liability of any person for causing or permitting a dematerialised instruction to be sent without authority; or to contain information which is incorrect; or to be expressed to have been sent by a person who did not send it, is not prejudiced by these provisions which can still be claimed outside the

[49] USR 2001 reg 23 (1) (b).
[50] Euroclear, 'CREST Terms and Conditions (September 2009)' [17.13].
[51] USR 2001 reg 36 (10).

system.[52] The liability of such person is similar to the liability of a person who causes a change in the issuer register of registered certificated securities, a transferee in a fraudulent transaction or a fraudster, as analysed in 3.4. The basis of the liability is in contract law. A person making a request to the Operator for a change in an operator register makes a representation to the Operator that the transfer as the basis for the change is genuine. The person is thus obliged to indemnify the Operator against the liability resulting from the change of the Operator register.[53] The Operator retains the right to recover from a third party any sum that he may be ordered to pay a true owner for the loss from an induced amendment of the Operator register or forged dematerialised instruction.[54]

It is the reservation of a true owner's right against any party other than the Operator which leads some commentators to argue that a transferee may still be liable to a true owner under the general law on the issue.[55] A transferee gets good title in the CREST system but the title may be inferior to that of a true owner under general law. It is argued that it is the finality of the CREST system that justifies the statutory estoppel against a true owner and insulates a transferee while outside the CREST system it is still governed by general law.[56] Interpretation in this way would cause unnecessary uncertainty.

Indeed there is no reference to the title of a true owner or a transferee, or the nature of a true owner's entitlement for compensation from the Operator in the statute. A transferee gets good title through estoppel, the same as negotiability of certificated bearer securities and quasi-negotiability of certificated registered securities. It can be reasonably concluded that drafters do not intend to insulate a fraudster who causes the unauthorised transfer from liability to a true owner, but not to make a good faith transferee liable to a true owner. It is clear from the wording and policy of the USR 2001 that a good faith transferee gets good title on reliance of the system and loss from failure of the authentication system is shifted to a

---

52 ibid reg 36 (10).

53 See 3.4.2.2; E Micheler, *Property in Securities: A Comparative Study* (Cambridge Studies in Corporate Law, Cambridge University Press, Cambridge 2007) 106.

54 ibid reg 36 (8).

55 See 3.3 and 3.4.

56 J Benjamin, *Interest in Securities: A Proprietary Law Analysis of the International Securities Markets* (Oxford University Press, Oxford 2000) 213; M Yates and G Montagu, *The Law of Global Custody* (3rd rev edn, Tottel Publishing, London 2009) 244.

true owner who can get compensation from the Operator.

4.4.5 Policy

It is a change of paradigm in the resolution of title conflicts. It shifts the loss from the purchaser side to the prior holder side, as a major carve-out of the *nemo dat* maxim. The change is justified by several reasons. Firstly the pressing need of systemic finality and integrity is overwhelming. Secondly a true owner is in a better position to protect his title as a true owner is able to choose the intermediary, when intermediary fraud is more likely than third party fraud as intermediaries have dominant control over client assets. A transferee often has no way to ascertain the authenticity of title.[57] Thirdly systemic infrastructure is designed to be reliable and capable of effective prevention of fraud by strangers. Fourthly a prior holder is entitled to claim damages from the Operator. Fifthly financial regulation over the custody of securities and securities intermediaries is a deterrent of fraud.[58]

4.5 Change in Respect of Certificated Securities

4.5.1 Change in respect of Certificated Bearer Securities

Purchasers of uncertificated securities in the CREST system enjoy a high level of protection which is functionally equivalent to negotiability or the equitable *bona fide* acquisition rule, that a good faith purchaser gets good title if he is innocent. It is even more favourable than negotiability and the good faith acquisition rule, since a transferee will get title if he has no knowledge of any defect in the title. The duty to investigate any suspicious circumstance is less onerous,[59] supported by the statutory estoppel against a true owner that the true owner cannot deny anything inconsistent with a duly executed transfer.

Money market instruments are the majority of bearer securities in England. Before migration into the CREST system as eligible debt securities they were settled in the system operated by the Central

---

[57] E Micheler, 'Farewell Quasi-Negotiability? Legal Title and Transfer of Shares in a Paperless World' [2002] JBL 358, 371-72.

[58] Financial Services and Markets Act 2000 (Regulated Activities) Order 2001 SI 2001/544 art 45.

[59] Compare *Sheffield v The London Joint Stock Bank* (1888) 13 App Cas 333 (HL).

Moneymarkets Officer Service in which certificates were immobilised and instruments were non-fungible. Thus the status of bearer securities and eligibility for negotiability were unaffected theoretically.[60] With migration into the CREST and the introduction of an Operator register of each issue, money markets instruments are transformed into registered eligible debt securities, despite the minor difference from originally registered securities that an issuer of eligible debt securities is not obliged to keep records of the Operator register.[61] A problem is raised with dematerialisation that negotiability is lost with the elimination of certificates. It would be a departure from current law to accord negotiability to intangible rights incapable of physical possession and delivery. However it is hardly necessary to replicate negotiability in respect of eligible debt securities since a transferee is in a better position in the CREST system. A transferee gets good title and the duty to investigate suspicious circumstances is reduced with statutory intervention, which, as analysed above, actually achieves the same result of negotiability with regard to legal title in the CREST system. There is support for this position.[62] However other than the top tier of the CREST system negotiability is indeed lost and title conflicts are governed by general priority rules.[63]

4.5.2 Change in respect of Certificated Registered Securities

This is a major change in respect of title to registered securities. In a transfer of uncertificated registered securities against the will of a true owner to a good faith transferee, a transferee gets good title and a true

---

[60] J Donohue and C Atkins, 'Demystifying UK Settlement Systems' (1993) 12 Int Fin L Rev 27; J Donohue and C Atkins, 'Settling Trades in the UK Moneymarkets' (1993) 12 Int Fin L Rev 35; M Evans, 'Moving to a Dematerialised Capital Market: Short-Term Instruments, Long-Term Gain' (2003) 18 JIBLR 121; Bank of England, 'The Future of Money Market Instruments: A Consultation (November 1999)'; Bank of England, 'The Future of Money Market Instruments: Next Steps (March 2000)'; Bank of England, 'The Future of Money Market Instruments: Progress towards Dematerialisation and Settlement in CREST, An Interim Report (January 2001)'; J Benjamin, 'The Dematerialisation of Money Market Instruments' with commentary by G Morton in S Worthington (ed) *Commercial Law and Commercial Practice* (Hart Publishing, Oxford 2003).

[61] USR 2001 reg 22; Euroclear, 'CREST Rules (April 2012)' r 14(b) (5).

[62] Bank of England, 'The Future of Money Market Instruments: A Consultation (November 1999)'; see also M Yates and G Montagu, *The Law of Global Custody* (3rd rev edn, Tottel Publishing, London 2009) 20, 244.

[63] See Chapter Five.

owner is entitled to compensation against the Operator and damages against a fraudster. In a transfer of certificated registered securities a true owner retains title and a transferee or an issuer sustains the loss with claim for damages against a fraudster which is practically precarious. A transferee in a fraudulent transaction sustains the loss of fraud while a transferee in a transaction in securities of which certificates have been duly issued by an issuer as a result of a fraudulent transaction is entitled to claim damages from the issuer who sustains the loss of fraud.

4.6 Conclusion

In conclusion, uncertificated securities in the CREST system are all registered securities; title is operator register; transfer of title to uncertificated securities in the CREST system is by a change in the operator register with simultaneous debit on a transferor's operator account and credit on a transferee's operator account; a statutory estoppel is introduced which actually achieves the result of negotiability: a good faith purchaser of uncertificated securities at the top tier in the CREST system gets good title free from any defect of title of a transferor, valid against a true owner. Although uncertificated securities are registered securities, their transfer and title conflicts are dealt with more similarly to bearer securities and negotiability, due to demands of system finality and integrity which subordinates the property law bias for a true owner of registered securities. The paradigm change in loss allocation of property law with respect to uncertificated registered securities has changed the preference for a true owner. The policy is that a true owner is in a better situation to avoid fraud by choosing his intermediary when intermediary fraud is more likely an occurrence, backed up by system authentications and admission qualifications against fraud, and statutory compensation from the Operator available to true owners divested of title by fraud. A good faith purchaser also gets good title free of any equitable interest in the uncertificated securities which have major implications for securities holders other than the top tier of the CREST system, which will be dealt with in the Chapter on title conflicts under general priority rules.[64]

---

[64] See Chapter Five.

CHAPTER FIVE

TITLE CONFLICTS IN RESPECT OF INTERMEDIATED SECURITIES UNDER GENERAL PRIORITY RULES

Title conflicts in respect of intermediated securities can be examined in the perspective of title conflicts in respect of securities as a special kind of property, as in Chapter Three and Chapter Four, as well as in the perspective of general property rules. Title conflicts in respect of intermediated securities between a prior innocent holder and an innocent purchaser may be title conflicts between legal and equitable title, between legal title, and between equitable title, thus involve the priority rules throughout the property right system. The issue may arise in the following scenarios: a CREST-participant purchaser with a legal title against a prior legal title of another CREST-participant or a prior equitable title of a non-CREST-participant; a non-CREST-participant purchaser with an equitable title against a prior legal title of a CREST-participant, a prior equitable title of another non-participant via the CREST system, or a prior equitable title against another non-participant other than via the CREST system. With the statutory estoppel under the Uncertificated Securities Regulations 2001 SI 2001/3755 a legal title acquired in the CREST system overrides a prior legal title and equitable title, which only resolves part of the complexity. Conflicts between equitable title, i.e., title of holders other than direct participants of the CREST system, are still subject to priority rules on equitable interests.[1] This Chapter investigates the transfer of equitable title to intermediated securities, conflicts between equitable title and between equitable title and legal title regarding intermediated securities, under general priority rules.

---

[1] And it is held the statutory estoppel only operates within the CREST system and title conflicts may still be subject to the priority rules under general law, see J Benjamin, *Interest in Securities: A Proprietary Law Analysis of the International Securities Markets* (Oxford University Press, Oxford 2000) 213; M Yates and G Montagu, *The Law of Global Custody* (3rd rev edn, Tottel Publishing, London 2009) 244.

5.1 Transfer

It is necessary to examine the title transfer mechanism and time of transfer in respect of intermediated securities other than the top tier of the CREST system before examining the issue of title conflicts in respect of these intermediated securities. As equitable interests under trusts the transfer of intermediated securities is governed by the rules on the transfer of equitable interests. The nature and the subject matter of transfer of equitable interests will be examined. As the intermediated securities holding system is structurally similar to payment systems, credit transfer in payment systems will be examined. Matching or non-matching (a credit is valid only when there is a corresponding valid debit) is also an issue to be discussed as it reveals the nature of transfer of intermediated securities. The time of transfer of title to intermediated securities will also be introduced, together with the time of credit transfer of payment system. The main point is that a transfer of an equitable interest is the extinction of the original equitable interest and the creation of a new equitable interest, rather than the passing of the original equitable interest, which is true to the holding and transfer of intermediated securities.

5.1.1 Form of Transfer

As equitable choses in action, equitable interests may be transferred by assignment or trust, more specifically in four ways:

> "Now the equitable interest in property in the hands of a trustee can be disposed of by the person entitled to it in favour of a third party in any one of four different ways. The person entitled to it (1.) can assign it to the third party directly; (2.) can direct the trustees to hold the property in trust for the third party (see per Sargant J. in In re Chrimes); (3.) can contract for valuable consideration to assign the equitable interest to him; or (4.) can declare himself to be a trustee for him of such interest."[2]

Much discussion on the nature of transfer of equitable interests is on the point whether there is a disposition of existing equitable interest which needs to be in writing to be valid.

> "[A] disposition of an equitable interest or trust subsisting at the time of the disposition, must be in writing signed by the person disposing of the

[2] *Timpson's Executors v Yerbury* [1936] 1 KB 645 (CA) 664 (Romer LJ).

same, or by his agent thereunto lawfully authorised in writing or by will."[3]

There is little doubt that assignment of equitable interests is disposition of existing equitable interests within the Law of Property Act 1925 s 53 (1) (c).[4] What is controversial is whether transfer of equitable interests by trust is disposition under this article. It is far from settled. Leading cases on this issue are often decided with judges dissenting. It is recognised that a transfer of equitable interest often involves a surrender or extinction of the existing equitable interest which, however, does not prevents it from being a transfer or disposition of existing equitable interest.

5.1.1.1 *Grey v IRC*

In *Grey v IRC*[5], a beneficial owner directed the trustee nominee to hold his equitable interest for others. The direction to the trustee was held to be disposition within Law of Property Act 1925 s 53 (1) (c) with dissenting opinions. It has detailed discussions on assignment, novation, transfer and disposition.

Assignment and novation

Assignment can only transfer rights but not liabilities under contracts. Novation can transfer the whole package of rights and liabilities under contracts with the consent of all parties, a transferor, a transferee and, a debtor in particular.[6] An old debt is replaced by a new debt under novation.

Assignment; language is insignificant

Assignment of equitable interests may be done by any form of words without specific requirements as long as there is clearly an intention to make an assignment. Assignment of an equitable interest may be by a direction, command, request, or permission to the trustee. It is immaterial what form of language is used as long as a trustee is informed of the intention of an original equitable owner that the equitable interest be held for another.[7] A direction to terminate an equitable interest is a grant or

[3] Law of Property Act 1925 s 53(1)(c).
[4] M Smith, *The Law of Assignment: The Creation and Transfer of Choses in Action* (Oxford University Press, Oxford 2007) 214-15.
[5] [1958] Ch 690 (CA), affd *Grey v IRC* [1960] AC 1 (HL).
[6] *Halsbury's Laws of England* (vol 9, 4th edn, Butterworths, London 1998) [1036].
[7] *Timpson's Executors v Yerbury* [1936] 1 KB 645 (CA) 665 (Romer LJ).

assignment of equitable interest and thus a disposition.[8]

Direction different from assignment or not?

One dissenting judge holds that a direction of the equitable owner to the trustee to hold for others is considered to be different from assignment as it terminates the equitable interest.

> "...judged against the general background of the characteristics of equitable interests, I think on the whole that a direction of the kind given in the present case by Mr. Hunter (a direction of the equitable owner to the trustee nominee to hold his equitable interest for others) is something distinct, not only in form, but also in substance, from an assignment; that it no more is or involves a disposition of a subsisting equitable interest than does a formal declaration of trust by an absolute proprietor of personal property, and accordingly that, like such a declaration of trust, it may take effect without writing. In form there can be no doubt that it is more closely analogous to such a declaration of trust than it is to an assignment. Indeed it is, in form, such a declaration, since it declares the trusts upon which the legal owner is to hold thc property as, admittedly, it is within the province of the beneficial owner to do."[9]

> "It was a direction to the trustees which, by reason of the power to direct, which he had, put an end to his beneficial rights. Was it, therefore, a disposition by him of an equitable interest subsisting at the time of the disposition? That is the one question which can be shortly and simply stated. I would answer the question negatively..."[10]

Indeed in the Chancery Division it is held that a direction to the trustee is the same as declaring oneself as a trustee both of which are deliberate choices different from assignment, as the direct passing of the equitable interests from the transferor to the transferee is lacking.[11]

Disposition by assignment or trust

It is held that there is a transfer of an equitable interest whether by way of assignment or by way of direction to trustees to hold on trust for a donee or donees.

> "But whatever language may be employed in cases where general principles have been under consideration the short question which here

[8] *Grey v IRC* [1960] AC 1 (HL) 16 (Lord Radcliffe).
[9] *Grey v IRC* [1958] Ch 690 (CA) 710 (Lord Evershed).
[10] ibid 716 (Lord Evershed).
[11] *Grey v IRC* [1958] Ch 375, 381-83 (Upjohn J).

> emerges is whether what Mr. Hunter did purported to amount to a 'disposition' by him. The word 'disposition' is a word of wide signification. ... Hunter possessed a subsisting equitable interest in the shares: his purpose and object when he gave his oral direction was to deprive himself immediately and irrevocably of his subsisting personal beneficial interest so that others could and should become beneficially entitled. It was a necessary part of his purpose that he should deal with his personal interest: he terminated it and informed his trustees that they should no longer hold for him but should hold on the substituted trusts which he declared. I cannot resist the conclusion that this was a purported 'disposition' by him of his interest. In Inland Revenue Commissioners v. Buchanan, a question arose whether a surrender is a disposition. Lord Goddard C.J. said: 'I think it clearly is a disposition. A person can dispose of his interest in a fund or in a chattel or in anything else in a variety of ways, but if, having an interest in a fund, although the interest may not then be in possession, he surrenders that interest, it seems to me that he disposes of that interest.'"[12]

A direction from an owner of an equitable interest to a trustee to hold the equitable interest on trust for another operates as a complete transfer or disposition of the interest.[13] It is argued that a direction, which terminates an equitable interest, or creates a new equitable interest, may not be a transfer of the equitable interest, but is still a disposition. Disposition is wider than transfer.[14]

It is unanimously confirmed in the House of Lords that a disposition has its natural meaning under which a direction to a trustee to hold the equitable interests for another is a disposition. The Lords come to the conclusion by exploring the legislative history of the Law of Property Act 1925.[15]

5.1.1.2 *Oughtred v IRC*[16]

In *Oughtred v IRC*, a mother was entitled to life interest and her son was entitled to absolute reversion in the trust property, both as equitable

[12] *Grey v IRC* [1958] Ch 690 (CA) 720-21 (Morris LJ).
[13] *Re Chrimes* [1917] 1 Ch 30, 36 (Sargant J).
[14] *Grey v IRC* [1958] Ch 690 (CA) 722 (Ormerod LJ); J McGhee (ed), *Snell's Equity* (31st edn, Trusts, Wills and Probate Library, Sweet and Maxwell, London 2005) 485; see also J Hackney, 'Usucapio and the Law of Trusts' in J Getzler (ed) *Rationalizing Property, Equity and Trusts: Essays in Honour of Edward Burn* (Lexis-Nexis UK, London 2003).
[15] *Grey v IRC* [1960] AC 1 (HL) 12-15 (Viscount Simonds), 16-17 (Lord Radcliffe).
[16] [1960] AC 206 (HL).

owners. The mother was meanwhile one of the trustees. An oral agreement between mother and son was made to give the mother the absolute reversion interest of the son. It was disputed whether the transaction was a disposition of existing equitable interests to be bound by the writing requirement. It was held such a transaction was not a disposition of existing equitable interests with dissenting opinions.

The conclusion that it is not a disposition of an existing equitable interest rests on the following: it was a release to the trustees of the settlement and a winding up of the trust for both mother and son. There was no transfer from the co-trustees to the mother.

> "It follows that, in my view, this transfer cannot be treated as a conveyance of the son's equitable reversion at all. The trustees had not got it: he never transferred or released it to them: how then could they convey it? With all respect to those who think otherwise, it is incorrect to say that the trustees' transfer was made either with his authority or at his direction. If the recital as to Mrs. Oughtred's rights was correct, as I think that it was, he had no remaining authority to give or direction to issue. A release is, after all, the normal instrument for winding up a trust when all the equitable rights are vested and the legal estate is called for from the trustees who hold it. What the release gave the trustees from him was acquittance for the trust administration and accounts to date, and the fact that he gave it in consideration of the legal interest in the shares being vested in his mother adds nothing on this point."[17]

Dissenting opinion holds that any act which operates as a transfer should be treated as a transfer. A direction to a trustee to convey an equitable interest to another by an equitable owner is a conveyance from the equitable owner to the other party, even though through a trustee. It is a substantive approach disregarding the apparent form of transactions. "The fact that the disputed transfer was made on the winding up of the trust does not, in my view, prevent it from being also a transfer on sale."[18]

> "He did not convey this reversionary interest direct to her, nor did he convey it to the trustees of the settlement. But he authorised the trustees to convey it to her-not in the shape of a reversionary interest as such-but by way of enlarging her life interest into absolute ownership. It is clear to me that, by the transfer so made by his authority, she acquired his reversionary interest as effectively as if he had conveyed it direct to her. ...In my opinion, every conveyance or transfer by which an agreement for sale is

[17] *Oughtred v IRC* [1960] AC 206 (HL) 228 (Lord Radcliffe).
[18] ibid 243 (Lord Jenkins).

> implemented is liable to stamp duty on the value of the consideration. It is not necessary for the instrument of implementation to be between the same parties as the agreement for sale, nor for it to relate to the selfsame property as the agreement for sale. Suffice it that the instrument is the means by which the parties choose to implement the bargain they have made. … Thus, when an equitable owner of shares (registered in the name of a nominee) agrees to sell them to a purchaser, and it is implemented by a transfer by the nominee to the purchaser, the transfer is a conveyance upon sale of any property-although, of course, the parties to the agreement are different from the parties to the transfer. And when two people are equitable co-owners of shares-and one of them agrees to sell his interest to the other-and it is implemented by a transfer of the shares by the trustees (with the authority of the one) to the other, the transfer is a conveyance upon sale of any property-although, of course, the property which is transferred is different from the property in the agreement."[19]

5.1.1.3 A sub-trust

In the case of a beneficial owner creating a sub-trust for another it is argued that there is a new equitable interest under a new trust rather than a disposition of existing equitable interest. This is not well settled as the case of a direction to the trustee.[20]

5.1.1.4 Disposition; transfer; assignment; novation

It is not settled what the nature of a disposition of an equitable interests exactly is. As choses in action an equitable interest may be assigned, or by a beneficiary declaring himself as trustee or directing a trustee to hold for another. Judicial discussion is centred on whether a transaction is disposition under the Law of Property Act 1925 s 53 (1) (c). Assignment falls within the scope without much doubt. Whether a transfer by a direction to a trustee is a disposition is not settled. Opinion against a disposition emphasises the fact that an equitable interest is extinguished when an original owner declares himself a trustee or directs a trustee to hold for another. Opinion in favour of a disposition emphasises the result that another party gets the equitable interest. An equitable owner, declaring himself a trustee for another of the equitable interest, creates a sub-trust which is apparently not a disposition of existing equitable interest. However it is unanimously recognised there is an extinction of the original

[19] ibid 232-33 (Lord Denning).

[20] D Hayton, P Matthews and C Mitchell, *Underhill and Hayton Law of Trusts and Trustees* (17th edn, LexisNexis Butterworths, London 2007) 294.

equitable interest and creation of a new equitable interest, obviously in the case of transfer by trust. Thus it can be concluded that transfer of equitable interests by trust is novation by nature.

5.1.2 Credit Transfer in Payment Systems

There are many similarities between electronic payment systems and securities holding systems. A client of a bank with a cash account with the bank is entitled to claim payment against the bank. An investor with a securities account with his intermediary is entitled to dispose of securities, which is a claim against the intermediary but valid against third parties. The difference is that the claim of a bank client against the bank is purely contractual while the claim of an investor against his intermediary is contractual but meanwhile recognised as proprietary, i.e., valid against third parties, in particular circumstances such as the intermediary insolvency.[21] The transfer mechanism is also similar with debits and credits on relevant cash accounts and securities accounts. It will thus be inspiring to examine the credit transfer in payment systems to understand the transfer of intermediated securities in intermediated holding systems. It is settled law that credit transfer is novation.

Credit transfers are done in three ways, two banks become each other's correspondent banks maintaining accounts for each other and request each other to make payment on its own behalf at the request of clients of each; in a clearing system, a clearing house maintains accounts for participating banks and makes credits or debits on the accounts of participating banks; or a common correspondent bank shared by banks acting as a clearing house for banks makes credits and debits on the accounts of banks.[22]

It is held that there is no assignment of credit from a payor to a payee. It is rather a debit of the account of a payor which initiates a process to enable a commitment to credit the account of a payee, through the payor's

---

[21] CW Mooney, 'Beyond Negotiability: A New Model for Transfer and Pledge of Interests in Securities Controlled by Intermediaries' (1990) 12 Cardozo L Rev 305, 403; RD Guynn and others, 'Modernizing Securities Ownership, Transfer and Pledging Laws (International Bar Association 1996)'; JH Sommer, 'A Law of Financial Accounts: Modern Payment and Securities Transfer Law' (1998) 53 Bus Law 1181, 1193.

[22] PR Wood, *Regulation of International Finance* (2nd edn, Law and Practice of International Finance Series, Sweet & Maxwell, London 2007) 342-45; RM Goode and E McKendrick, *Goode on Commercial Law* (4th edn, LexisNexis, London 2009) 505-07.

bank, intermediary bank or banks, and the payee's bank.[23]

> "An account transfer means the process by which some other person or institution comes to owe money to the Libyan Bank or their nominee, and the obligation of Bankers Trust is extinguished or reduced pro tanto. 'Transfer' may be a somewhat misleading word, since the original obligation is not assigned (notwithstanding dicta in one American case which speak of assignment); a new obligation by a new debtor is created."[24]

It is confirmed in *R v Preddy*[25] that there is no transfer of property but the extinction of the original debt and the creation of a new debt.

> "Let it be assumed that the lending institution's bank account is in credit, and that there is therefore no difficulty in identifying a credit balance standing in the account as representing property, i.e. a chose in action, belonging to the lending institution. The question remains however whether the debiting of the lending institution's bank account, and the corresponding crediting of the bank account of the defendant or his solicitor, constitutes obtaining of that property. The difficulty in the way of that conclusion is simply that, when the bank account of the defendant (or his solicitor) is credited, he does not obtain the lending institution's chose in action. On the contrary that chose in action is extinguished or reduced pro tanto, and a chose in action is brought into existence representing a debt in an equivalent sum owed by a different bank to the defendant or his solicitor. In these circumstances, it is difficult to see how the defendant thereby obtained property belonging to another, i.e. to the lending institution."[26]

This is so even though there is correlation between the creation of a new debt and the extinction of the old debt, as the old debt can no longer be identified.

> "In truth the property which the defendant has obtained is the new chose in action constituted by the debt now owed to him by his bank, and represented by the credit entry in his own bank account. This did not come into existence until the debt so created was owed to him by his bank, and

---

[23] RM Good and E McKendrick, *Goode on Commercial Law* (4th edn, LexisNexis, London 2009) 505-07; EP Ellinger, E Lomnicka and R Hooley, *Ellinger's Modern Banking Law* (4th edn, Oxford University Press, Oxford 2006) 546-57.

[24] *Libyan Arab Foreign Bank v Bankers Trust Co* [1989] QB 728, 750 (Staughton J).

[25] [1996] AC 815 (HL).

[26] *R v Preddy* [1996] AC 815 (HL) 834 (Lord Goff of Chieveley).

so never belonged to anyone else. True, it corresponded to the debit entered in the lending institution's bank account; but it does not follow that the property which the defendant acquired can be identified with the property which the lending institution lost when its account was debited."[27]

In the case of credit transfer the nature of credit as choses in action and its transfer a novation is established in law. The nature of credit transfer as novation can be seen more clearly in interbank credit transfers by a series of novation through intermediary banks. The debtor also changes from a payor's bank to a payee's bank.

5.1.3 Transfer of Intermediated Securities other than the Top tier of the CREST System

Intermediated securities held with an intermediary are characterised as equitable interests except securities held by participants in the CREST system as legal title. The transfer of intermediated securities other than the top tier in the CREST system is thus transfer of equitable interests. By either of the four ways of transfer equitable interests it is a disposition and thus writing is required. Transfer through the CREST system is exempted from the writing requirement. [28] It is uncertain whether transfer of intermediated securities other than on the top tier of the CREST system, i.e., of equitable interests, is still governed by the writing formality. Statutory clarification will be welcome.[29]

Whether there is a disposition, in a transfer of intermediated securities, there is an extinction of original title to intermediated securities of a transferor and creation of a new title to intermediated securities of a transferee, which makes it a novation. In most circumstances in a centralised securities market an investor instructs his intermediary to dispose of intermediated securities without knowing the purchaser, with a debit of his securities account with his intermediary,[30] which can be seen

[27] ibid 834 (Lord Goff of Chieveley), see also 841 (Lord Jauncey of Tullichettle).

[28] Companies Act 2006 s 770 (1)and Uncertificated Securities Regulations 2001 SI 2001/3755 reg 2, displacing Law of Property Act 1925 ss 53 (1) (c) and 136.

[29] Trust Law Committee Working Party, 'Equitable Problems in the Securities Markets'; J Benjamin, *Interest in Securities: A Proprietary Law Analysis of the International Securities Markets* (Oxford University Press, Oxford 2000) 73.

[30] T Prime, *International Bonds and Certificates of Deposit* (Butterworths, London 1990) 232-33; L Thévenoz, 'New Legal Concepts regarding the Holding of Investment Securities for a Civil Law Jurisdiction – The Swiss Draft Act' [2005]

as a surrender of the equitable title to the trustee. A purchaser instructs his intermediary to acquire securities, with a credit on his securities account with his intermediary, without knowing the seller.[31] It is hard to identify the specific securities from a seller to a purchaser. This process is by nature a novation. This is so where a seller and purchaser hold securities accounts with the same intermediary. It is more clear when a seller and a purchaser hold securities accounts with different intermediaries, a transfer involves a series of novation and the debtor has changed from the seller's intermediary to the purchaser's intermediary.

5.1.3.1 No matching

Theoretically corresponding to a credit there is a debit in an account somewhere in the whole holding system, as the whole issue of a security is fixed at a point of time, though it is difficult to identify the exact account of a debit, due to the normal practice of multilateral netting and clearing in the securities settlement process.[32] A credit of securities in a transaction may be traceable to debits in multiple accounts held with different intermediaries at different tiers in the holding chain. Normally a credit of a unit of securities can be matched by a valid debit of a unit of securities when everything goes smoothly. English law does not require matching, namely for a credit to be valid there is no requirement that a valid debit must be identified. This is further support for the proposition that a transfer of intermediated securities is novation.

Matching is based on the traditional property law thinking that when a specific thing is acquired there must be a disposition of it. Non-matching systems lays less emphasis on the specificity of securities which is closer to reality, and recognises the indirect nature of the proprietary right of an investor to securities as a claim against his intermediary. Matching systems are more costly because of support arrangements and reduced

---

Rev dr unif 301, 309; PR Wood, *Regulation of International Finance* (2nd edn, Law and Practice of International Finance Series, Sweet & Maxwell, London 2007) 321-22.

[31] PR Wood, *Set-off and Netting, Derivatives, Clearing Systems* (2nd edn, Law and Practice of International Finance Series, Sweet & Maxwell, London 2007) 335, 338; PR Wood, *Regulation of International Finance* (2nd edn, Law and Practice of International Finance Series, Sweet & Maxwell, London 2007) 345-49.

[32] PR Wood, *Set-off and Netting, Derivatives, Clearing Systems* (Law and Practice of International Finance Series Volume 4, 2nd edn, Sweet & Maxwell, London 2007) 96-100.

efficiency but more effective in detecting a defective debit and preventing inflation, i.e., more securities credited to securities accounts than actually issued. Non-matching systems are more efficient but run greater risk of inflation.[33] However inflation does happen as a result of a defective debit in both matching and non-matching systems. A matching system responds with allocating loss to the specific account where a defective debit is made. A non-matching system often responds with a loss sharing rule to relevant accounts of an intermediary.[34]

Non-matching under English law recognises the fact that there is no transfer in an individual transaction. A seller disposes of his securities to the pool of securities on organised exchanges while a purchaser gets his securities from the pool of securities on organised exchanges, under the process of settlement and netting. There is transfer in the market as a whole from the seller side to the purchaser side but normally there is no need to identify the specific securities in a specific transaction.

5.1.3.2 Time of transfer; earlier than credit

Intermediated securities are represented by credits to securities accounts and it is natural to provide that an investor acquires intermediated securities on a credit of securities to his securities account with his intermediary, as in the Geneva Securities Convention.[35] It is necessary to confirm the status of a credit as acquiring intermediated securities for countries which require additional procedures for a transfer. English law is less bothered with formalities. Under the trust analysis of English law an investor acquires intermediated securities once the securities are identifiable in the control of his intermediary, even before a credit is made.[36] The credit to the securities account is not a constitutive act of transfer. Absent a credit an investor may still be able to claim to have acquired intermediated securities otherwise.[37]

This is the same with the time of payment in the payment system. The

---

[33] Law Commission, 'The UNIDROIT Convention on Substantive Rules regarding Intermediated Securities: Further Updated Advice to HM Treasury (May 2008)' [2.48].

[34] ibid [3.5]-[3.10].

[35] Art 9.

[36] Law Commission, 'The UNIDROIT Convention on Substantive Rules regarding Intermediated Securities: Further Updated Advice to HM Treasury (May 2008)' [4.49].

[37] ibid [4.50].

time of transfer of payment within a bank from a payor to a payee is the time when a bank accepts the payment order and decides to debit the payor's account and credit the payee's account, i.e., the time the funds is available to the payee, irrespective whether the bank's internal accounting processes have been completed, or the decision has been implemented by debit or credit.[38]

With interbank payment it is the same position that a payment is completed when a payee's bank unconditionally accepts that the payee is its creditor,[39] or when a payee' bank is notified that that funds are available for the payee.[40] The payment process is fundamentally the same either within the same bank or through different banks, at least from the perspective of customers.[41] The difference is that a decision of a bank to make payment in inter-bank payment is once-and-for-all and normally irrevocable once communicated to another bank while a decision to make in-house payment within the same bank can be deferred or revoked in the same day.[42]

That the time of transfer of intermediated securities is the time the intermediated securities become identified in an intermediary or when the intermediary decides to allocate the securities to the securities account of a client reinforces the point that transfer of intermediated securities as equitable interests is novation. The reason is that the transfer of intermediated securities is a separate creation of interests in the intermediated securities for a transferee, in most circumstances, distinct from the intermediated securities a transferor disposes of, either in a transfer with the same intermediary, or through tiers of intermediaries.

5.1.4 Conclusion

An equitable interest may be disposed of by assignment, contract for consideration, a direction to the trustee to hold the equitable interest for another, or by a beneficiary declaring oneself a trustee for another.

[38] *The Brimnes* [1973] 1 WLR 386, affd [1975] QB 929; *Momm v Barclays Bank International Ltd* [1977] 1 QB 790, 803 (Kerr J).

[39] RM Good and E McKendrick, *Goode on Commercial Law* (4th edn, LexisNexis, London 2009) 508.

[40] *Royal Products Ltd v Midland Bank Ltd* [1981] 2 Lloyd's Rep 194; PR Wood, *Set-off and Netting, Derivatives, Clearing Systems* (2nd edn, Law and Practice of International Finance Series, Sweet & Maxwell, London 2007) 296.

[41] *Royal Products Ltd v Midland Bank Ltd* [1981] 2 Lloyd's Rep 194.

[42] *Momm v Barclays Bank International Ltd* [1977] 1 QB 790, 793-94 (Kerr J).

Disposition covers transfer by assignment and by trust. The formal distinction between assignment and trust highlights the fact there is an equitable interest throughout the transfer by assignment while there is an extinction and creation of equitable interests, as in novation. Thus as equitable interests transfer of intermediated securities is novation, as seen in transaction patterns that a sellers sells to the markets and a purchasers buys from the market without knowing the identity of each other and the non-matching practices. The similarity of transfer of intermediated securities to credit transfer in payment systems is further support for the position that the nature of intermediated securities is a claim and their transfer is novation.

5.2 Title Conflicts in Respect of Intermediated Securities under the Priority Rules

An examination of the priority between legal interests, between equitable interests, between a legal interest and an equitable interest, i.e., throughout legal and equitable property rights, is necessary. The basic rule of first in time will be introduced. The modifying rule based on the merits of title, i.e., the priority of a legal title over a prior equitable title, and the priority of an equitable title over a prior mere equity, the better equity rule between equitable title, will be introduced; other modifications of postponement and the rule of *Dearle v Hall*, will be analysed. The application of priority rules to intermediated securities will be examined.

5.2.1 The General Rule: Time and Nature

Priority rules can be found in both case law and statutes. The general principles are established in case law and exceptions in statutes. The basic rule is that competing interests rank according to the order of creation if they are equal, i.e., first in time subject to the nature of property rights. The order of creation rule is the last criterion to refer to.

5.2.1.1 Nature of rights

The nature of rights means that rights are legal, equitable, or mere equities. Rights can be graded on the basis of their contents and validity. Legal rights are stronger than equitable rights, equitable rights are stronger than mere equities. It is known as the *bona fide* purchaser rule, that an equitable interest is defeated by a legal right, and a mere equity is defeated by an equitable interest. The nature of rights also functions among rights of the same genre, i.e., among equitable interests, and among mere equities, and the conduct of parties has an impact on the merits of their rights. Legal rights are relatively fixed and the conduct of parties generally does not affect their rights. Thus the basic rule on legal title is the first in time rule, i.e., the *nemo dat* rule, subject to common law estoppel and statutes. Registration can be seen as modifying the nature of rights by conferring great validity and merit on a registered right regardless of whether the competing rights are legal, or equitable. The notice rule in *Dearle v Hall*[43] can also be seen as part of the rule of the nature of rights by conferring greater merit upon an equitable right being communicated to the obligor of the equitable right.[44]

5.2.1.2 First in time

The first in time rule is found both at law and in equity. At law it is generally known as the *nemo dat quod non habet* rule that no one can give more than what he has. Thus only an owner can give title. Then the title of an owner wins. This the first in time rule at law, since legal interests are uniform and there is no issue of comparative merits of legal interests. The *nemo dat* rule is subject to common law estoppel and statutory exceptions. In equity it is more directly expressed as *qui prior est tempore potior est jure*, or he who is earlier in time is stronger in law, provided that the equities of the claimants are equal.[45] Equitable interests are diverse in content and effect.[46] The priority on equitable interests is based on the merits of equitable interests, known as the issue of better equity.

---

[43] *Dearle v Hall* (1828) 3 Russell 1, 38 ER 475.
[44] *Phillips v Phillips* (1861) 4 De G F & J 208, 45 ER 1164; *Re Samuel Allen & Sons Ltd* [1907] 1 Ch 575; *Macmillan Inc v Bishopsgate Investment Trust plc (No 3)* [1995] 1 WLR 978 (Ch) 999-1000 (Millett J); J McGhee (ed), *Snell's Equity* (31st edn, Trusts, Wills and Probate Library, Sweet and Maxwell, London 2005) 55; M Smith, *The Law of Assignment: The Creation and Transfer of Choses in Action* (Oxford University Press, Oxford 2007) 415.
[45] *Brace v Duchess of Marlborough* (1728) 2 P Wms 491, 495; 24 ER 829, 832; *Macmillan Inc v Bishopsgate Investment Trust plc (No 3)* [1995] 1 WLR 978 (Ch) 1000 (Millett J); J McGhee (ed), *Snell's Equity* (31st edn, Trusts, Wills and Probate Library, Sweet and Maxwell, London 2005) 56.
[46] See 2.3.

> "As between persons having only equitable interests, if their equities are equal, '*qui prior est tempore potior est jure*.' This form of stating the rule is not so obviously incorrect as the former. And yet even this enunciation of the rule (when accurately considered) seems to me to involve a contradiction. For when we talk of two persons having equal or unequal equities, in what sense do we use the term 'equity?' For example, when we say that A. has a better equity than B., what is meant by that? It means only that, according to those principles of right and justice which a Court of Equity recognises and acts upon, it will prefer A. to B., and will interfere to enforce the rights of A. as against B. And therefore it is impossible (strictly speaking) that two persons should have equal equities, except in a case in which a Court of Equity would altogether refuse to lend its assistance to either party as against the other. If the Court will interfere to enforce the right of one against the other on any ground whatever, say on the ground of priority of time, how can it be said that the equities of the two are equal; i.e., in other words, how can it be said that the one has no better right to call for the interference of a Court of Equity than the other? To lay down the rule therefore with perfect accuracy, I think it should be stated in some such form as this:—'As between persons having only equitable interests, if their equities are in all other respects equal, priority of time gives the better equity; or, *qui prior est tempore potior est jure*.'"[47]

The timing factor is the last factor to resort to when there is no other ground for preferring one of the competing rights.

> "I have made these observations, not of course for the purpose of a mere verbal criticism on the enunciation of a rule, but in order to ascertain and illustrate the real meaning of the rule itself. And I think the meaning is this: that, in a contest between persons having only equitable interests, priority of time is the ground of preference last resorted to; i.e. , that a Court of Equity will not prefer the one to the other, on the mere ground of priority of time, until it finds upon an examination of their relative merits that there is no other sufficient ground of preference between them, or, in other words, that their equities are in all other respects equal; and that, if the one has on other grounds a better equity than the other, priority of time is immaterial."[48]

5.2.2 Good Faith Acquisition: Legal Title and Equitable Title; Equitable Title and Mere Equities

Overreach is the bona fide purchaser rule under English law, different from the civil law bona fide acquisition. The *bona fide* purchaser rule

---

[47] *Rice v Rice* (1853) 2 Drew 73, 77-78 (Sir RT Kindersley V-C); 61 ER 646, 647-48.

[48] *Rice v Rice* (1853) 2 Drew 73, 78 (Sir RT Kindersley V-C); 61 ER 646, 648.

applies between legal interests and equitable interests, that a good faith purchaser for value without notice of the prior equitable title gets a legal title free of the prior equitable title,[49] and between equitable interests and mere equities, that a good faith acquirer of an equitable interest for value without notice of a prior mere equity does get an equitable interest free of the prior mere equity.[50]

"A mere equity is not a right of property but a right, usually of a procedural nature, which is ancillary to some right of property, and which limits or qualifies it in some way."[51] For examples, the right to have a transaction set aside for fraud, misrepresentation, or undue influence, to claim a remedy arising from a proprietary estoppel, or to have a document rectified for mistake, as by inserting a repairing covenant.[52] It is short of equitable interests but more than mere personal rights. It is often ancillary to equitable property interests. It is inferior to equitable interests in case of competition.

The good faith acquisition of a legal title overriding a prior equitable title or the good faith acquisition of an equitable title overriding a prior mere equity appears to be confusing. It is however consistent with the first in time rule and the rule of merits of rights. The first in time rule means that rights rank according to the time they are created, if the rights are equal, i.e., both are legal rights, both are equitable interests, or both are mere equities. As to the competition between rights of unequal nature, i.e., equitable and legal, mere equities and equitable interests, the good faith purchaser rule applies, that is a good faith purchaser of a legal interest

[49] J Ulph, *Commercial Fraud, Civil Liability, Human Rights and Money Laundering* (Contract Law Library, Oxford University Press, Oxford 2006) 735-41.

[50] *Phillips v Phillips* (1861) 4 De G F & J 208, 45 ER 1164; D O'Sullivan, 'The Rule in Phillips v Phillips' (2002) 118 LQR 296; M Pawlowski and J Brown, 'Mere Equities and Third Parties in Leasehold Law' [2010] L& T R 100-04.

[51] J McGhee (ed), *Snell's Equity* (31st edn, Trusts, Wills and Probate Library, Sweet and Maxwell, London 2005) 23.

[52] See *Rice v Rice* (1853) 2 Drew 73, 61 ER 646; *Phillips v Phillips* (1861) 4 De G F & J 208, 45 ER 1164; *Cave v Cave* (1880) 15 Ch D 639; *Westminster Bank Ltd v Lee* [1956] Ch 7; *National Provincial Bank v Ainsworth* [1965] AC 1175 (HL) 1237-38 (Lord Upjohn); J McGhee (ed), *Snell's Equity* (31st edn, Trusts, Wills and Probate Library, Sweet and Maxwell, London 2005) 23; D Hayton, P Matthews and C Mitchell, *Underhill and Hayton Law of Trusts and Trustees* (17th edn, LexisNexis Butterworths, London 2007) 67; M Smith, *The Law of Assignment: The Creation and Transfer of Choses in Action* (Oxford University Press, Oxford 2007) 91-94; M Pawlowski and J Brown, 'Mere Equities and Third Parties in Leasehold Law' [2010] L& T R 100,104.

defeats a prior equitable interest, a good faith purchaser of an equitable interest defeats a prior mere equity.

There is doubt as to the practice of treating mere equities and equitable interests differently based on a simple formal distinction which is actually not easy to make. It is argued that the distinction of mere equities and equitable interests is merely an artificial refinement of the discretion of weighting the merits of equitable interests.[53] Indeed there is uncertainty in the priority between equitable rights due to the diversity of equitable interests in terms of creation, content and validity. Equitable interests can arise by contract or by operation of law, can range from mortgage to vendor's lien, can be valid against specific parties or general parties. It is not so uniform and standardised as property rights at common law. The distinction of equitable interests and mere equities is not clear and much less so than the distinction of legal interests and equitable interests. The scope of mere equities is hard to delineate. The *bona fide* purchaser rule is fundamentally speaking the better equity rule, i.e., the equitable interest with better merits prevails.

Equitable title in intermediated securities will not be subject to mere equities such as preemption of third parties under this rule. A purchaser of an equitable or legal interest is most likely to have no notice of mere equities given the nature of mere equities.[54] A purchaser of intermediated securities will normally qualify as good faith acquirer and will not be subject to prior mere equities.

5.2.3 Equitable Interest: Better Equity

It is not easy to define which of two competing equitable interests has better equity. Firstly, equitable title acquired from a beneficiary or a trustee is considered to be of greater weight than equitable title arising otherwise. Other than equitable title acquired from a beneficiary or a trustee, the manner under which equitable interests arise is irrelevant, for example an equitable vendor's lien and an equitable mortgage are held to be of no difference in equity.[55] Secondly, legal title is often relevant, that

---

[53] D O'Sullivan, 'Distributing the Risk of Contract Fraud' (2001) 117 LQR 381, 386.

[54] *Smith v Jones* [1954] 1 WLR 1089; D Hayton, P Matthews and C Mitchell, *Underhill and Hayton Law of Trusts and Trustees* (17th edn, LexisNexis Butterworths, London 2007) 67.

[55] *Rice v Rice* (1853) 2 Drew 73, 61 ER 646.

acquisition of legal title after acquiring an equitable title obviously equips the equitable title with better equity, or more exactly under the legal title trumps a prior equitable title rule. Thirdly, an equitable title with better title to legal title is with better equity, such as an equitable title acquired out of a legal title overriding a prior equitable title, which is in fact the sheltering effect of the good faith acquisition rule.

5.2.3.1 Getting equitable title from the trustee or from a beneficiary

In *Wilmot v Pike*[56], the first mortgagee got an equitable mortgage from the borrower who was the equitable owner, the second mortgagee got an equitable mortgage from the trustee who was the legal owner. It was held that the equitable title from the trustee has better equity.

> "if a first incumbrancer has a declaration of trust only by the borrower, and none by the trustee, and the second incumbrancer has a formal mortgage of the equity of redemption, and the trustee is a party to the deed, and declares himself a trustee for the second incumbrancer, will not that declaration by the trustee give the second priority over the first? I think the second would, in that case, have a better right to call for the legal estate than the first; and if it would be so in the case of a stranger, I think the trustee cannot be precluded by his situation as trustee from claiming the benefit of the legal estate without notice, leaving every trust of which he had notice untouched by his present claim. I have referred to the cases of Stanhope v. Earl Verney (2 Eden, 81) and Maundrell v. Maundrell (10 Ves. 271; and see 1 Sugd. Vend. 782, 11th ed.), from which it appears that, as to the trusts of a term, a declaration in form by a trustee, that he will stand possessed of the term, is held equivalent to an assignment, so as to give the preference to the party who gets the declaration over one who has a good equitable interest, but not in the same form. I believe that attention to this distinction will clear up nearly all that is apparently conflicting in the reported cases. A declaration of trust by a trustee, in whom the legal estate is, has always been considered of great weight in the determination of equitable rights."[57]

Absence of action of a trustee in favour of either equitable interest

In *Assaf v Fuwa*[58], there were two equitable interests. The first one was out of a contract to purchase land from a mortgagor with an equity of

[56] (1845) 5 Hare 14; 67 ER 808.

[57] *Wilmot v Pike* (1845) 5 Hare 14, 22-23 (Sir James Wigram V-C); 67 ER 808, 812; see also *Rooper v Harrison* (1855) 2 K & J 86; 69 ER 704; *Taylor v London and County Banking Co, London and County Banking Co v Nixon* [1901] 2 Ch 231 (CA) 262-63 (Stirling LJ).

[58] [1955] AC 215.

redemption, the second was out of conveyance of the land from the same mortgagor. The legal title lay in the mortgagee. Thus both interests were equitable. There was no action on the part of the mortgagee in favour of either of the two. Thus the subsequent one was held to have no better title to call the legal title and the first in time took priority.

> "It has accordingly been held that if a purchaser for value takes an equitable title only, or omits to get in an outstanding legal estate, and a subsequent purchaser for value without notice procures, at the time of his purchase, the person in whom the legal title is vested to declare himself a trustee for him, or even to join as party in a conveyance of the equitable interest (although he may not formally convey or declare of trust of the legal estate), still the subsequent purchaser gains priority."[59]

Creation of equitable interests other than under trusts irrelevant to better equity: a vendor's lien and an equitable mortgage

> "Each of the parties in controversy has nothing but an equitable interest; the plaintiff's interest being a vendor's lien for unpaid purchase-money, and the defendant *Ede* having an equitable mortgage. Looking at these two species of equitable interests abstractedly and without reference to priority of time, or possession of the title deeds, or any other special circumstances, is there anything in their respective natures or qualities which would lead to the conclusion that in natural justice the one is better or more worthy or more entitled to protection than the other? Each of the two equitable interests arises out of the forbearance by the party of money due to him. There is, however, this difference between them, that the vendor's lien for unpaid purchase-money is a right created by a rule of equity without any special contract; the right of the equitable mortgagee is created by the special contract of the parties. I cannot say that in my opinion this constitutes any sufficient ground of preference, though if it makes any difference at all, I should say it is rather in favour of the equitable mortgagee inasmuch as there is no *constat* of the right of the vendor to his lien for unpaid purchase-money until it has been declared by a decree of a Court of Equity, whereas there is a clear *constat* of the equitable mortgagee's title immediately on the contract being made. But I do not see in this any sufficient ground for holding that the equitable mortgagee has the better equity."[60]

The merits upon the different categories of equitable interests are inapplicable to equitable title to intermediated securities which are uniform in nature as beneficial title under trusts. However difference may

---

[59] *Assaf v Fuwa* [1955] AC 215, 229-30 (Lord Porter).

[60] *Rice v Rice* (1853) 2 Drew 73, 79 (Sir RT Kindersley V-C); 61 ER 646, 649-50.

be established based on different tiers of intermediaries, known as upper-tier priority.[61]

5.2.3.2 Better right to legal interest: with later acquired legal interest

An equity with better right to legal interest is with better equity, which can be a later acquired legal interest.[62]

> "I take it to be the rule in equity, that where a man is a purchaser without notice, he shall not be annoyed in equity, not only where he has a prior legal estate, but where he has a better title or right to call for the legal estate than the other…"[63]

> "Equality means the non-existence of any circumstance which affects the conduct of one of the rival claimants, and makes it less meritorious than that of the other. Equitable owners who are upon an equality in this respect may struggle for the legal estate, and he who obtains it, having both law and equity on his side, is in a better situation than he who has equity only. …The doctrine applies in favour of all equitable owners or incumbrancers for value without notice of prior equitable interests, who get in the legal estate from persons who commit no breach of trust in parting with it to them…"[64]

Getting legal title without involving a breach of trust; Limitation of application: no trusts; shares

There is a limitation to getting priority to an equitable title through acquiring legal title. A good faith purchaser of an equitable interest, without notice of the prior equitable interest, cannot gain priority by subsequently getting legal estate from the trustee, if he is guilty of taking part in a new breach of trust.[65]

The rule is only helpful where legal title can be acquired from third

---

[61] CW Mooney, 'Beyond Negotiability: A New Model for Transfer and Pledge of Interests in Securities Controlled by Intermediaries' (1990) 12 Cardozo L Rev 305, 380.

[62] J Mowbray and others, *Lewin on Trusts* (18th edn, Thomson Sweet & Maxwell, London 2008) 1193, 1195.

[63] *Wilkes v Bodington* (1707) 2 Vern 599, 600; 23 ER 991, 993.

[64] *Bailey v Barnes* [1894] 1 Ch 25 (CA) 36-37 (Lindley LJ).

[65] *Saunders v Dehew* (1692) 2 Vern 271, 23 ER 775; *Bailey v Barnes* [1894] 1 Ch 25 (CA) 37 (Lindley LJ); D Hayton, P Matthews and C Mitchell, *Underhill and Hayton Law of Trusts and Trustees* (17th edn, LexisNexis Butterworths, London 2007) 1230.

parties other than a trustee. For example, in *Taylor v Russell*[66], a legal mortgage was prior to two equitable mortgages. The second equitable mortgagee, later finding the legal mortgage and the first equitable mortgage, got a legal mortgage from the prior legal mortgagee. The second equitable mortgagee was entitled to rely on the legal title to prevail over the first equitable mortgagee. There was no breach of trust since the legal mortgagee was not a trustee for the first equitable mortgagee, even though the legal mortgagee was the trustee for a stranger not involved in the case.

Another important example is with shares, legal title of which has to be obtained by registration with an issuer. Securities are a kind of property where the act of an issuer is necessary to perfect the transfer of legal title.[67] The execution of transfer form and delivery of securities certificates confer equitable title on a transferee while registration on the issuer register is required for full legal title. An equitable mortgagee got the shares from a trustee of shares without notice of the trust, afterwards had notice of the trust, then registered with the issuer and became a legal mortgagee. It was held that the legal mortgage defeated the equitable interest of the beneficiary as there was no breach of trust involved in getting the legal title.[68]

The policy of the special rule on shares lies in the formalities of the transfer of shares which requires the act of an issuer other than a transferor:

> "A transferor who delivers to a transferee a share certificate together with an executed transfer may still retain the legal estate for the time being, but he has done everything in his power to vest it in the transferee, while the transferee for his part has it within his own power to vest the legal estate in himself without further recourse to the transferor. As between the transferee who has given value on the one hand and the transferor and those claiming under him on the other, this rather than the time when the transferee actually obtains the legal title is to my mind the appropriate time for the question of notice to be tested.
>
> …

---

[66] [1891] 1 Ch 8 (CA).

[67] JE Martin, *Modern Equity* (18th edn, Sweet & Maxwell, London 2009) 129.

[68] *Dodds v Hills* (1865) 2 H & M 424, 71 ER 528; See also *Blackwood v London Charted Bank of Australia* (1874) 5 PC 92 (Judicial Committee) 111; *Mumford v Stohwasser* (1874) 18 Eq 556, 563 (Sir Jessel MR); *Harpham v Shacklock* (1881) 19 Ch D 207, 214 (Jessel MR); *Bailey v Barnes* [1894] 1 Ch 25 (CA) 36-37 (Lindley LJ); *Perham v Kempster* [1907] 1 Ch 373.

> To expose him to the further risk of being bound by an adverse claim of which he had no notice when he advanced his money, and from which he would have been free if he had obtained registration, is in my judgment commercially unacceptable."[69]

Notice after acquisition of equitable interest and before or at the time of acquisition of legal interest

A purchaser of an equitable interest for value without notice of a prior equitable interest, who later acquires legal estate, will prevail over the prior equitable interest, even if at the time of acquiring the legal estate has notice of the prior equitable interest.[70]

> "A transferee or incumbrancer for valuable consideration who takes in the first instance a merely equitable interest, without notice of any prior interest, can subsequently perfect his title, even after notice of the prior interest, by acquiring the legal estate, subject to the exceptions suggested in Taylor v. Russell 13 , Mumford v. Stohwasser 14, Harpham v. Shacklock 15, and other cases, which may perhaps be stated as follows: The transferee must not get in the legal estate from a person whom he knows or ought to know to be a trustee of the estate upon express trusts for a prior incumbrancer."[71]

> "...There is nothing more familiar than the doctrine of equity that a man, who has bonâ fide paid money without notice of any other title, though at the time of the payment he, as purchaser, gets nothing but an equitable title, may afterwards get in a legal title, if he can, and may hold it; though during the interval between the payment and the getting in the legal title he may have had notice of some prior dealing inconsistent with the good faith of the dealing with himself."[72]

Equitable holders of intermediated securities would not acquire legal title unless they become direct participants of the CREST system. A subsequent equitable interest would not gain priority in this way. It is the prior equitable interest which wins.

---

[69] *Macmillan Inc v Bishopsgate Investment Trust plc (No 3)* [1995] 3 All ER 747 (Ch) 773 (Millett J).

[70] J McGhee (ed), *Snell's Equity* (31st edn, Trusts, Wills and Probate Library, Sweet and Maxwell, London 2005) 69.

[71] *Powell v London and Provincial Bank* [1893] 1 Ch 610, 615-16 (Wright J); affd [1893] 2 Ch 555 (CA).

[72] *Blackwood v London Charted Bank of Australia* (1874) 5 PC 92 (Judicial Committee) 111.

5.2.3.3 Beneficiary under a new trust

If a purchaser has the legal interest conveyed to a trustee for him, and neither he nor the trustee has notice of a prior equity, the purchaser will take free from it, for his right to the legal estate is the better.[73]

In *Thorndike v Hunt*[74], a trust fund was paid into the court which was affected with the breach of trust by the trustee, and the payment was a trust for the winning party. The court was equity's darling for the purpose of good faith acquisition. There was a change of trust and thus a change of legal title which defeats the prior equitable title under the prior trust. The beneficiary under the new trust was held to have priority over the beneficiary under the prior trust. The later equitable title had better equity than the prior equitable title.

This line of cases can be explained by the *bona fide* purchaser of the legal estate rule that a change of trust means that legal title is acquired which defeats a previous equitable interest, thus the new equitable interest depends on the robustness of the legal title of the trustee under the new trust. It also operates when an acquirer first acquires the legal title, then alienates to another, and only retains the equitable interest. As suggested in the famous case of *Macmillan Inc v Bishopsgate Investment Trust plc (No 3)*

> "It is not necessary that the purchaser should obtain the legal estate and have the same vested in himself. It is sufficient if he has the legal estate transferred to a trustee or nominee for him. Provided that neither he nor his nominee has notice of the prior equitable interest, he will take free from it, for he has the better right to the legal estate. … Lehman Bros would be treated as obtaining the better right to the legal estate when it deposited the shares in the DTC system. The effect of doing so was to divest DIT, the former registered owner, of legal title to the shares, and to vest it in CEDE & Co, a nominee company for Lehman Bros International Ltd, as an indirect nominee for Lehman Bros."[75]

If a transaction is via the CREST system between a prior holder and a purchaser whose intermediary is a CREST-participant, there is a change of legal title. It can be seen that the purchaser gets legal title first and then has

---

[73] J McGhee (ed), *Snell's Equity* (31st edn, Trusts, Wills and Probate Library, Sweet and Maxwell, London 2005) 69.

[74] (1859) 3 De G & J 563, 563; 44 ER 1386, 1386; see also *Stanhope v Earl Verney* (1761) 2 Eden 81, 28 ER 826.

[75] [1995] 3 All ER 747(Ch) 770 (Millett J).

the legal title vested in its intermediary and retains equitable title himself. Although it is the intermediary who is entered in the operator register of securities in the CREST system, it can be seen through legal fiction that the intermediary gets legal title and transfers the legal title to the client, and the client then vests the legal title in the intermediary and retains the equitable interest, as suggested in the case of *Macmillan Inc v Bishopsgate Investment Trust plc (No 3)* above. This is precisely the application of the principle. Even absent the statutory estoppel the rule of the good faith acquisition and sheltering would give priority to a legal title and a subsequent equitable title over a prior equitable title. By the sheltering effect lower-tier clients can be sheltered. In the O to P3 transaction, P3 will be sheltered by the title of I n2 against O. (See the diagram and explanation below).

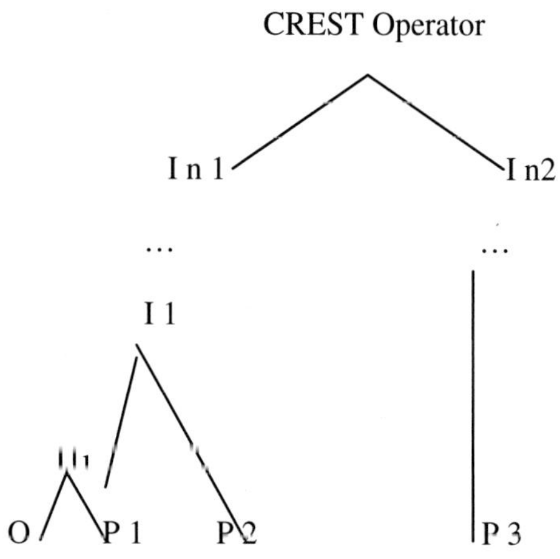

I means intermediary. I n1 and I n2 are the top tier intermediaries who are participants in the CREST system and hold legal title to securities. I 1 and I 1i are lower tier intermediaries who hold equitable title to securities.

A prior owner (O) holds equitable title with his intermediary (I 1i). This diagram shows the title conflicts between a prior owner and a purchaser (P) in three situations where, due to the fraud of a third party, the title of the prior owner is misappropriated to a purchaser: firstly where the prior owner (O) and the purchaser (P1) share the same intermediary and there is no change of legal title in the operator register; secondly where the prior owner (O) and the purchaser (P2) do not share the same intermediary and there is no change of legal title in the operator register; and thirdly where the prior owner (O) and the purchaser (P3) do not share the same intermediary and there is a change of legal title in the operator register.

5.2.3.4 Extension of the rule of good faith acquisition and sheltering

The good faith acquisition rule under English law is basically the principle of giving priority to rights with greater merits, i.e., a legal title over a prior equitable title. The good faith acquisition rule can be extended and indeed priority is given to an equitable title with better equity over a prior equitable title. And rights acquired out of a preferred right are similarly sheltered against a prior right. Thus in a transaction with no change of legal title in the CREST system, that is where a seller and a purchaser share the same intermediary who is not a direct participant of the CREST system and only holds an equitable title (O to P1), or the top tier of intermediary involved in a transaction is not a direct participant of the CREST system and holds only an equitable title (O to P2), both of which are lower tier transactions not involving a change of title on the top tier of the CREST system, it is still possible to argue that the purchaser enjoys priority as the top intermediary in the specific transaction enjoys better title than the prior holder and grants the intermediary of the purchaser and the purchaser better title. The purchaser has the better title vested in his intermediary who (perhaps through a number of intermediaries) has the better title vested in the top intermediary: in the O to P 1 transaction, I I1 and thus P 1 has a better title than O; in the O to P 2 transaction, I 1 and thus P 2 has a better title than O. (See the diagram and explanation above). The idea of upper-tier priority is also in conformity with the reality in the market. As the enjoyment and exercise of rights in intermediated securities depend on the intermediary chain, a break of the chain at an upper tier will inevitably prohibit the enjoyment and exercise of rights downwards the chain.[76] Extension of the rule of good faith acquisition and sheltering is a persuasive argument though it is not current law.

---

[76] CW Mooney, 'Beyond Negotiability: A New Model for Transfer and Pledge of Interests in Securities Controlled by Intermediaries' (1990) 12 Cardozo L Rev 305, 380.

5.2.4 Postponement

The principle of giving priority to rights with greater merits is subject to the limitation that the conduct of a holder of right with greater merits may postpone his right to a right with weaker merits. It is postponement of the rights without changing the nature of the rights *per se*. "The question is not what circumstances may as between two equities give priority to the one over the other, but what circumstances justify the Court in depriving a legal mortgagee of the benefit of the legal estate."[77] It depends upon court discretion of specific circumstances in individual cases. There is thus much uncertainty.

Protection of a legal estate may be lost against a later equitable interest by fraud[78], or negligence so gross as to amount to evidence of fraud[79], or estoppel similar to negligence[80], on the part of a legal owner. Fraud is not within the discussion on title conflicts between innocent parties. Gross negligence[81] or estoppel[82] is difficult to establish.

5.2.4.1 Postponement between equitable interests by conduct

Fraud, estoppel, and negligence are also factors to postpone an

---

77 *Northern Counties of England Fire Insurance Co v Whipp* (1884) 26 Ch D 482 (CA) 487 (Cotton, Bowen, and Fry LJJ); see also J Mowbray and others, *Lewin on Trusts* (18th edn, Thomson Sweet & Maxwell, London 2008) 1193-94.

78 *Midland Bank Trust Co Ltd v Green* [1980] Ch 590 (CA), revd [1981] AC 513 (HL).

79 *Hewitt v Loosemore* (1851) 9 Hare 449, 68 ER 586; *Ratcliffe v Barnard* (1871) 6 Ch App 652 (CA); J McGhee (ed), *Snell' s Equity* (31st edn, Trusts, Wills and Probate Library, Sweet and Maxwell, London 2005) 78; D Hayton, P Matthews and C Mitchell, *Underhill and Hayton Law of Trusts and Trustees* (17th edn, LexisNexis Butterworths, London 2007) 1228; M Smith, *The Law of Assignment: The Creation and Transfer of Choses in Action* (Oxford University Press, Oxford 2007) 422-24.

80 J McGhee (ed), *Snell's Equity* (31st edn, Trusts, Wills and Probate Library, Sweet and Maxwell, London 2005) 78.

81 *Colyer v Finch* (1856) 5 HLC 905, 10 ER 1159; *Northern Counties of England Fire Insurance Co v Whipp* (1884) 26 Ch D 482 (CA); *Grierson v National Provincial Bank of England* [1913] 2 Ch 18.

82 *Dixon v Muckleston* (1872) 8 Ch App 155 (CA)160 (Lord Selborne LC); *Northern Counties of England Fire Insurance Co v Whipp* (1884) 26 Ch D 482 (CA) 492 (Cotton, Bowen, and Fry LJJ); J McGhee (ed), *Snell's Equity* (31st edn, Trusts, Wills and Probate Library, Sweet and Maxwell, London 2005) 78.

equitable interest with better equity to another equitable interest. Fraud is not part of the discussion on title conflicts between innocent parties. It is relatively easier to establish estoppel and negligence in litigation to postpone an equitable interest with better equity to a subsequent equitable interest than in litigation to postpone a prior legal interest to a subsequent equitable interest. An equitable interest may be postponed because a holder of a prior equitable interest or his trustee is guilty of inequitable behaviour. There must be some tangible and distinct events to take away any preexisting admitted equitable title.[83] The prior equitable interest holder "has acted in such a way as to make it inequitable for him in insisting on his equity as against the later."[84]

5.2.4.2 Evaluating of conducts

In *National Provincial Bank of England v Jackson*[85], a brother deceived his two sisters as equitable owners of freehold property and got their signatures to deeds. The brother then established an equitable charge over the property to a bank. The deeds to the property were not sealed. The sisters were deceived by the brother and had some fault in enabling him as owner. The bank had negligence for not investigating title represented by the unsealed deeds. In comparison of the equities of the equitable owner sisters and the equitable mortgagee bank, it was held that the acts of the sisters were not sufficient to postpone their equities to the bank.[86]

5.2.4.3 Title deeds

Leaving title deeds in the hand of another is a frequent scenario for establishing negligence or estoppel as creating a false appearance to the world that someone else is the owner. However leaving title deeds in the hand of a trustee or a fiduciary is not negligence. Failure to ask for or retain the title deeds to unregistered land is inequitable behaviour to postpone an equitable interest to a subsequent equitable interest.[87] In

---

[83] *Shropshire Union Rlys and Canal Co v R* (1875) 7 HL 496 (Divisional Court) 514 (Lord O'Hagan).

[84] *National Provincial Bank of England v Jackson* (1886) 33 Ch D 1 (CA) 13 (Cotton LJ).

[85] (1886) 33 Ch D 1 (CA).

[86] *National Provincial Bank of England v Jackson* (1886) 33 Ch D 1 (CA).

[87] *Farrand v Yorkshire Banking Co* (1888) 40 Ch D 182.

Lloyds Bank v Bullock[88] a vendor of land left title deeds to a purchaser before being paid. The vendor had an equitable interest in the land. The purchaser created an equitable mortgage by depositing the title deeds (short of registration which was necessary for legal mortgage). The prior equitable interest was postponed to the subsequent equitable interest as the prior right holder was to blame for leaving the title deeds with the purchaser before purchaser money was paid, while the subsequent right holder had no duty to investigate the title.[89] Negligence is sufficient to postpone an equitable interest to a subsequent equitable interest. No need for gross negligence is required as for postponing a legal interest to an equitable interest.[90]

5.2.4.4 Fiduciary relations

Equitable interests under trusts are treated more benignly than other equitable interests. An equitable interest under a trust will not be postponed simply because the property is vested in a trustee.[91] This is the fundamental *raison d'être* of the trust mechanism. A beneficiary or a client of solicitors does not lose priority by the improper or negligent acts of his trustee or solicitor, unless the beneficiary or client has notice of or is privy to the impropriety or negligence.[92]

Where a vendor conveys land to a purchaser without receiving the purchase money, yet signs a conveyance containing a receipt for it, his equitable lien for the unpaid purchaser-money will be postponed to a subsequent equitable mortgagee who obtains the title deeds without notice of the lien.[93] The owner is negligent in leaving the title deeds with another

---

[88] [1896] 2 Ch 192.

[89] ibid.

[90] *National Provincial Bank of England v Jackson* (1886) 33 Ch D 1 (CA); *Taylor v Russell* [1891] 1 Ch 8(CA); *Taylor v London and County Banking Co, London and County Banking Co v Nixon* [1901] 2 Ch 231 (CA) 262-263 (Stirling LJ).

[91] J McGhee (ed), *Snell's Equity* (31st edn, Trusts, Wills and Probate Library, Sweet and Maxwell, London 2005) 81.

[92] *Oliver v Hinton* [1899] 2 Ch 264 (CA); *Capell v Winter* [1907] 2 Ch 376; D Hayton, P Matthews and C Mitchell, *Underhill and Hayton Law of Trusts and Trustees* (17th edn, LexisNexis Butterworths, London 2007) 1228.

[93] *Rice v Rice* (1853) 2 Drew 73, 61 ER 646; *Lloyds Bank v Bullock* [1896] 2 Ch 192,197 (Chitty J); *Heid V Reliance Finance Corp Pty Ltd* (1984) 154 CLR 326; *Australian Guarantee Corp (NZ) Ltd v CFC Commercial Finance Ltd* [1995] 1 NZLR 129; J McGhee (ed), *Snell's Equity* (31 edn, Trusts, Wills and Probate Library, Sweet and Maxwell, London 2005) 81-82.

person. But if there is an additional relation of a fiduciary nature, not simply of mortgagor and mortgagee, such as trustee and beneficiary, client and solicitor, a holder of an equitable interest is not negligent in leaving title deeds with a fiduciary and does not suffer from the breach of the duty by the fiduciary, as long as the equitable owner has no ground to suppose that there is bad faith of the fiduciary.[94] The favour to beneficiaries under trusts or other fiduciary relations is due to the fiduciary relation, which prevents the establishment of negligence or fraud. The duty of a beneficiary in a fiduciary relation to be alert to the fiduciary is less onerous than the duty of holders of equitable interests other than in a fiduciary relationship. A beneficiary is not in a position to be alert to his fiduciary since trust and reliance are fundamental to the fiduciary relation.

5.2.4.5 Conclusion

It is hard to postpone a prior equitable title to a subsequent equitable title, if the prior holder is innocent, due to the general law preference for vested title, in particular for a prior equitable title in fiduciary relations. The same as in the principle of granting priority to a subsequent equitable title with later acquired legal title over a prior equitable title, there is a limitation that acquisition of legal title does not involve a breach of trust of a prior equitable title. The enhanced preference for equitable title under trusts is an important point, which on one hand safeguards beneficiaries but on the other hand may hinder transactions, as will be seen in intermediated securities.

In respect of intermediated securities, under the better equity rule a good faith purchaser may get priority under the rule of good faith acquisition and sheltering, though subject to uncertainty. Now it is time to examine the priority as regards intermediated securities under the postponing rule.

As been explained, the conduct of a prior holder of an equitable interest or a trustee may operate to postpone a prior equitable interest. A major inequitable conduct is to leave title deeds in another person to arm him as the apparent owner and to deal with third parties. However, it is not inequitable for a beneficiary to leave the title deeds with his trustee. There can hardly be any postponing event between two innocent holders of intermediated securities with equitable title under case law. Firstly, a prior

[94] *Taylor v London and County Banking Co, London and County Banking Co v Nixon* [1901] 2 Ch 231 (CA) 260-261 (Stirling LJ).

holder cannot be blamed for holding securities with an intermediary and leaving the proof of title, i.e., the securities account, with his intermediary. This is simply the standard model of holding intermediated securities. However the point is open to argument that there is a strong policy of the need of transaction finality in the market. Secondly, an investor in intermediated securities is characterised as a beneficiary under a trust and misappropriation of securities by its intermediary does not postpone the beneficiary's equitable interest as a result of the presence of fiduciary relation. In conclusion between competing innocent equitable interests in intermediated securities without a change of legal title in the CREST system, it is hard to prefer a later title under postponement. This is one case of inconsistency between the policy of protecting equitable interests under trusts and the need of transaction safety as a result of incorporating intermediated securities into the trusts law analysis.

5.2.5 The *Dearle v Hall*[95] Rule

The rule in *Dearle v Hall* applies to successive dealings with choses in action, including an equitable interest in any property, real or personal.[96] Thus the priority of equitable interests is determined by the time of receipt of notice by the trustee, as a kind of choses in action.[97]

5.2.5.1 The rationale

The rationale of the notice rule is that giving notice serves to inform a trustee that an assignor is no longer the holder of the equitable interest. Otherwise the assignor who still appears to be the holder of the equitable interest to the trustee and others may commit a fraud with this position. Thus an assignee who does not give notice to the trustee actually facilitates the fraud of the assignor and should be postponed to a subsequent assignee who gives notice to the trustee.[98] The notice rule in *Dearle v Hall* governs successive dealings in choses in action. It has some bearing on title

---

[95] (1828) 3 Russ 1, 38 ER 475.

[96] *Dearle v Hall* (1828) 3 Russ 1, 38 ER 475, [1824-34] All ER Rep 28, 28 (Sir Thomas Plumer MR); J McGhee (ed), *Snell's Equity* (31st edn, Trusts, Wills and Probate Library, Sweet and Maxwell, London 2005) 83.

[97] *Stocks v Dobson* (1853) 4 De G M & G 11, 17 (Turner LJ); 43 ER 411, 415.

[98] *United Bank of Kuwait plc v Sahib* [1997] Ch 107 (CA); J McGhee (ed), *Snell's Equity* (31st edn, Trusts, Wills and Probate Library, Sweet and Maxwell, London 2005) 84.

conflicts if a prior holder is seen as the first transferee.[99]

The notice rule is out of the essence of choses in action as claims enforceable against an obligee or a trustee. Choses in action cannot be possessed as chattels and the only way of control is giving notice to the obligee or trustee, as established in *Dearle v Hall*:

> "Personal property passes by delivery of possession. In the case of the transfer of a chose in action consisting of a right to the produce of a fund in which other person have the legal interest it is not possible for the transferor to transfer the possession of the fund which must remain with those other persons, but there is a mode of dealing with it which a court of equity considers tantamount to possession, namely, by giving notice to the legal depositary of the fund. By such notice the legal holders are converted into trustees for the transferee and are charged with responsibility towards him, and the transferor is deprived of the power to carry the same security repeatedly into the market and induce third persons to advance money on it under the erroneous belief that it still belongs to him absolutely, free from incumbrance. That precaution is always taken by diligent purchasers and incumbrancers. If it is not taken, there is neglect, and the solicitor who conducts the business for the transferee is responsible for that neglect. He who contracts for a chose in action and does not give notice gives personal credit to the individual with whom he deals, but to perfect his title, to give a complete right *in rem* and not merely a right against him who conveys his interest, notice is necessary."[100]

Failure to give notice by a transferee is held as negligence as a transferor is still the apparent owner of the chose in action and may induce another to act to his detriment. The negligent transferee should bear the loss. The notice rule can be explained by the better equity rule or the postponing rule. A transferee who gives notice is believed to have better equity, or a transferee who fails to give notice is negligent in not giving notice.

> "The maxim '*Qui prior est in tempore potior est in jure*' as an equitable rule admits of exception, and gives way when the question does not lie between bare and equal equities. If there appears to be, in respect of circumstances independent of priority of time, a better title in a subsequent purchaser than in the purchaser who preceded him in date, the case ceases to be a balance of equal equities, and the preference which priority of date

[99] *Macmillan Inc v Bishopsgate Investment Trust plc (No 3)* [1995] 3 All ER 747 (Ch) 762 (Millett J).

[100] *Dearle v Hall* (1828) 3 Russ 1; 38 ER 475; [1824-34] All ER Rep 28, 29 (Sir Thomas Plumer MR).

> might otherwise have given is done away with and counteracted. In a court of equity a plaintiff cannot be heard who asks the interposition of the court to indemnify him against the effects of his own negligence at the expense of another who has used all diligence, and, if he is to suffer loss, will suffer it by reason of the negligence of the very person who prays relief against him."[101]

5.2.5.2 Notice

An assignee who has actual or constructive notice of a previous assignment when he advances his money or acquires his security cannot gain priority over it by being the first to give notice.[102] However, knowledge of previous assignment acquired after he advances his money does not prevent an assignee from claiming priority for being the first to give notice even though with knowledge of previous assignment.[103] This is in line with the better equity rule that notice of a prior equitable interest, after acquiring equitable estate but before acquiring legal estate, does not prevent an acquirer from claiming priority with legal estate.

5.2.5.3 Inapplicable to shares

The *Dearle v Hall* rule is inapplicable to shares as companies are not bound to take notice of equitable interests under trusts.[104]

Shares as special choses in action

Shares are originally and by nature choses in action. However shares have long since enjoyed special status and have special rules on transfer, exempt from the general rules on assignment of choses in action.[105] There are fundamental differences between shares and typical choses in action.[106]

---

[101] *Dearle v Hall* (1828) 3 Russ 1; 38 ER 475; [1824-34] All ER Rep 28, 29 (Sir Thomas Plumer MR).

[102] *Timson v Ramsbottom* (1837) 2 Keen 35, 48 ER 541; *Spencer v Clarke* (1878) 9 Ch D 137; *Re Weniger's Policy* [1910] 2 Ch 291; J McGhee (ed), *Snell's Equity* (31st edn, Trusts, Wills and Probate Library, Sweet and Maxwell, London 2005) 83.

[103] *Mutual Life Assurance Society v Langley* (1886) 32 Ch D 460 (CA).

[104] Companies Act 2006 s 126; J Mowbray and others, *Lewin on Trusts* (18th edn, Thomson Sweet & Maxwell, London 2008) 1206-08.

[105] *Macmillan Inc v Bishopsgate Investment Trust plc (No 3)* [1995] 3 All ER 747 (Ch) 761 (Millett J).

[106] *Société Générale de Paris v Walker* (1884) 14 QBD 424 (CA) 447 (Cotton LJ), affd (1885) 11 App Cas 20 (HL).

A shareholder has legal rights against the company instead of equitable rights. A shareholder can bring legal proceedings against the company to enforce his rights. Shares are capable of legal transfer and governed by statutes. Shares as legal rights are different from choses in action which can only be transferred in equity. This was the position in the 1880s when the leading case *Société Générale de Paris v Walker* [107] was decided. There has been little change except statutory intervention. An agreement between a beneficiary and a trustee is effective as between themselves but is not binding upon a company.[108] Companies are not obliged to take notice of trusts or beneficial title in shares. A beneficial owner of shares cannot turn a company into a trustee by giving notice; but unless a company can be turned into a trustee, the notice rule does not work, and a beneficiary cannot gain priority over a prior equitable interest in shares by giving notice.[109]

Company duty

A holder of beneficial interest in shares has no rights against the company to have him registered. There is an issue of protecting a beneficial interest in shares against a legal owner. It is a crucial issue whether a notice of beneficial interest to the company can bind the company and prevent the company from registering a transfer by the legal owner in breach of the trust. There are two competing interests, i.e., the interest of an equitable owner or mortgagee and the duty of a company to keep a register of equitable interests in shares.[110] There is no such duty for a company.

> "The person having the beneficial interest in the shares has, as against the company, no right to them; he has as against the company no right to have them registered in his own name. But it is necessary to consider another matter, viz., the effect of a notice given to a company by a cestui que trust or equitable mortgagee of shares in it, and in particular it is necessary to consider whether after such a notice the company can properly decline to permit the registration of a transfer by the registered holder of the shares. It is obvious that the question is one of the utmost importance not only to equitable owners and mortgagees of shares, but also to companies; for

---

[107] ibid.

[108] *Société Générale de Paris v Walker* (1885) 11 App Cas 20 (HL) 30 (Earl of Selborne).

[109] ibid.

[110] *Société Générale de Paris v Walker* (1884) 14 QBD 424 (CA) 452 (Lindley LJ), affd (1885) 11 App Cas 20 (HL).

> whilst on the one hand, if the notice is valueless, an equitable owner or mortgagee will be at the mercy of the registered owner, yet on the other, if the notice operates as a stop on the transfer of the shares, companies must be careful to preserve such notices and not to disregard them. A very onerous duty will be thrown upon companies, for they will in this case not only have to keep a register of shareholders and of transfers, but in some shape or other a register of notices of equitable interests."[111]

5.2.5.4 Intermediated securities

The *Dearle v Hall* rule is inapplicable to shares as a special kind of choses in action the transfer of which is governed by statutes.[112] In the context of intermediated securities it is applicable to equitable title in intermediated securities in theory since equitable title to intermediated securities is different from legal title to the underlying securities. There are several issues to be clarified however before coming to the conclusion whether application of the *Deale v Hall* rule to equitable interests in intermediated securities is satisfactory. What is notice in the transfer of intermediated securities, to whom to give notice?

Transfer of intermediated securities is through debits and credits on the relevant books of a transferor, relevant intermediaries and a transferee. The simplest case would be the case where a transferor a transferee share the same intermediary, a debit on the securities account of the transferor and a credit on the securities account of the transferee, both made by their common intermediary, would constitute notice to the trustee. However the interest of the transferor is also known to the intermediary and the notice is prior in time. The *Dearle v Hall* rule cannot help transferees. Consider more complex cases where a transferor and a transferee have securities accounts with different intermediaries, a transfer is done through debits on the securities account of the transferor, the intermediary of the transferor and upper-tier intermediaries until there is a top-tier intermediary which debits the securities account of the upper-tier intermediary on the side of the transferor and credits the securities account of the upper-tier intermediary of the side of the transferee until the account of the transferee. In these cases notice of the equitable interest of the transferee can be seen as given to each tier of intermediary. Again notice of an equitable interest

[111] *Macmillan Inc v Bishopsgate Investment Trust plc (No 3)* [1995] 3 All ER 747 (Ch).

[112] Companies Act 2006 s 126; J Birds and others (eds), *Boyle & Birds' Company Law* (7th edn, Jordan, Bristol 2009) 294, 400.

of a transferor can be seen as having been given by debits to each tier of intermediary, always prior to credits as notice of an equitable interest of a transferee.

Thus even characterising the good faith acquirer issue as successive dealings artificially, the holding and transfer mechanism of intermediated securities makes it necessary to give notice to relevant intermediaries of an equitable title. Intermediated securities cannot be transferred without relevant intermediaries as trustees. Notice of a transferor's interests is always prior to notice to a transferee's notice. The notice rule on priority cannot help a transferee against a transferor.

5.2.6 Analysis of Priority Rules

5.2.6.1 General remarks

Novation and priority

The argument that transfer of equitable interests is novation by nature finds support in the priority rules on equitable interests. The priority rule on equitable title is not designed for transfer of equitable interests from the beginning but on co-existent equitable interests. The better equity approach and the postponement by party conducts both presume the parallel interests in co-existence of each other. The subsequent equitable interest is a new interest, or more exactly, a new claim against the trustee or fiduciary. A typical situation of competing equitable interests is a mortgagor creating successive equitable mortgages. A prior equitable mortgage is not extinguished but is still valid and in competition with a subsequent mortgage. It is not an issue of loss and gain as the transfer of specific tangibles. This basic position is recognised in the priority rule on competing title, which is a comparative approach.

The first in time rule and the greater merits rule

The priority rule across the whole system of legal rights, equitable rights and mere equities is the first in time rule, modified by the nature and merits of rights. Merits of rights depend upon the nature of rights subject to the postponing conducts of right holders, which governs legal title subject to statutory exceptions as well as equitable title and mere equities.

5.2.6.2 The good faith purchaser rule under English law

As regarding title conflicts between innocent parties, a purchaser of legal estate has priority over a prior equitable estate; a purchaser of equitable interest has priority over a prior mere equity. There is no general rule of protecting a good faith acquirer of rights as against a prior right of the same nature. In most civil law countries property rights can only be legal and a good faith purchaser enjoys priority against a prior legal right. There is a fundamental difference between the good faith purchaser rule in English law and typical civil law. Under English law between legal rights the *nemo dat* principle is the rule and the protection of good faith purchaser is only in statutory exceptions and customs. Statutory carve-outs are mainly in commercial context, regarding mercantile agents and hire purchasers where possession is regularly separate from ownership and the goods are in regular commercial circulation. Hence the security of transaction is of utmost importance. Negotiable instruments are a product of customs. The principle that a good faith acquirer of legal title gets clean title and defeats a prior equitable title and a good faith purchaser of equitable title gets clean title and defeats a prior mere equity, has several underlying policies. Firstly, it is a result of the difference of the natures of rights. Secondly, as to a good faith acquirer of legal title it is held to be an issue of jurisdiction in that a court of equity has no jurisdiction to deprive a legal owner of his legal right.

Nature or merits of rights

Trust is considered as typical of situations where one has the best public title to an asset while the true ownership is vested in another.[113] A trustee is the true owner with apparent title but is obliged to turn the benefit of ownership to a beneficiary. As the trustee obligation and the beneficiary entitlement are not visible to outsiders to a trust, a purchaser of the legal title to the asset without notice of the beneficiary entitlement deserves priority over the beneficiary. A purchaser of the equitable title or interests to the asset without notice of the beneficiary entitlement is subject to the prior equitable interest. There is common sense in the different treatment of legal and equitable title. Legal title is public and strong while equitable title is hidden and weak. Creation of equitable

[113] PR Wood, *Principles of International Insolvency* (2nd edn, Law and Practice of International Finance Series, Sweet & Maxwell, London 2007) 278.

interests is less formal and flexible.[114] Naturally an equitable title is overriden by a legal title acquired without notice of the equitable title.

Jurisdiction

It is also argued that the rule that a good faith acquirer of legal estate defeats a prior equitable interest is a result of the historical parallel co-existence of courts of common law and equity. It is a matter of jurisdiction and constitutional law. Common law courts used to decide on legal rights and equity courts on equitable rights with separate authority. A court of equity could not enforce an equitable right against a legal right.[115]

In a leading case it is held that a court of equity had no jurisdiction to deprive a legal owner of legal rights:

> "I propose simply to apply myself to the case of a purchaser for valuable consideration, without notice, obtaining, upon the occasion of his purchase, and by means of his purchase deed, some legal estate, some legal right, some legal advantage; and, according to my view of the established law of this Court, such a purchaser's plea of a purchase for valuable consideration without notice is an absolute, unqualified, unanswerable defence, and an unanswerable plea to the jurisdiction of this Court. Such a purchaser, when he has once put in that plea, may be interrogated and tested to any extent as to the valuable consideration which he has given in order to shew the *bona fides* or *mala fides* of his purchase, and also the presence or the absence of notice; but when once he has gone through that ordeal, and has satisfied the terms of the plea of purchase for valuable consideration without notice, then, according to my judgment, this Court has no jurisdiction whatever to do anything more than to let him depart in possession of that legal estate, that legal right, that legal advantage which he has obtained, whatever it may be. In such a case a purchaser is entitled to hold that which, without breach of duty, he has had conveyed to him."[116]

> "My view of the principle is, that when once you have arrived at the conclusion that the purchaser is a purchaser for valuable consideration without notice, the Court has no right to ask him, and has no right to put him to contest the question, how he is going to defend himself, or what he is going to rely on. He may say, honestly and justly, 'I am not going to tell

---

[114] See 2.4.1; Calnan, 'Reforming Priority Law' [2006] JIBFL 4.

[115] Law Commission, 'The UNIDROIT Convention on Substantive Rules regarding Intermediated Securities Further Updated Advice to HM Treasury (May 2008)' [5.68]; J Hackney, 'Usucapio and the Law of Trusts' in J Getzler (ed) *Rationalizing Property, Equity and Trusts: Essays in Honour of Edward Burn* (Lexis-Nexis UK, London 2003).

[116] *Pilcher v Rawlins* (1872) 7 Ch App 259, 268-69 (Sir James LJ).

> you. I have got the deeds; I defend them, and you will never be able to make me produce them, and you will never be able to produce secondary evidence of them. I am not obliged to produce them at all; probably before you get half way through your action of ejectment you will find a jus tertii which you will not dispose of; the estate is in the hands of a legal tenant to whom I have let it, and no one can determine that tenancy without notice, and no one can give that notice but myself; I will not give that notice, and no Court has any power to compel me to give it. I have a right to rely, as every person defending his position has, on the weakness of the title of the person who is seeking to displace me.' That seems to be exactly the position of such a purchaser as this."[117]

Both the nature of rights theory and the jurisdiction theory support the argument that the good faith purchaser rule is not a general rule under English law as in civil law, but only operates between legal title and equitable title or equitable title and mere equities.

5.2.6.3 Priority between legal rights, and between equitable interests

The *nemo dat* rule still dominates the priority between rights of the same category. The notion of protecting vested rights is so deeply entrenched that it is never replaced by a general good faith purchaser rule shielding a good faith purchaser of rights from prior rights of the same quality. This may be attributed to the responsive approach across the English legal system which tends to order specific remedies in specific cases. Another explanation may be from the socio-legal perspective that the frequency of fraud is not serious enough to tip the balance from in favour security of title to in favour of security of transaction.

First in time among equitable title

The preference for a prior right is true both at law and in equity, i.e., both between legal rights and between equitable rights. There is even greater tendency to prefer a prior equitable interest to a subsequent equitable interest, especially an equitable interest under a trust. A good faith purchaser of an equitable interest cannot take the equitable interest free of a prior equitable interest, unless the later equitable interest has better equity or the prior equitable interest is postponed by the conduct of the equitable owner. There is no good faith acquisition between equitable interests with equal equities or merits. It is stringent to achieve better equity for a later equitable interest. For example, getting legal title after

---

[117] ibid 269-70 (Sir James LJ).

getting equitable title cannot involve a breach of trust, which is of limited application in respect of equitable interests under trusts. It is also difficult to establish a postponing conduct on the part of a prior equitable owner and a trustee of a prior equitable owner. The standards of establishing negligence on the part of a beneficial owner are harder to satisfy as the duty of due diligence of a beneficial owner is lower in dealing with his trustee. There may be several reasons. Firstly, the favour for a prior equitable title against a later one has something to do with the fiduciary nature and the social function of trusts in the past, in addition to the general characteristics of equitable interests. Secondly equitable interests are not designed for transfer on a regular basis, such as shares on exchanges, but are personal and involve a strong degree of privity between the acquirer of an equitable interest and the trustee, the security of transaction is less a concern in this context.[118]

Protection of equitable owners as weak parties

It is argued that it is unfair for a beneficiary to suffer from the improper conduct of a trustee in which the beneficiary has trust and reliance. Most beneficiaries used to be weak parities in society, such as infants and women, benefiting under the shelter of trusts. It is against the policy of the mechanism of trusts to require a beneficiary to keep a close eye on the trustee.

> "...whenever you have an equitable owner who is the absolute owner, that is to say, entitled to the whole equitable interest, such a person ought not to have a trustee at all holding the indicia of legal ownership; or, if he chooses, for his own purpose, to have such a trustee, he must be in danger of suffering for every act of improper conduct by that trustee; and that therefore, if the person entitled absolutely to the equitable interest in a share in a railway company, chooses for his own purpose to have that share standing in the name of a trustee for him, he will be bound not merely by a valid legal transfer of that share by the trustee, but by any equitable dealing or contract which the trustee may choose to enter into. My Lords, that is a very serious proposition, It goes not merely to shares, but it goes to land, and to every other species of property; and it goes to say that, whereas there is a large, well-known, recognised, and admitted system of trusts in this country, that system of trusts is to be cut down and moulded and reduced to this, that it is to be a system applicable only to infants, married women, or persons with limited interests; and that wherever the limited interest has ceased, and the equitable interest has become entire and

[118] D O'Sullivan, 'Distributing the Risk of Contract Fraud' (2001) 117 LQR 381, 386.

> complete without any limit, there the equitable owner is under some measure of obligation with regard to his duty of watching his trustee, an obligation which does not lie upon a limited owner. I find no authority for such a proposition, and I feel satisfied that your Lordships will not be disposed to introduce, for the first time, that as a rule of law."[119]

An equitable owner has to put the indicia of title in the custody of the trustee who is the legal owner. An equitable owner is not negligent for leaving the indicia of title in the trustee. If a trustee breaches the trust and misappropriates the trust property, there are two circumstances. If a person dealing with a trustee gets a legal title, for the sake of the integrity of transactions the equitable interest is tramped by the legal title. If a person dealing with a trustee gets an equitable interest in the property, the prior equitable interest cannot be subordinated. One of the policies is the protection of beneficiaries who, often weak parties in society, have confidence and trust in the trustee and, such as children, married women in the past. It is proposed that a beneficiary is not in an alert position of trustees and obliged to keep a close eye on the conduct of trustees. There is a preference for the existing beneficiaries.

Lack of compelling necessity of commercial circulation

Equitable interests were not intended to be in frequent circulation. It was at the beginning a way of allocating property over time, i.e., for the benefit of generations to enjoy. Before the exploration of trusts for commercial use equitable interests were not in regular commercial circulation. Equitable interests, though proprietary, are personal obligations against the trustee by nature. The conflict of the security of title and security of transaction in respect of equitable interests are less fierce than that in respect of legal title. A purchaser of an equitable interest normally has sufficient knowledge of the trustee, or pays less value than acquiring legal title, if he gets an equitable interest from a trustee who acts against the equitable interest of another beneficiary in breach of trustee obligations. Even regarding legal title the security of transaction is in principle subordinated to the security of title under English law.

Absent a general rule of favouring a later equitable interest acquired in good faith, it is up to judicial discretion to compare the merits of equitable interests in individual cases. Indeed it is raised that whether the priority is a comparison of the merits of competing equitable interests, or it is the

---

[119] *Shropshire Union Rlys and Canal Co v R* (1875) 7 HL 496 (Divisional Court) 507 (Lord Cairns).

compelling need of transaction which makes it desirable to introduce a general rule of protecting a good faith purchaser of equitable interests against prior equitable interests, as legal title in commercial transactions.[120]

5.2.6.4 Priority in intermediated securities

Normally a good faith acquirer of intermediated securities can get good title against a good faith prior holder when a legal title is acquired, or when an equitable interest is acquired and there is a change of legal title in the CREST system. A good faith acquirer of equitable title without a change of legal title in the CREST system cannot get good title against a prior equitable title, though it is possible by arguing for an extension of the rule of good faith acquisition and sheltering, that is a change of an equitable title at an upper-tier defeats a prior lower-tier title and confers priority upon a subsequent title. The priority of title of a good faith acquirer depends on too many issues: whether legal title or equitable title is acquired; whether there is a change of legal title between a prior owner and a good faith acquirer; and perhaps the level of the tiers of a prior owner and a good faith acquirer. There is much uncertainty.

In addition even if it is possible to get good title under the good faith acquirer rule of legal title over a prior equitable title, there are uncertainties as what is good faith and notice. The scope of notice is wide and relatively easy to establish, which is not in favour of a purchaser.

The lack of sufficient protection of good faith acquirers of intermediated securities under the current law on title conflicts is nothing new. The priority system under English law is complex and there is an entrenched tendency of preferring a vested right, against the need for transaction safety. The situation of intermediated securities does highlight this issue for the following reasons.

Firstly, equitable title to intermediated securities is in regular circulation and indeed the value of intermediated securities lies in liquidity to a large extent. Thus equitable interests in intermediated securities are typical cases of the circulation of equitable interests in financial and commercial trusts, in contrast with the traditional family and charity trusts under which equitable interests were infrequently transferred. Transfer of equitable interests is on a standard basis rather than on an individual basis. Conflicts of equitable title are not between individual parties on a discrete

[120] Jenks, 'The Legal Estate' (1908) 24 LQR 147; D O'Sullivan, 'Distributing the Risk of Contract Fraud' (2001) 117 LQR 381.

basis, as between two equitable mortgagees in old cases. Secondly, investors in intermediated securities as beneficiaries are not weak parities like infants or the elder. They are reasonable individual investors. Thirdly, the personal and fiduciary relationship between an account holder and his intermediary is attenuated compared with the fiduciary or even altruistic nature of the trustee-beneficiary relationship in traditional family trusts.

The policy of preferring a prior equitable interest against a later equitable interest finds weaker basis in the context of intermediated securities. Rather commercial need and market liquidity call for that the priority be given to a later equitable interest acquired in good faith.

Intermediated securities are a new case highlighting some of the issues of commercial use of trusts, developed in the context of family and charity.[121] The use of trusts for commercial exploration is a major change in the function of the trusts. The static function of allocating property over time of trusts is subordinated to the dynamic function of making use of property. Equitable interests which used to be relatively stable and not in regular circulation are no longer so. Rather they are designed to be in circulation such as unit trusts. Unit trusts are statutory and enjoy special rules on the transfer and priority of title.[122] Other novel equitable interests in regular circulation not governed by special statutes are still subject to the general priority rules. In addition beneficiaries are not necessarily weak parties under the shelter of trusts as it used to be. The fact that beneficiaries under commercial and financial trusts are professional investors or rational individuals makes the policy of the law of preferring the weak party outdated.

However, the result of title conflicts in respect of intermediated securities under general law on priority is not radically different from certificated securities. Though a good faith acquirer of intermediated securities cannot get title as a holder in due course of bearer securities, he is not radically worse than a good faith acquirer of registered certificated

---

[121] For commercial use of trusts and trusts law in commercial relations, see PD Finn (ed), *Equity and Commercial Relationships* (The Law Book Company, Sydney 1987); J Mummery, 'Commercial Notions and Equitable Potions' in S Worthington (ed) *Commercial law and Commercial Practice* (Hart Publishing, Oxford 2003); D Hayton, P Matthews and C Mitchell, *Underhill and Hayton Law of Trusts and Trustees* (17th edn, LexisNexis Butterworths, London 2007); D Hayton, H Pigott and J Benjamin, 'The Use of Trusts In International Financial Transactions' [2002] JIBFL 23.

[122] Financial Services and Markets Act 2000 ss 242-261; KF Sin, *The Legal Nature of the Unit Trust* (Clarendon Press, Oxford 1997).

securities. There are situations where a good faith acquirer of intermediated securities does get good title against a prior title, for example, via the sheltering effect of the statutory estoppel. A good faith acquirer of certificated registered securities can not get title against a prior holder, as explained in Chapter Three.

5.2.7 Need for Change?

Acquirers of legal title to intermediated securities in the CREST system enjoy special statutory protection which is the highest degree of negotiability ever known under English law, which reaffirms the rule of good faith acquisition and sheltering under general law. An equitable title acquired after a change in legal title in the CREST system is sheltered from a prior equitable title. An equitable title not sheltered by the statutory estoppel or the rule of good faith acquisition and sheltering is subject to the priority rule on equities, i.e. the better equity and postponement rule. A subsequent equitable title may be granted priority over a prior equitable title, under an extension of the rule that the equity with better right to legal title wins, i.e., a change of title at a high-tier intermediary as trustee. The principle of postponement is largely inapplicable.

The disparity of the status of legal title and equitable title, and of equitable title via or not via the CREST system, to intermediated securities has been identified and recognised by legal experts as might cause unacceptable legal uncertainty, despite the growth of intermediated securities markets. It is considered necessary to clarify the issue before problems break out on a large basis.[123]

The complexity of priority is attributed to the introduction of priority rules on equitable title, as well as between equitable and legal title, as a result of treating title to intermediated securities as equitable title. Thus there are arguments in favour of characterising interests in intermediated securities as legal interests rather than as equitable interests. There are two ways proposed for achieving legal title. One approach is to introduce a new kind of rights in intermediated securities legally detached from the underlying securities. Holders of intermediated securities at each tier get

[123] Law Commission, 'The UNIDROIT Convention on Substantive Rules regarding Intermediated Securities: Further Updated Advice to HM Treasury (May 2008)' [5.65]; Financial Markets Law Committee, 'The FMLC Report on Property Interests in Indirectly Held Investment Securities: An Analysis of the Need for and Nature of Legislation in the UK' [2005] Rev dr unif 339.

legal title to intermediated securities held with their intermediaries. Of course the intermediated securities at lower tiers depend on the soundness and integrity of intermediated securities at upper tiers and the underlying securities. It is however possible to define title to intermediated securities at a specific tier as legal title.

Another approach is to characterise the custody of securities not as trust but as bailment.[124] Under bailment a bailor retains legal title and a bailee does not take legal title. However bailment is designed for chattels and based on possession. The argument is that the essence of delivery of possession under bailment is the actual control over chattel. The idea of control can be extended to the context of intermediated securities where intermediated securities keep control of intermediated securities and serve as bailees. There are indeed cases where bailment was held to be valid where the bailee has no actual possession.[125]

However characterising title to intermediated securities as legal title throughout the holding system would not solve the problem. Resolution of title conflicts in favour of a prior title is not because of title to intermediated securities is equitable. The problem is that conflicts of legal title are not treated in favour of a purchaser under the general priority rule on legal title. There is no general principle of good faith acquirer rule under English law between rights of the same category. The good faith acquirer rule is to prefer a later legal title to a prior equitable title, instead of preferring a later legal title to a prior legal title. In case of certificated securities, a good faith acquirer of bearer securities benefit from the negotiability of bearer securities; a good faith acquirer of registered securities is subject to a prior legal title. Resolution of title conflicts under general English law is inconsistent with market expectations of preferring the right last in time, but friendly to the vested rights, both in common law and in equity. It is thus not an issue of whether title to intermediated securities is equitable or legal. It is an issue of the priority rule under general law.

As explained that the trust mechanism can accommodate most property

---

[124] A Beaves, 'Global Custody-A Tentative Analysis of Property and Contract' in N Palmer and E McKendrick (eds), *Interests in Goods* (2nd edn, Lloyds of London Press, London 1998); MF Khimji, 'Intermediary Credit Risk-A Comparative Law Analysis of Property Rights in Indirectly Held Securities' [2005] JBL 287; Law Commission, 'The UNIDROIT Convention on Substantive Rules regarding Intermediated Securities: Further Updated Advice to HM Treasury (May 2008)' [5.95].

[125] NE Palmer, *Bailment* (2nd edn, Sweet & Maxwell, London 1991) 13-15.

law issues in intermediated securities consistent with market expectations, such as recognition of the property interests of holders of intermediated securities, insulation of client assets in intermediary insolvency, and fiduciary duties on intermediaries. One point that is unsatisfactory is the disparity of protection of good faith acquirer of intermediated securities other than the top tier of the CREST system, which is not the fault of equity as analysed.

5.2.8 Conclusion

Title, legal and equitable, is ranked by merits and time of creation. A legal title acquired in good faith for value overrides a prior equitable title due to the greater merits of legal title. Equitable title is ranked by their merits, subject to party conduct. The departure of law on title conflicts is safeguarding the vested title, in particular in respect of equitable title, which is inconsistent with market expectation of finality. This issue has long been present in English law. The result of its application to intermediated securities of protecting purchasers and transaction finality is not satisfactory but nothing new. Indeed it is uncommon that in modern society where transactions are so frequent that the security of transaction has never found greater favour than the security of title in English law. This is particularly so in the financial markets where liquidity constitutes the value of financial assets. Even in the financial markets only bearer securities enjoy negotiability while registered securities never have had negotiable status. The fundamental point is whether finality in respect of intermediated securities is such a strong policy that deserves a statutory intervention and how vested title can effectively be safeguarded meanwhile.

5.3 Conclusion

Transfer of intermediated securities as equitable interests is novation. Title conflicts in respect of intermediated securities as equitable interests are dealt with in favour of a prior title as a principle subject to the rule of good faith acquisition and sheltering. Certain policies underlying the priority rules on equitable interests are inconsistent with intermediated securities.

CHAPTER SIX

TITLE CONFLICTS: THE WAY FORWARD

6.1 Introduction

The law on title conflicts in respect of intermediated securities is not uniform or certain. At the top tier of the CREST system, a purchaser who is not fraudulent gets a legal title free of any prior adverse legal and equitable right or interest under the statutory estoppel. Other than that, under the priority rules on securities, apparently negotiability of certificated bearer securities is inapplicable to intangible book entry securities due to the absence of physical certificates, according to the mainstream view. Estoppel against the issuer of registered securities cannot avail a purchaser of intermediated securities either, due to the absence of physical certificates.[1] Under the general property law on priority, if a purchaser acquires a legal title as a participant in the CREST system his title is valid against a prior legal title under the statutory estoppel, and a prior equitable title, under the statutory estoppel as well as under the law of equity. If a non-participant purchaser acquires an equitable title, his equitable title is inferior to a prior legal title, superior to an equitable title before the change of legal title, but inferior to an equitable title after the change of legal title. It is the result of the *nemo dat* rule and the complexity of priority between legal property rights and equitable property rights as well as between equitable property rights. This uncertainty proves unsatisfactory. However the lack of consistent protection of good faith purchasers is nothing new but a tradition of English law which values the vested rights of an owner over a purchaser more than other legal systems, despite the need for security of transaction. Exceptions are provided by statutes where security of transaction is

---

[1] Though it is open to debate that the underlying policy of negotiability and estoppel against the issuer of registered securities can be resorted to in favour of a purchaser, see 6.3.4.

deemed to be of essential necessity.

Before any proposal can be made on the English law regarding title conflicts, it may help to examine the practices of other countries and international uniform law. The need for enhancing protection of purchasers of intermediated securities, i.e., the balance between the protection of purchasers as well as the current owners will be scrutinised. The two approaches for achieving such protection, i.e., the traditional *bona fide* acquisition and the new credit based approach, together with relevant national laws, will be presented. The approaches will then be analysed in terms of general policy as well as English law. Finally possible responses and their results under English law will be suggested.

There is almost unanimous support for protecting good faith purchasers over true owners by national legislations and international instruments.[2] The fundamental idea is still the persistent need of transaction security in individual transactions on a micro level. In addition there is a macro level of transaction security known as systemic integrity in the securities settlement system, that the failure of an individual transaction caused by a prior investor tracing back the title to securities may invalidate a series of onward transactions. Systemic integrity depends on the acquisition of securities capable of being relied on for onward transactions. This is true to all organised markets.[3] Market practices of rapid conclusion and execution of transactions through impersonal organised markets requires a high level of confidence of an acquirer in the rights he acquires. Meanwhile market structures of securities holding and transfer prevent an acquirer from being able to identify a seller or check the authenticity of title of securities he acquires. Imposing a general duty of inquiry or investigation would be futile or inappropriate.[4] Thus a purchaser of intermediated securities who is not fraudulent deserves protection against prior proprietary claims in intermediated securities.

---

[2] CR Reitz, 'Reflections on the Drafting of the 1994 Revision of Article 8 of the US Uniform Commercial Code' [2005] Rev dr unif 357, 364-65; Swiss Federal Intermediated Securities Act art 29 (1); UNIDROIT, 'Draft Official Commentary on the Draft Convention on Substantive Rules regarding Intermediated Securities (UNIDROIT 2009 CONF 11/2-Doc 5)' [17-9].

[3] In the intermediated holding system it is more difficult for an acquirer to check the title of securities he acquires.

[4] Geneva Securities Convention Art 17 (b); UNIDROIT, 'Draft Official Commentary on the Draft Convention on Substantive Rules regarding Intermediated Securities (UNIDROIT 2009 CONF 11/2-Doc 5)' [17-9].

6.2 How Can a Purchaser Be Protected

There are generally two models of protecting an innocent purchaser who has no knowledge of any defect in the title he acquires, i.e., the traditional *bona fide* acquisition rule under the property law model and the credit based approach or the claim model, as it solely focuses on the credit as acquisition of title.

6.2.1 The Traditional *Bona Fide* Acquisition Rule[5]

Countries applying the traditional property law regime to intermediated securities and with a general *bona fide* acquisition rule tend to extend the *bona fide* acquisition rule to intermediated securities. The property law model is often related to the direct holding system or the transparent model where an issuer, or a central securities depository keeps securities accounts for individual investors at all tiers, and individual investors have ownership over specific underlying securities or as co-owners to a pool of specific underlying securities, consistent with the specificity requirement of property rights, or more accurately, rights *in rem*. This model tries to incorporate intangible intermediated securities into the property law designed for tangibles through legal fiction, by treating intangible book entries as certificates as proof of title, and credit or registration as constructive possession. Transfer of intermediated securities is treated as transfer of moveables from a seller to a purchaser which is normally buttressed by the requirement of matching, that a credit is valid only if there is a valid corresponding debit. With such legal characterisation of intangible book entry securities as tangibles and credit or registration as constructive possession, it is thus theoretically legitimate to apply the *bona fide* acquisition rule to intermediated securities. Now that it is established that the *bona fide* purchaser rule can be extended to intermediated securities, a further issues arises concerning what constitutes *bona fide*. There are certain conditions to be met to qualify as a *bona fide* purchaser out of concerns to protect the property rights of a true owner and prevent fraud. Given the features of intermediated securities markets and their distinctions from traditional markets of tangibles, it merits consideration whether it is necessary to modify the test of *bona fide* with regard to

---

[5] Cv Bar and E Clive (eds), *Principles, Definitions and Model Rules of European Private Law: Draft Common Frame of Reference (DCFR)* (vol 5, Sellier. European Law Publishers, Munich 2009) 4824-77.

intermediated securities. *Bona fide* for the purpose of the *bona fide* purchaser rule is often equivalent to no knowledge of any circumstance of irregularity in the title a purchaser acquires. Due to the anonymity of transactions in intermediated securities and need of systemic integrity, it is reasonable that the test of *bona fide* be relaxed with regard to the acquisition of intermediated securities.

The Swiss Federal Intermediated Securities Act (FSIA) extends the *bona fide* acquisition rule under civil law to intermediated securities on the basis of the proprietary nature of intermediated securities.[6] It protects a person who acquires intermediated securities or rights in intermediated securities for value and in good faith in respect of the acquisition even where the transferor has no power or authority to transfer the intermediated securities; or the credit of intermediated securities to the transferor's securities account is reversed.[7] A new requirement of for value is added. *Bona fide* follows the definition under general law that it is presumed but failure to pay necessary notice to suspicious circumstance is not *bona fide*.[8]

French law has a good faith rule protecting good faith acquirers of moveables against prior owners, but not to intermediated securities, mainly because possession is not available in respect of intermediated securities. It is suggested that the rule can be extended to intermediated securities by interpreting registration with possession. The test of good faith continues to apply.[9]

Under German law, most intermediated securities are treated as moveables and governed by the traditional good faith acquirer rule. Intermediated securities treated as claims are also governed by a special rule of good faith acquirer rule.[10]

---

[6] Code civil Suisse du 10 décembre 1907 (Etat le 1er janvier 2013) arts 933, 934, 935, 973; H Kuhn, B Graham-Siegenthaler and L Thévenoz (eds), *The Federal Intermediated Securities Act (FISA) and the Hague Securities Convention (HSC)* (Stämpfli's Commentary, Stämpfli Publishers Ltd., Berne 2010) 451.

[7] FISA art 29 (1).

[8] Code civil Suisse du 10 décembre 1907 (Etat le 1er janvier 2013) art 3.

[9] A Maffei, 'De la nature juridique des titres dematerialisés intermédiés en droit francais' [2005] Rev dr unif 237, 248-49; UNIDROIT, 'UNIDROIT Committee of Governmental Experts for the Preparation of a draft Convention on Substantive Rules regarding Intermediated Securities. Informal Working Group on Article 14 of the draft Convention-Response to the Questionnaire Concerning Acquisition by an Innocent Person (submitted by the delegation of France)-January 2008 (UNIDROIT 2008-Study LXXVIII-Doc 107 Rev)'.

[10] UNIDROIT, 'Informal Working Group on Article 14 of the draft Convention-

The *bona fide* acquisition is applicable to tangibles. It assumes the gain at the loss of another. It favours the purchaser and attributes loss to the true owner. Contractual claims are not within the rule of good faith acquirer as there is nothing such as possession of tangibles to rely on. By incorporating the book entry securities into the property law framework the *bona fide* acquisition is extended to the acquisition of intermediated securities.

6.2.2 The New Credit Based Approach

The credit approach develops a new regime, on the basis of the characteristics of property rights in intermediated securities. As property rights in intermediated securities are contractual claims enforceable against intermediaries, different from property rights over tangibles; and the transfer of intermediated securities is through debits and credits which are by nature novation without correlation between debits and credits in individual transactions, different from the transfer of tangibles, it is absurd to introduce the good faith purchase rule designed for property rights over tangibles into intermediated securities. Furthermore, opposition against extending the good faith purchaser rule to intermediated securities argues that the good faith acquirer rule presupposes something tangible and specific, capable of transfer and possession;[11] the good faith rule focuses on the identity of specific property being transferred which is not the case of intermediated securities which are uniform and fungible, established by credits on securities accounts;[12] and the rights in intermediated securities are subject to the rights of other co-holders. [13]

Comments on the questionnaire concerning 'good faith acquisition' (submitted by the German delegation) (UNIDROIT 2007-Study LXXVIII-Doc 98)'; P Scherer and R Gallei, 'UNIDROIT Draft Convention and German Securities Law: Friend or Foe?' (2009) 24 JIBLR 470; E Micheler, *Property in Securities: A Comparative Study* (Cambridge Studies in Corporate Law, Cambridge University Press, Cambridge 2007) 213-15.

[11] CW Mooney, 'Beyond Negotiability: A New Model for Transfer and Pledge of Interests in Securities Controlled by Intermediaries' (1990) 12 Cardozo L Rev 305, 310-15; JS Rogers, 'Policy Perspectives on Revised UCC Article 8' (1996) 43 UCLA L Rev 1431, 1453.

[12] JS Rogers, 'Negotiability, Property and Identity' (1990) 12 Cardozo L Rev 471, 484; UNIDROIT, 'UNIDROIT Seminar on Intermediated Securities-Paris, France, 31 January-1st February 2006 (UNIDROIT 2006-Study LXXVIII-SEM 3)' 19.

[13] JS Rogers, 'Policy Perspectives on Revised UCC Article 8' (1996) 43 UCLA L

The term transfer is misleading as it implies something identical from a transferor to a transferee.[14] It is suggested that a credit to a securities account should be the sole focus as creating securities rights in favour of an account holder, regardless of a corresponding debit, therefore eliminating any transfer.[15] This is obviously the fact in non-matching systems where a credit is valid without the need for identifying a corresponding debit.

6.2.2.1 Credit, settlement finality and irrevocability of transfer of securities

For the sake of transaction security and system integrity, it is widely recognised that an account holder should be able to rely on the entries in his securities accounts with his intermediary as good against any conflicting claim. This is known as transferee priority over a transferor.[16] In addition to the micro view of a transferor and a transferee on an individual basis, there are other polices in favour of a transferee on a macro basis, i.e., the finality of securities transactions and the integrity of the holding and transfer system. It is submitted that the issue of good faith should be substituted by the mandatory financial regulation over securities intermediaries. A wronged transferor should turn to his intermediary for redress instead of to a good faith transferee.[17] A further back-up of insurance mechanisms should be in place to counteract the effect of a failed intermediary who cannot satisfy the claims of clients. A good faith transferee should be protected against a prior adverse claim to securities. The policy lies in the design of the intermediated holding system which

---

[14] UNIDROIT, 'The UNIDROIT Study Group on Harmonised Substantive Rules Regarding Indirectly Held Securities: Position Paper (August 2003) (UNIDROIT 2003-Study LXXVIII-Doc 8)' 21.

[15] ibid; L Thévenoz, 'New Legal Concepts regarding the Holding of Investment Securities for a Civil Law Jurisdiction-The Swiss Draft Act' [2005] Rev dr unif 301, 309.

[16] UNIDROIT, 'The UNIDROIT Study Group on Harmonised Substantive Rules Regarding Indirectly Held Securities: Position Paper (August 2003) (UNIDROIT 2003-Study LXXVIII-Doc 8)' 21; L Thévenoz, 'New Legal Concepts regarding the Holding of Investment Securities for a Civil Law Jurisdiction-The Swiss Draft Act' [2005] Rev dr unif 301, 307.

[17] EFMLG (European Financial Markets Lawyers Group), 'Harmonisation of the Legal Framework for Rights Evidenced by Book-entries in respect of Certain Financial Instruments in the European Union (June 2003)' 26-27.

assumes anonymity and good title. Any abnormal title should be stopped where it occurs. This is important for preventing systemic risk.[18] The finality of transaction on organised securities markets is in the final analysis the security of transaction. The good faith acquisition rule or negotiability is a way of achieving finality or the security of transactions on markets in bearer securities.[19] When markets change and book entry securities replace bearer certificated securities it is time to introduce a new approach to achieve finality and transaction security rather than sticking to the old good faith acquisition rule or negotiability. The new rule proposed is that a credit to securities account confers title upon an acquirer who is not fraudulent. A new test to protection should be introduced to replace the test of good faith for clarity.[20]

6.2.2.2 Inflation and loss sharing

Focusing on the credit side solely does raise the issue that excessive securities may be created as both the rights of a prior owner and a purchaser may be kept intact. The good faith rule based on Roman law means the acquisition of property rights by an acquirer to the loss of a true owner. Focusing on the credit side only without considering the debit side may well keep intact both the rights of an acquirer and a transferor.[21] It is proposed that the issue of excessive securities can be dealt with a reasonable loss sharing rules. It should work in this way that whenever an intermediary finds its actual holding of securities cannot cover the client holding and its house holding, a loss sharing rule among all clients of the intermediary will come into play.[22] The essence is to allocate the loss of the system among more relevant account holders rather than to a specific account holder. It is often not feasible or unfair in the context of liquid

---

[18] JS Rogers, 'Policy Perspectives on Revised UCC Article 8' (1996) 43 UCLA L Rev 1431, 1461.

[19] ibid 1468.

[20] UCC art 8-502; ibid 1469.

[21] UNIDROIT, 'Study Group for the Preparation of Harmonised Substantive Rules on Transactions on Transnational and Connected Capital Markets. Restricted Study Group on Item 1 of the Project: Harmonised Substantive Rules regarding Securities Held with an Intermediary. Summary Report 3rd Session (13-16 November 2003) (UNIDROIT 2003-Study LXXVIII-Doc 11)'21.

[22] UNIDROIT, 'UNIDROIT Seminar on Intermediated Securities-Bern, Switzerland, 15-17 September 2005-Rome 2005 (UNIDROIT 2005-Study LXXVIII-SEM 1)' Appendix 5.

markets and multilateral netting to identify a specific account holder.

6.2.2.3 Insurance

A sound loss sharing scheme has to be supported by further back-up mechanisms. Otherwise the risk of loss from intermediary failure would deter investors from holding through intermediaries. For example in the US intermediaries are required to maintain inventory securities and where an insolvent intermediary fails to maintain enough inventory securities, clients of the intermediary are protected under the Securities Investor Protection Act of 1979. The compulsory insurance scheme is believed to be the foundation of the strong preference for purchasers of the US at the cost of prior holders.[23]

6.2.2.4 A protected purchaser under US law[24]

The US approach is to go directly to the essence by stating a protected purchaser acquires its interests in the security free of any adverse claim, as long as he who gives value; does not have notice of any adverse claim to the security; and obtains control of the security.[25] No reference is made to the good faith purchaser rule. But it inherits the structure of the good faith purchaser rule of establishing good faith on the mind of a purchaser, i.e., whether a purchaser has notice, and whether a purchaser gives value. And a new requirement is added of obtaining control.[26] Notice is defined in the statute to avoid the uncertainty in case law.[27]

---

[23] SEC Rules 15c 3-3, UCC art 8-504; Securities Investor Protection Act of 1970; SL Schwarcz, 'Indirectly Held Securities and Intermediary Risk' [2001] Unif L Rev 283, 295; CR Reitz, 'Reflections on the Drafting of the 1994 Revision of Article 8 of the US Uniform Commercial Code' [2005] Rev dr unif 357, 362.

[24] RA Hakes, 'UCC Article 8: Will the Indirect Holding of Securities Survive the Light of Day?' (2002) 35 Loy LA L Rev 661; CW Mooney, SM Rocks and RS Schwartz, 'An Introduction to the Revised UCC Article 8 and Review of Other Recent Developments with Investment Securities' (1994) 49 Bus Law 1891; JS Rogers, 'Policy Perspectives on Revised UCC Article 8' (1996) 43 UCLA L Rev 1431; V Combs, 'The Law of Intermediated Securities: UCC versus UNIDROIT' (2006) 58 Ala L Rev 399.

[25] UCC art 8-303.

[26] JS Rogers, 'Policy Perspectives on Revised UCC Article 8' (1996) 43 UCLA L Rev 1431.

[27] UCC art 8-105; JS Rogers, 'Policy Perspectives on Revised UCC Article 8' (1996) 43 UCLA L Rev 1431, 1471.

In addition to the substantive defense available to a purchaser, a protected purchaser is protected against any action based on an adverse claim. Any adverse action against a purchaser is normally precluded.[28] This is one additional step besides the substantive defence of good faith acquisition in an action based on an adverse claim. The burden of proof is meanwhile shifted to the claimant to prove that the purchaser should be protected if any action is allowed.[29] It is hard for a claimant to prove that a purchaser does not satisfy the protected purchaser status.

The eminent preference for purchasers at the cost of entitlement holders leads to the back-up of the securities investor protection scheme which awards damages to wronged entitlement holders of an insurance nature.[30]

According to the credit based approach, in the indirect holding system a holder of intermediated securities relies on his intermediary for the enjoyment and realisation of his rights in intermediated securities. The focus on the system integrity and finality of transaction calls for enhanced security of transaction. It is at the cost of a holder of intermediated securities where his intermediary misappropriates his securities, which cannot be ignored either. The inherent conflict of interests in the indirect holding system merits further consideration.

6.3 English law

6.3.1 Is It Necessary to Introduce Additional Protection for Purchasers

Firstly a purchaser can be sheltered against prior adverse proprietary claims by the market structure of anonymous trading and multilateral netting. Considered as a barrier to investigating title by a purchaser it is meanwhile a barrier to tracing title by a prior holder. Before the substantive and procedural bar, there is the structural protection insulating

[28] UCC art 8-503; RA Hakes, 'UCC Article 8: Will the Indirect Holding of Securities Survive the Light of Day?' (2002) 35 Loy L A L Rev 661, 754-55.

[29] RA Hakes, 'UCC Article 8: Will the Indirect Holding of Securities Survive the Light of Day?' (2002) 35 Loy L A L Rev 661, 712; Law Commission, 'The UNIDROIT Convention on Substantive Rules regarding Intermediated Securities: Further Updated Advice to HM Treasury' (May 2008) [4.111].

[30] Security Investor Protection Act of 1979; RA Hakes, 'UCC Article 8: Will the Indirect Holding of Securities Survive the Light of Day?' (2002) 35 Loy L A L Rev 661, 734.

a purchaser from most possible prior adverse claims of a proprietary nature. Securities are traded and settled on organised exchanges where it is hard to trace the flow of specific securities by a prior holder. Though it is possible either to identify the flow through matching or tracking the movement of securities, either is impractical if not impossible.[31] Simply speaking a wronged holder of securities entitlement can hardly identify where his assets are to make a claim. Secondly a purchaser can be protected by financial regulation over securities intermediaries against fraud. This is the same rationale of protecting bank depositors against bank fraud and bank insolvency. Deposits belong to banks, not depositors. Banks are under strict regulation to insure that claims of depositors can be satisfied most of the time.[32] Though there are many similarities between payment systems and securities holding systems, a major difference is that securities held by intermediaries for clients belong to clients. Financial regulation rules are in place to prevent securities intermediaries from misappropriating client securities by intermediaries. Even if misappropriation does happen it does not matter much if an intermediary is solvent and capable to pay damages. What is crucial is in the insolvency context. Bank failure would have a systemic effect as banks take deposits from the public and are interconnected with each other. Thus there is heavy regulation to prevent bank failures. Securities intermediaries are less systemically important. It is easier to allow failure of securities intermediaries.[33] Enhanced financial regulation over securities intermediaries would serve to prevent misappropriation of client assets by intermediaries but not without cost. Thirdly a purchaser can be protected against adverse claims by a procedural bar as adopted in the US UCC Article 8 that a wronged owner normally has to turn to his intermediary for remedy. Fourthly a purchaser can be protected against prior adverse proprietary claims by a substantive defense if he qualifies as a protected purchaser or a good faith purchaser.

Under current UK law, the first layer and second layer of protection[34]

---

[31] RA Hakes, 'UCC Article 8: Will the Indirect Holding of Securities Survive the Light of Day?' (2002) 35 Loy L A L Rev 661, 711.

[32] PR Wood, *Regulation of International Finance* (2nd edn, Law and Practice of International Finance Series, Sweet & Maxwell, London 2007) 667; PR Wood, *Principles of International Insolvency* (2nd edn, Law and Practice of International Finance Series, Sweet & Maxwell, London 2007) 729.

[33] PR Wood, *Regulation of International Finance* (2nd edn, Law and Practice of International Finance Series, Sweet & Maxwell, London 2007) 667.

[34] For example, Financial Services and Markets Act 2000 (Regulated Activities)

are available, the third layer is absent, and the fourth layer is uncertain and precarious. This raises the issue whether it is necessary to introduce the third layer of protection and clarify the fourth layer. Empirical evidence shows that the market of intermediated securities has seen growth despite the lack of sufficient protection of property law:

> "Financial regulation reduces the risk of loss by reducing both the chances of impropriety and the possibility that the intermediary at fault will be insolvent and consequently unable to remedy the loss in full. Netting in clearing and settlement systems makes it difficult for claimants to trace securities (or their proceeds) into the hands of a purchaser. Litigation concerning the availability of legal protection to purchasers of intermediated securities is rare."[35]

There is indeed uncertainty in the title a purchaser gets under current English law, a legal title is good against any prior title, an equitable title is inferior to a prior legal title, superior to an equitable title prior to the change of legal title through the CREST system, and inferior to an equitable title subsequent to the change of legal title through the CREST system. However it can be seen that chances that a purchaser gets a title inferior to a prior title are slim and the competition of title is outside the CREST system. There is no major effect on systemic integrity.

Meanwhile protection of purchasers cannot be achieved without cost. In the insolvency of a fraudulent intermediary either a purchaser or a prior owner or owners have to suffer the loss. In the property law model of good acquisition, an individual prior owner whose account has been debited wrongfully suffers the loss while in the credit based model account holders of the fraudulent intermediary share the loss. There is no consensus on loss sharing as to which category of account holders share the loss,[36] i.e., account holders of the relevant issue of securities, or all account holders of the intermediary, or all account holders of the intermediary except those account holders whose securities are kept in segregated accounts with the upper-tier intermediary.[37] Even though loss sharing seems more reasonable

---

Order 2001 SI 2001/544; Financial Services and Markets Act 2000 (Carrying on Regulated Activities by Way of Business) Order 2001 SI 2001/1177.

[35] Law Commission, 'The UNIDROIT Convention on Substantive Rules regarding Intermediated Securities: Further Updated Advice to HM Treasury (May 2008)' [5.5].

[36] Ibid [4.180]; M Yates and G Montagu, *The Law of Global Custody* (3rd rev edn, Tottel Publishing, London 2009) 37.

[37] See *Barlow Clowes International Ltd (in liq) v Vaughan* [1992] 4 All ER 22;

than the good faith acquisition model, it is not acceptable to account holders whose securities are not secure. The credit based model which overprotects a purchaser has to be buttressed by insurance schemes awarding compensation to account holders of an insolvent intermediary,[38] for example the US model.

The great favour for purchaser is too radical for English priority rules. English law has been cautious of making carve-outs of the *nemo dat* principle, due to its respect for vested property rights, which can only be subjected to really demanding policies. Commercial need is one of those and is carefully drafted to limited categories of property. Loss sharing has been rejected for its complexity and uncertainty in that which parties may be involved, for example, in successive sales of goods through multiple parties.[39] A preliminary issue arises whether intermediated securities are a special kind of property which deserve a special rule protecting purchasers against prior claims, as another exception from the *nemo dat* rule. Despite the protection in place through inherent market structures and financial regulation, the rarity of relevant litigation, as well as the need for sufficient guarantee to prior securities holders, calls for an express rule protecting purchasers of intermediated securities have found favour with leading experts and official reports.[40] Assume that it is necessary to introduce

---

latest Lehman judgements; Law Commission, 'The UNIDROIT Convention on Substantive Rules regarding Intermediated Securities: Further Updated Advice to HM Treasury (May 2008)' [4.182]-[4.183]; PR Wood, *Set-off and Netting, Derivatives, Clearing Systems* (2nd edn, Law and Practice of International Finance Series, Sweet & Maxwell, London 2007) 345-47; J Benjamin, *Financial Law* (Oxford University Press, Oxford 2007) 436.

[38] SL Schwarcz, 'Indirectly Held Securities and Intermediary Risk' [2001] Unif L Rev 283, 295; there is an insurance scheme for financial services under the Financial Services and Markets Act 2000 pt xv, Financial Services and Markets Act 2000 (Compensation Scheme: Electing Participants) Regulations 2001 SI 2001/1783, which are however limited to eligible categories of services, see I MacNeil, *An Introduction to the Law on Financial Investments* (Hart Publishing, Oxford 2005) 200-03. And there is opposition against enhanced insurance schemes as deterring cost for financial service providers, see K McCormick and S Melzack, 'Depositor Protection: An Increased Burden for the Financial Services Sector?' [2008] JIBFL 185; P Hertz and others, 'The All-American Dream: Developing Effective Resolution Arrangements for Investment Banks in the UK' [2009] JIBFL 466, 468-69.

[39] *Ingram v little* [1961] 1 QB 31; J Ulph, 'Conflicts of Title and the Obligations of the Seller' in E McKendrick (ed) *Sale of Goods* (LLP, London 2000) 170.

[40] Law Commission, 'The UNIDROIT Convention on Substantive Rules regarding Intermediated Securities: Further Updated Advice to HM Treasury (May 2008)'

enhanced protection of purchasers in an express and certain way, further issues arise whether it is necessary to introduce a procedural bar of limiting proprietary claims of an account holder to his intermediary only, rather than a purchaser; as to substantive defense, which model to adopt, the traditional *bona fide* acquisition model, or the credit based model, or a peculiar English model; given the complexity of priorities between legal and equitable title under the unique trusts analysis, is it necessary to delineate a rule protecting purchasers of intermediated securities against prior proprietary claims specifically or protecting purchasers of equitable interests against prior equitable proprietary interests generally?

6.3.2 A Procedural Bar

A procedural bar prohibits an account holder from bringing a proprietary claim in intermediated securities against an identified purchaser as a principle. Only exceptionally the account holder may only bring an action if (i) its intermediary is insolvent; (ii) the insolvent intermediary does not have sufficient assets to satisfy the account holder's claim; (iii) the intermediary violated its obligation to maintain sufficient securities; and (iv) the purchaser colluded with the intermediary in violating this obligation.[41]

This is considered too radical a departure on title conflicts from the traditional *bona fide* acquisition or negotiability. It forces account holders to turn to their intermediary first. It also shifts the burden of proving innocence by a purchaser to a true owner by requiring the owner to prove the collusion or fault of the purchaser. Obviously there are major barriers to establishing that a purchaser is not innocent by a true owner. It has few followers, for example it is not adopted in either the Swiss FISA or the Geneva Securities Convention.

In the UK, there is no appetite for introducing such a procedural bar. It is widely accepted that a rule in the same structure and with the same policy of negotiability or *bona fide* acquisition would be sufficient and practical.[42] That is a purchaser can be liable to an adverse claim from a

[5.6].

[41] UCC art 8-503(d) and (e).

[42] Law Commission, 'The UNIDROIT Convention on Substantive Rules regarding Intermediated Securities: Further Updated Advice to HM Treasury (May 2008)' [4.113]; Financial Markets Law Committee, 'The FMLC Report on Property Interests in Indirectly Held Investment Securities: An Analysis of the Need for and

prior owner but can raise a defense that can shelter him from the adverse claim. This is similar to the negotiability and the *bona fide* purchaser of legal title overriding a prior equitable interest under English law, though modifications may be introduced to the test of a holder in due course or *bona fide* in consideration of the situation of the intermediated securities markets.

6.3.3 A Substantive Defense of *Bona Fide* Acquisition

6.3.3.1 Property based or credit based

Though the contractual nature of intermediated securities as claims against an intermediary is recognised under the trust analysis as equitable interests, and the exact nature of disposition of intermediated securities as well as equitable interest as novation is recognised,[43] it is not necessarily that the credit based approach be adopted. As with equitable interests, though it is a claim and its disposition a novation, a subsequent equitable interest is never given priority over a prior equitable interest. The fact that the two equitable interests are not the same as a tangible thing does not mean that they are completely independent of each other. With the same trustee over the same property the two equitable interests are competing claims in competition between two innocent parties. English law has developed rules to compare the merits of the competing claims, as seen in the priority rules over equitable interests, such as better equity and postponement by party conducts. It is consistent with the responsive, flexible, and generalisation-averse approach of English law. Interests in intermediated securities are claims but meanwhile proprietary. Thus it is not necessary that the credit approach be adopted. Support for the property model is based on the proprietary aspect of intermediated securities.

6.3.3.2 Scope of a *bona fide* acquisition rule; intermediated securities or equitable interests in general

It is necessary to clarify that it is desirable to introduce a bona fide acquisition rule only to intermediated securities, not to equitable interests in general. It would be too radical a change to too large an area of law. Firstly the *nemo dat* principle has always been the rule under English law,

Nature of Legislation in the UK' [2005] Rev dr unif 339.

[43] See 5.1.

between legal title as well as between equitable title. It would be absurd to introduce a general exception to equitable title while leaving legal title intact. There have been calls for a general rule reversing the *nemo dat* principle which have never seen the light of day.[44] This shows the entrenched attitude of English law on this aspect. Secondly the *bona fide* purchaser rule under English law by which a legal title defeats a prior equitable title is not *bona fide* acquisition in the general sense as in civil law, or negotiability under English law, but based on the greater merits of legal title. There is no sense of extending the current *bona fide* purchaser rule under English law to equitable interests in general. Thirdly it is expedient to characterise intermediated securities other than those in the CREST system as equitable interests under trusts to achieve proprietary protection to holders of intermediaries, with the unique effect of trusts of awarding proprietary effects to contractual claims. Indeed the account holder–intermediary relationship roughly mirrors the beneficiary–trustee relationship in most aspects and there is no major difficulty in incorporating intermediated securities into the trust laws analysis. However intermediated securities are not typical beneficial or equitable interests under trusts, as analysed elsewhere,[45] in that there is no policy of protecting weak parties as in family trusts; the value of intermediated securities depends on currency and liquidity which is not the case of typical trust of holding property in a static state; and intermediated securities are not hidden interests in property as typical equitable interests under trusts but autonomous and independent assets though intermediated securities are derivative interests from the underlying securities. It deserves further analysis whether it is necessary to clarify the legal nature of intermediated securities in a single statute as in the US rather than applying the trusts law analysis as it carries too much sediment of the past which may be inconsistent with the new situation of intermediated securities. However the common law and the trust law are noted for their capability and flexibility of accommodating new situations and catching up with the evolution of society, armed with the case law and judiciary. The Law Commission is in support of continuing the trust law analysis rather than introducing a new kind of property as to intermediated securities, but it is necessary to introduce a rule of good faith acquisition of intermediated securities.

---

[44] RM Goode and E McKendrick, *Goode on Commercial Law* (4th edn, LexisNexis, London 2009) 481-82.

[45] See 5.2.6.

6.3.3.3 Qualification for protection

Holder in due course and good faith acquisition under English law

If a rule similar to negotiability or good faith purchaser of legal title over equitable title be introduced in respect of intermediated securities, an issue arises what test a purchaser has to satisfy, i.e., the test of holder in due course under negotiability, or under the good faith purchaser of legal title over equitable title, or a new statutory test. The difference between the tests under negotiability and the good faith purchaser of legal title lies in the duty imposed on a purchaser. A holder in due course is a holder who gives value, acts in good faith and has no notice of any defects in the title of the transferor.[46] Good faith is honesty or equivalent to no notice. Notice is actual or imputed notice, excluding constructive notice. Imputed notice is actual or constructive notice of a purchaser's agent, counsel, or solicitor of a purchaser imputed to the purchaser.[47] Under the good faith purchaser of legal title rule, a good faith purchaser pays sufficient value, has no notice of equitable interests at the time he gives value and the transfer.[48] The burden is believed to be on a purchaser as defendant. Notice of an equitable interest can be actual notice, constructive notice or imputed notice. Constructive notice is notice which would have been acquired if inquiries which ought to have been made had been made. A narrow view of constructive notice is held to be applicable to commercial transactions in property other than land,[49] including securities.[50] The difference between the test of protection under negotiability and the good faith acquisition of legal title is that a holder in due course is not tainted by constructive notice and is generally under lightened scrutiny.

---

[46] Bills of Exchange Act 1882 s 27 (2). Law Commission, 'The UNIDROIT Convention on Substantive Rules regarding Intermediated Securities: Further Updated Advice to HM Treasury (May 2008)' [5.19].

[47] Law of Property Act 1925 s 199 1 (ii) (b).

[48] Law Commission, 'The UNIDROIT Convention on Substantive Rules regarding Intermediated Securities: Further Updated Advice to HM Treasury (May 2008)' [5.26]-[5.36].

[49] *Manchester Trust Ltd v Furness, Withy & Co Ltd* [1895] 2 QB 539 (CA); *Polly Peck International plc v Nadir (No 2)* [1992] 4 All ER 769 (CA).

[50] *Macmillan Inc v Bishopsgate Investment Trust plc (No 3)* [1995] 1 WLR 978 (Ch).

The Geneva Securities Convention

The rule in the Geneva Securities Convention is similar. It does not introduce a procedural bar to proprietary claims against purchasers but introduces an innocent acquirer rule which is largely a replication of the traditional good faith acquisition rule without referring to good faith. It provides that

> "1. Unless an acquirer actually knows or ought to know, at the relevant time, that another person has an interest in securities or intermediated securities and that the credit to the securities account of the acquirer, designating entry or interest granted to the acquirer violates the rights of that other person in relation to its interest: (a) the right or interest of the acquirer is not subject to the interest of that other person; (b) the acquirer is not liable to that other person; and (c) the credit, designating entry or interest granted is not rendered invalid, ineffective against third parties or liable to be reversed on the ground that the credit, designating entry or interest granted violates the rights of that other person.
> 2. Unless an acquirer actually knows or ought to know, at the relevant time, of an earlier defective entry: (a) the credit, designating entry or interest is not rendered invalid, ineffective against third parties or liable to be reversed as a result of that defective entry; and (b) the acquirer is not liable to anyone who would benefit from the invalidity or reversal of that defective entry.
> 3. Paragraphs 1 and 2 do not apply to an acquisition of intermediated securities, other than the grant of a security interest, made by way of gift or otherwise gratuitously."[51]

It protects a purchaser against adverse proprietary claims who pays value and does not actually knows or ought to know any defect in the title he acquires. Knowledge of an organisation is knowledge of the individual responsible for a matter to which the interests or fact is relevant.[52] The effort to introduce an autonomous standard of an innocent purchaser is abandoned.[53] There is however a policy consensus that there should not be

[51] Geneva Securities Convention art 18.

[52] Geneva Securities Convention art 17 (c).

[53] UNIDROIT, 'Draft Official Commentary on the Draft Convention on Substantive Rules regarding Intermediated Securities (UNIDROIT 2009 CONF 11/2-Doc 5)' [17-3]; UNIDROIT, 'UNIDROIT Committee of Governmental Experts for the Preparation of a draft Convention on Substantive Rules regarding Intermediated Securities. Informal Working Group on Article 14 of the draft Convention. PRELIMINARY NOTE-November 2007 (UNIDROIT 2007-Study LXXVIII-Doc 96)'; CW Mooney, 'The (UNIDROIT) Geneva Securities Convention on Intermediated Securities' [2009] JIBFL 596, 598; T Keijser and M

a duty to investigate the title on an acquirer as long as he is honest or not fraudulent.[54] When deciding whether an acquirer ought to know the defect of title, consideration should be taken of the *sui generis* context of intermediated securities, where it is often impossible to know the counterparty or title even after due diligent investigation or inquiry.[55]

The Law Commission supports the standard of the good faith acquisition under English law,[56] for it is moderate and will not create a double standard on the same issue in different areas. The author thinks it necessary to be moderate without giving too much favour to purchasers without a strong and effective insurance scheme in place,[57] or before the operator compensation scheme at the top tier of the CREST system can be extended throughout the system.

6.3.4 Judicial Approach; Estoppel

Statutory intervention under English law must take international instruments into consideration. The position of the Geneva Securities Convention is to clarify the protection to a purchaser of intermediated securities free of adverse claims if he is not fraudulent. The EU Commission is in the legislative process on a Securities Law Directive with respect to the property law, corporate law and conflict of laws of intermediated securities, or book entry securities. The approach of the EU Commission would be similar to the Geneva Securities Convention. If there is no domestic action before the adoption of any international instrument, a purchaser may still be protected in litigation by arguing for estoppel.

Much has been said of estoppel as a flexible and effective weapon. It has been the fundamental weapon under common law to subordinate a

Parmentier, 'The Geneva Securities Convention: The Debates of the Diplomatic Conference' [2010] JIBFL 230, 232.

[54] UNIDROIT, 'Draft Official Commentary on the Draft Convention on Substantive Rules regarding Intermediated Securities (UNIDROIT 2009 CONF 11/2-Doc 5)' [17-3].

[55] Geneva Securities Convention art 17 (b); UNIDROIT, 'Draft Official Commentary on the Draft Convention on Substantive Rules regarding Intermediated Securities (UNIDROIT 2009 CONF 11/2-Doc 5)' [17-9].

[56] Law Commission, 'The UNIDROIT Convention on Substantive Rules regarding Intermediated Securities: Further Updated Advice to HM Treasury (May 2008)' [5.109].

[57] Financial Services and Markets Act 2000 pt xv.

vested title to a later title of a purchaser as exemption from the *nemo dat* rule and achieve the compelling policy of commercial needs of transaction safety. It has been used to protect purchasers of chattels under common law, some of which have been codified in statutes.[58] It has been the basis of the evolution of negotiability.[59] It has been the chief way of granting damages to purchasers of certificated registered securities.[60] Though there are different grounds of estoppel in different property, i.e., possession of chattel, possession of certificates of bearer securities, possession of certificates of registered securities, the essence is that there are certain indicia of title which deserves reliance by a purchaser who deserves protection of such reliance for the sake of transaction safety, while a true owner or someone else is negligent in creating apparent ownership inconsistent with reality with the indicia of title or in a better position to prevent or avoid such apparent ownership. Under the statutory exception regarding chattels, an owner of chattel voluntarily leaving the chattel in the possession of another in commercial transactions is estopped from denying the fact that the possessor has title against a *bona fide* purchaser, for the protection of purchasers and transaction security. Under negotiability, a holder of bearer securities voluntarily leaving the bearer securities in the hands of another, or involuntarily losing possession of bearer securities, is estopped from denying that the possessor has title against a *bona fide* purchaser, on the basis that negotiable instruments and bearer securities are quasi-currency designed to be in circulation where finality and transaction safety are fundamental. Under estoppel, an issuer of registered securities issuing a certificate upon registration of a fraudulent transfer is estopped from denying that the holder carried on the certificate is the true holder to a transferee of the certificate, or a transferee a direct victim of fraud submitting a transfer for registration is estopped from denying that the transfer is valid against the issuer. The high-level safeguard of the true owner of registered securities originates from the nature of registered securities of a kind of participation or membership in the entity of the issuer, which is similar to the high-level safeguard of beneficiaries under fiduciary relations under postponement between equitable interests.

Estoppel has been used in equity to postpone a prior equitable title to a subsequent equitable title otherwise equal. For example a holder of a prior equitable title leaving the indicia of title in another is estopped against a

---

[58] See 3.1.
[59] See 3.3.
[60] See 3.4.

holder of a later equitable title if the other person commits fraud with the indicia of title, though estoppel in this way is more difficult to establish against a holder of equitable title under a fiduciary relation such as a trust, who is under a higher level of protection.[61]

Estoppel has also been the key tool for achieving finality in the CREST system under the statutory framework. A participant of the CREST system, by accessing to the system, is estopped by statutes and system rules from denying that he sends an instruction of disposition of securities expressed to have been sent by him, that the content of the instruction is correct, that he has the authority to send the instruction, and he gives warranty of title. Such estoppel prevents any defect in a disposition of title as long as a purchaser has no knowledge of any defect in such a disposition of title. The requirement of systemic finality and integrity is achieved by imposing the estoppel upon a participant of the CREST system upon participation in the system that by participation a participant agrees to be bound by the estoppel. Potential loss to a participant as prior holders of securities is counteracted by the preventive authentication measures of the system as well as financial regulation against fraud and damages against the system-Operator when fraud does happen, as back-up measures for the high level finality at the top level of the CREST system, currently unavailable other than the top tier.

With the compelling policy of protecting a purchaser of intermediated securities and the systemic integrity, it would be persuasive to argue that a purchaser deserves protection over a prior owner who chooses to hold securities through an intermediary and chooses the specific intermediary. A prior owner is thus estopped from asserting title against a purchaser by accessing the intermediated holding system, choosing his intermediary and holding securities through his intermediary.[62] A general rule of protecting a purchaser of equitable title without notice of a prior equitable title might be established through case law in litigations.

Another possibility is arguing for the rule of good faith acquisition and sheltering as well as its extension, which is in fact upper-tier priority, as analysed in 5.2.3.4.

---

[61] See 5.2.4.
[62] See 4.4 and 5.2.4.5.

6.4 Conclusion

Under the current indirect holding model there is a balance to be struck between the protection of a purchaser and a prior owner. A purchaser has to be confident in the title he acquires while an owner has to feel safe that his title is not lost. Currently much emphasis is laid over the protection of purchasers while protection of prior owners is reduced to a back-up position by loss sharing and mandatory insurance schemes. There is certainly rationality in the policy of promoting the liquidity and integrity of the system which however has to be curtailed by the viability of the system. In extending over-protection of purchasers, intermediated securities are treated as currency as money in payment systems where banks are presumed to be always solvent and bank insolvency is rare and there is often a deposit insurance scheme. This in turn requires heavier financial regulation over securities intermediaries to prevent their insolvency and guarantee that claims against intermediaries of investors are normally satisfied. Mandatory securities insurance schemes are also essential to the viability of the system.[63] Otherwise the intermediated securities system, even achieving sufficient protection for purchasers, would finally lose favour with investors who can be both purchasers and prior owners on different occasions.

Over protection of purchasers is not a tradition of English law as explained. Furthermore English law is averse to heavy regulation and mandatory insurance due to cost considerations. Thus a modest approach would be desirable, i.e., either to introduce a substantive defense of bona fide acquisition of intermediated securities or to simply leave the issue to judicial discretion in litigation where estoppel, or the rule of good faith acquisition and sheltering or the extension of rule of good faith acquisition and sheltering, might help purchasers.

---

[63] And there are challenges to the cost of financial regulation or mandatory insurance schemes, K McCormick and S Melzack, 'Depositor Protection: An Increased Burden for the Financial Services Sector?' [2008] JIBFL 185; P Hertz and others, 'The All-American Dream: Developing Effective Resolution Arrangements for Investment Banks in the UK' [2009] JIBFL 466, 469.

CONCLUSION

English law has no major theoretical barrier to recognising proprietary interests in intermediated securities other than legal title on the Operator register of securities. Without a property-claim dichotomy, equipped with equity and trusts, English law is ready to recognise indirect proprietary interests in intangible subject matter held with another, such as intangible book entry intermediated securities held by an investor with his intermediary, as equitable title under trusts.

With its readiness to recognise proprietary interests or title, English law is ready to cope with sorting out title conflicts. A central theme is relative title and the determination of priority of title upon their comparative merits. A fundamental policy is non intervention with vested title which always remains the maxim. The competing policy of transaction safety only gains priority exceptionally by statutory intervention, customs and common law estoppel. With certificated securities, title conflicts between an innocent prior holder and an innocent purchaser in respect of bearer securities are resolved in favour of the purchaser under negotiability through estoppel, where the quasi-currency nature of bearer securities presses for transaction safety; such title conflicts in respect of registered securities are however in favour of a prior holder, with loss to be distributed between an issuer and a purchaser through estoppel, as a proof of the persistence of the principle of guarding vested title, despite the pressing need of transaction safety.

With uncertificated securities title conflicts in respect of legal title are resolved with preference for a purchaser over a prior holder by statutory estoppel, given the need of systemic finality and integrity, with support of system authentication measures and operator compensation to prior holders divested of title involuntarily. Other than legal title in intermediated securities, conflicts of equitable title in intermediated securities are subject to general law on priority. There is much interaction between statutes and case law. Under the principle of giving priority to rights with greater merits and first in time, resolution of title conflicts in respect of intermediated securities under general priority rules would be precarious.

Under the statutory estoppel, a legal title defeats a prior legal title; under the statutory estoppel or equity a legal title defeats a prior equitable title. Under the statutory estoppel and equity, an equitable title defeats a prior equitable title between which there is a change of legal title; otherwise conflicts between two equitable title are in favour of the prior equitable title, under the maxim of protecting the vested title[1] which is more prominent in favour of beneficiaries under fiduciary relations. The law on title conflicts regarding intermediated securities is not satisfactory but not radically different from that applying to certificated registered securities under English law.

Internationally there is overwhelming support for title conflicts in respect of intermediated securities in favour of innocent purchasers over innocent prior owners based on systemic finality and integrity of securities markets. Besides the *bona fide* acquisition rule subordinating a prior legal title to a subsequent legal title for the sake of transaction safety in most legal systems, there is a further step of establishing a procedural barrier to a subsequent legal title against a prior legal title. The basis of the zealous protection of rights last in time over rights first in time is that a credit confers rights independent of a prior debit in the context of intermediated securities, rather than a loss and gain of specific tangibles. However the issue is characterised, the fundamental issue of loss persists. The credit based approach of title conflicts with overwhelming preference for purchasers while leaving prior holders at greater risks of losing title, tries to allocate loss to a group of relevant prior holders rather than individual prior holders, backed by preventive financial regulation over intermediaries and remedial mandatory insurance schemes in case of intermediary insolvency.

A balance has to be struck between protecting a vested title and a subsequent title, i.e., security of title and security of transaction. English law has a tradition of giving priority to the former with its generally responsive and mild approach, as shown by its reluctance to reverse the *nemo dat* maxim. Tilting the point towards the purchaser side needs effective mechanisms for counteracting the adverse impact upon prior holders, such as the statutory estoppel and the corresponding Operator compensation as regards legal title in the CREST system. It is widely believed that it would be sufficient to introduce a statutory *bona fide* acquisition rule in respect of intermediated securities of giving priority to an equitable title to a prior equitable title and legal title, without going as

[1] As analysed in 5.2.1.2.

far as establishing a procedural barrier against prior adverse claims. Before any statutory action is taken, estoppel under common law and equity would be a valuable tool for arguments in favour of transaction security, as shown in cases of certificated bearer securities and certificated registered securities, as well as the statutory estoppel in case of legal title to intermediated securities.

A Further Thought: The *In Rem-In Personam* Dichotomy

Title to intermediated securities is an ingenious manipulation of property and contract, i.e., rights *in personam* and rights *in rem*. Its similarity to the structure of payment systems is an illustration in point. The major difference between rights of a customer of a bank and rights of a client of a securities intermediary is that the former is a pure claim while the latter is a claim when things are normal and proprietary when things go wrong, for example intermediary insolvency. The fact that most bank customers feel they retain title or ownership over their money is rested upon the assumption that banks do not fail and their claims can always be satisfied. Though banks do fail but it is rare. Banks are under heavy financial regulation and there is often a mandatory depositor scheme. The trend of treating title to intermediated securities as claims against intermediaries presupposes a sound network of intermediaries which will not fail. The illusion that intermediaries, major intermediaries in particular, do not fail, has been shattered by the collapse of Lehman Brothers.

The Lehmans cases do highlight some of the disastrous property issues in intermediated securities hypothesised by commentators. Equitable title is indeed respected: securities held by Lehman for others are held to be under the beneficial ownership of clients of Lehman, as the courts rejected the administrators' application of a scheme of arrangement under insolvency law as this was only applicable to claims of creditors, but not applicable to assets held on trusts for others.[2] On the other hand equitable title is extremely difficult to identify over specific assets when there are numerous counterparties dealing with Lehman in various transactions, and clients' requests for the return of trusts assets have been rejected by courts due to the difficulty of identifying the ownership of assets held by Lehman.[3] The difficulty lies in several practices: identification of trust

---

[2] *Re Lehman Brothers International (Europe) (in administration) (No 2)* [2009] EWCA Civ 1161, [2009] All ER (D) 83 (Nov).

[3] *RAB Capital plc v Lehman Bros International (Europe)* [2008] EWHC 2335 (Ch),

assets in the regular course of transaction under the requirement of segregation, and the consensual disapplication of beneficial ownership under which clients of Lehman grant Lehman full ownership over trust assets to engage in security lending and repo in the name of Lehman.[4]

Thus one of the uncertainty of property law regarding intermediated securities, namely that whether a valid trust has been established in terms of the certainty of subject matter required for a valid trust where a client has its holding commingled with other client of the same intermediary with the upper-tier intermediary, which has been considered theoretically resolved by arguing for a trust over the commingled holding of all clients who enjoy equitable title as co-tenants, is raised again in complex cases involving multiple parties. The real strength of indirect equitable title to intangible book entry securities often commingled with the holding of others is tested by the Lehman cases. It is proprietary, but subject to the right of co-tenants, and perhaps creditors of the intermediary. Nominal holding of rights and actual realisation of rights are not always equivalent.[5]

The adventurous approach to blurring rights *in rem* and rights *in personam* has its merits of enhancing efficiency while prudence should not be totally ignored, especially when contractual arrangements with proprietary effect have systemic implications, as in the case of Lehman. Despite calls for caution on enhanced financial regulation[6] out of concerns

---

[2008] BCC 915.

[4] Furthermore, see *Re Lehman Brothers International (Europe) (in administration); Pearson v Lehman Brothers Finance SA* [2010] EWHC 2914 (Ch), [2010] All ER (D) 232 (Nov); *Re Lehman Brothers International (Europe) (in administration)* [2010] EWCA Civ 917, [2010] All ER (D) 15 (Aug). See also comments S Worthington, 'Pitfalls with Property Claims: Lehman Bros Again' [2009] JIBFL 321; A Al-Attar, 'Client Money' [2009] JIBFL 530; E Sjostrand, 'Cash Matters: Unsecured Creditor or Proprietary Interest? Analysis of the Recent Lehman Brothers Case' [2010] CRI 9; S Shivji, 'Financial Collateral: Trust Issues in the Administration of Lehman Brothers' [2010] JIBFL 11; LC Ho, 'Trusts Notwithstanding, Courts Remain Free to Find Scheme Jurisdiction' [2010] JIBFL 156.

[5] There have been government consultations on effective resolution of investment insolvency and quick return of client assets, see HM Treasury, 'Developing Effective Resolution Arrangements for Investment Banks (May 2009)'; HM Treasury, 'Establishing Resolution Arrangements for Investment Banks (December 2009)'.

[6] For example Financial Markets Law Committee response of 1 June 2009 to European Commission Consultation Paper: Legislation on Legal Certainty of Securities Holding and Dispositions (G2/PP D (2009)), as well as of 21 January 2011 to the European Commission Consultation Paper: Legislation on Legal

of rising cost for financial markets participants, it may be the appropriate time that the non-risk-averse approach of English law be more risk averse with regards to financial markets and the manipulation of rights *in rem* and rights *in personam* be carefully adjusted.

Certainty for Securities Holding and Dispositions, 5 November 2010 (G2 MET/OT/acg D(2010) 768690), opposing regulation of all intermediaries as a burden of cost; P Hertz and others, 'The All-American Dream: Developing Effective Resolution Arrangements for Investment Banks in the UK' [2009] JIBFL 466.

BIBLIOGRAPHY

Books

Halsbury's Laws of England (vol 6, 4th edn reissue, LexisNexis, London 2003)

Halsbury's Laws of England (vol 9, 4th edn, Butterworths, London 1998)

Halsbury's Laws of England (vol 16, 4th edn reissue, LexisNexis, London 2003)

AO Austen-Peters, *Custody of Investments: Law and Practice* (Oxford University Press, Oxford 2000)

HG Beale and others (eds), *Chitty on Contracts* (The Common Law Library, 2004)

AP Bell, *Modern Law of Personal Property in England and Ireland* (Butterworths, London 1989)

Cv Bar and E Clive (eds), *Principles, Definitions and Model Rules of European Private Law: Draft Common Frame of Reference (DCFR)* (sellier. European Law Publishers, Munich 2009)

J Benjamin, *Interest in Securities: A Proprietary Law Analysis of the International Securities Markets* (Oxford University Press, Oxford 2000)

—. *Financial Law* (Oxford University Press, Oxford 2007)

J Birds and others (eds), *Boyle & Birds' Company Law* (7th edn, Jordan, Bristol 2009)

WW Buckland and AD McNair, revised by FH Lawson, *Roman Law and Common Law: A Comparison in Outline* (1965 reprinted, 2nd edition, Cambridge University Press, Cambridge, 1952)

E Cooke, *The Modern Law of Estoppel* (Oxford University Press, Oxford 2000)

J Dalhuisen, *Dalhuisen on Transnational Comparative, Commercial, Financial and Trade Law Volume 2: Contract and Movable Property law* (4th edn, Hart Publishing, Oxford 2010)

PL Davies and others, *Gower and Davies' Principles of Modern Company Law* (8th edn, Sweet & Maxwell, London 2008)

EP Ellinger, *Negotiable Instruments* (International Encyclopedia of Comparative Law, Volume IX: Commercial Transactions and

Institutions, J.C.B Mohr (Paul Siebeck); Martinus Nijhoff Publishers, 2000)

EP Ellinger, E Lomnicka and R Hooley, *Ellinger's Modern Banking Law* (4th edn, Oxford University Press, Oxford 2006)

P Feltham, D Hochberg and T Leech, *Spencer Bower The Law Relating to Estoppel by Representation* (4th edn LexisNexis, London 2004)

PD Finn (ed), *Equity and Commercial Relationships* (The Law Book Company, Sydney 1987)

FD Finn, *Fiduciary Obligations* (The Law Books Limited, Sydney 1977)

N Foster and S Sule, *German Legal Systems and Laws* (4th edn, Oxford University Press, Oxford 2010)

RM Goode and L Gullifer, *Goode on Legal Problems of Credit and Security* (4th edn, Sweet & Maxwell, London 2008)

RM Goode and E McKendrick, *Goode on Commercial Law* (4th edn, LexisNexis, London 2009)

J Gordley, *Foundations of Private Law: Property, Tort, Contract, Unjust Enrichment* (Oxford University Press, Oxford 2006)

KR Handley, *Estoppel by Conduct and Election* (Sweet & Maxwell, London 2006)

DJ Hayton, *The Law of Trusts* (Fundamental Principles of Law, 4th edn, Sweet & Maxwell, London 2003)

D Hayton and C Mitchell, *Hayton and Marshall Commentary and Cases on the Law of Trusts and Equitable Remedies* (Sweet & Maxwell, London 2005)

D Hayton, P Matthews and C Mitchell, *Underhill and Hayton Law of Trusts and Trustees* (17th edn, LexisNexis Butterworths, London 2007)

H Kuhn, B Graham-Siegenthaler and L Thévenoz (eds), *The Federal Intermediated Securities Act (FISA) and the Hague Securities Convention (HSC)* (Stämpfli's Commentary, Stämpfli Publishers Ltd., Berne 2010)

I MacNeil, *An Introduction to the Law on Financial Investments* (Hart Publishing, Oxford 2005)

FW Maitland, *Equity: A Course of Lectures* (Cambridge University Press, Cambridge 1936, 1969 reprint) JE Martin, *Modern Equity* (18th edn, Sweet & Maxwell, London 2009)

J McGhee (ed), *Snell's Equity* (31st edn, Trusts, Wills and Probate Library, Sweet and Maxwell, London 2005)

A McKnight, *The Law of International Finance* (Oxford University Press, Oxford 2008)

E Micheler, *Property in Securities: A Comparative Study* (Cambridge Studies in Corporate Law, Cambridge University Press, Cambridge 2007)

J Mowbray and others, *Lewin on Trusts* (18th edn, Thomson Sweet & Maxwell, London 2008)

NE Palmer, *Bailment* (2nd edn, Sweet & Maxwell, London 1991)

JE Penner, *The Idea of Property in Law* (Oxford University Press, Oxford 1997)

RR Pennington, *The Law of the Investment Markets* (Blackwell Law, Oxford 1990)

RA Posner, *Economic Analysis of Law* (7th edn, Aspen Publishers, Austin 2007)

T Prime, *International Bonds and Certificates of Deposit* (Butterworths, London 1990)

KF Sin, *The Legal Nature of the Unit Trust* (Clarendon Press, Oxford 1997)

M Smith, *The Law of Assignment: The Creation and Transfer of Choses in Action* (Oxford University Press, Oxford 2007)

ELG Tyler and NE Palmer, *Crossley Vaines'Personal Property* (5th edn, Butterworths, London 1973)

J Ulph, M Tugendhat and J Glister, *Commercial Fraud, Civil Liability, Human Rights and Money Laundering* (Contract Law Library, Oxford University Press, Oxford 2006)

A Watson, *Roman Law & Comparative Law* (The University of Georgia Press, Athens 1991)

G Watt, *Trusts and Equity* (Oxford University Press, Oxford 2010)

PR Wood, *Comparative Law of Security Interests and Title Finance* (2nd edn, Law and Practice of International Finance Series, Sweet & Maxwell, London 2007)

—. *Conflict of Laws and International Finance* (2nd edn, Law and Practice of International Finance Series, Sweet & Maxwell, London 2007)

—. *International Loans, Bonds, Guarantees, Legal Opinions* (2nd edn, Law and Practice of International Finance Series, Sweet & Maxwell, London 2007)

—. *Principles of International Insolvency* (2nd edn, Law and Practice of International Finance Series, Sweet & Maxwell, London 2007)

—. *Regulation of International Finance* (2nd edn, Law and Practice of International Finance Series, Sweet & Maxwell, London 2007)

—. *Set-off and Netting, Derivatives, Clearing Systems* (2nd edn, Law and Practice of International Finance Series, Sweet & Maxwell, London 2007)

S Worthington, *Equity* (2nd edn, Clarendon Law Series, Oxford University Press, Oxford 2006)

M Yates and G Montagu, *The Law of Global Custody* (3rd rev edn, Tottel Publishing, London 2009)

Book Contributions

A Beaves, 'Global Custody-A Tentative Analysis of Property and Contract' in N Palmer and E McKendrick (eds), *Interests in Goods* (2nd edn, Lloyds of London Press, London 1998)

JH Beekhuis, 'Civil Law' in FH Lawson (ed) *Structure Variations in Property Law* (International Encyclopedia of Comparative Law vol VI Property and Trusts, Chapter 2, JCB Mohe (Paul Siebeck), Tubingen)

J Benjamin, 'The Dematerialisation of Money Market Instruments' with *comments* by G Morton in S Worthington (ed) *Commercial Law and Commercial Practice* (Hart Publishing, Oxford 2003)

C Bernasconi, R Potok and G Morton, 'General Introduction: Legal Nature of interests in Indirectly Held Securities and Resulting Conflict of Law Analysis' in R Potok (ed), *Cross Border Collateral: Legal Risk and the Conflict of Laws* (Butterworths, London 2002)

J Hackney, 'Usucapio and the Law of Trusts' in J Getzler (ed) *Rationalizing Property, Equity and Trusts: Essays in Honour of Edward Burn* (Lexis-Nexis UK, London 2003)

D Hayton, 'The Irreducible Core Content of Trusteeship' in AJ Oakley (ed) *Trends in Contemporary Trust Law* (Clarenden Press, Oxford 1996)

AM Honoré, 'Ownership' in AG Guest (ed) *Oxford Essays in Jurisprudence* (Oxford University Press, Oxford 1961)

T Honoré, 'Trusts: The Inessentials' in J Getzler (ed) *Rationalizing Property, Equity and Trusts: Essays in Honour of Edward Burn* (Lexis-Nexis UK, London 2003)

H Kötz, 'The Modern Development of Trust Law in Germany' in D Hayton (ed) *Modern International Developments in Trust Law* (Kluwer Law International, The Hague 1999)

FH Lawson, 'Common Law' in FH Lawson (ed) *Structure Variations in Property Law* (International Encyclopedia of Comparative Law vol VI Property and Trusts, Chapter 2, JCB Mohe (Paul Siebeck), Tubingen)

B Lurger, 'Assignment' in JM Smits (ed) *Elgar Encyclopedia of Comparative Law* (Edward Elgar, Chelteham 2006)

E McKendrick, 'Sale of Goods' in P Birks (ed) *English Private Law*

(Oxford University Press, Oxford 2000)

JM Milo, 'Property and Real Rights' in JM Smits (ed) *Elgar Encyclopedia of Comparative Law* (Edward Elgar, Chelteham 2006)

J Mummery, 'Commercial Notions and Equitable Potions' in S Worthington (ed) *Commercial law and Commercial Practice* (Hart Publishing, Oxford 2003)

NE Palmer, 'Possessory Title' in NE Palmer and E McKendrick (eds), *Interests in Goods* (2nd edn, Lloyds of London Press, London 1998)

J Payne, 'Intermediated Securities and the Right to Vote in the UK' in L Gullier and J Payne (eds), *Intermediated Securities: Legal Problems and Practical Issues* (Hart Publishing, Oxford 2010)

F Reynolds, 'Agency and Representation' in P Birks (ed) *English Private Law* (Oxford University Press, Oxford 2000)

E Simpson, 'The Conflict of Interest' in P Birks and A Pretto (eds), *Breach of Trust* (Hart Publishing, Oxford 2002)

W Swadling, 'The Law of Property' in P Birks (ed) *English Private Law* (Oxford University Press, Oxford 2000)

J Ulph, 'Conflicts of Title and the Obligations of the Seller' in E McKendrick (ed) *Sale of Goods* (LLP, London 2000)

D Waters, 'Convergence and Divergence: Civil Law and Common Law' in D Hayton (ed) *Extending the Boundaries of Trusts and Similar Ring-Fenced Funds* (Kluwer Law International, The Hague 2002)

T Watkin, 'Changing Concepts of Ownership in English Law during the Nineteenth and Twentieth Centuries' in M Dixon and GH Griffiths (eds), *Contemporary Perspectives on Property, Equity and Trusts Law* (Oxford University Press, Oxford 2007)

D Wright, 'The Remedial Aspects of Equitable Property' in P Jackson and DC Wilde (eds) *Contemporary Property Law* (Ashgate Dartmouth, Aldershot 1999)

Journal Articles

A Al-Attar, 'Client Money' [2009] JIBFL 530

R Barham, 'CREST: the Phoenix from the Ashes of Taurus' (1993) 8 JIBL 426

J Benjamin, 'Computerisation and Negotiability Part 1' [1995] JIBFL 253

W Blair, 'Negotiability and Estoppel' (1988) 3 JIBL 8

R Calnan, 'Reforming Priority Law' [2006] JIBFL 4

V Combs, 'The Law of Intermediated Securities: UCC versus UNIDROIT'

(2006) 58 Ala L Rev 399
G Davies, 'Using Intermediated Securities as Collateral: Equitable Interests with Inequitable Results' [2007] JIBFL 70
J Donohue and C Atkins, 'Demystifying UK Settlement Systems' (1993) 12 Int Fin L Rev 27
—. 'Settling Trades in the UK Moneymarkets' (1993) 12 Int Fin L Rev 35
M Evans, 'The Sun Sets on Daylight Exposure: A UK Perspective on Securities Settlement' [2001] JIBFL 515
M Evans, 'Moving to a Dematerialised Capital Market: Short-Term Instruments, Long-Term Gain' [2003] JIBLR 121
JS Ewart, 'Negotiability and Estoppel' (1900) 16 LQR 159
Financial Markets Law Committee, 'The FMLC Report on Property Interests in Indirectly Held Investment Securities: An Analysis of the Need for and Nature of Legislation in the UK' [2005] Rev dr unif 339
D Fox, 'Relativity of Title at Law and in Equity' (2006) 65 CLJ 330
RM Goode, 'The Nature and Transfer of Rights in Dematerialised and Immobilised Securities' [1996] JIBFL 167
—. 'Are Intangible Assets Fungible?' [2003] LMCLQ 379
K Gordon, 'The Certainties of Trust' [2006] TM 218
RA Hakes, 'UCC Article 8: Will the Indirect Holding of Securities Survive the Light of Day?' (2002) 35 Loy L A L Rev 661
D Hayton, 'The Development of the Trust Concept in Civil Law Jurisdictions' [2000] JTCP 159
—. 'Exploiting the Inherent Flexibility of Trusts' [1999] JTCP 69
P Hertz and others, 'The All-American Dream: Developing Effective Resolution Arrangements for Investment Banks in the UK' [2009] JIBFL 466
LC Ho, 'Trusts Notwithstanding, Courts Remain Free to Find Scheme Jurisdiction' [2010] JIBFL 156
M Hughes, 'Bond Issues A Banking Lawyer's Perspective' [2000] JIBFL 263
E Jenks, 'The Legal Estate' (1908) 24 LQR 147
T Keijser and M Parmentier, 'The Geneva Securities Convention: the Debates of the Diplomatic Conference' [2010] JIBFL 230
MF Khimji, 'Intermediary Credit Risk-a Comparative Law Analysis of Property Rights in Indirectly Held Securities' [2005] JBL 287
M Kirby, 'Crest and Securities Law Reform' [2000] JIBFL 3
K Löber and P Paech, 'Interconnecting Law of Securities Holding and Transfer—A Chance for Seamless International Improvements' [2007] JIBFL 9

A Maffei, 'De la nature juridique des titres dematerialisés intermédiés en droit francais' [2005] Rev dr unif 237

FR Malan, 'Share Certificates, Money and Negotiability' (1977) 94 The South African LJ

K McCormick and S Melzack, 'Depositor Protection: An Increased Burden for the Financial Services Sector?' [2008] JIBFL 185

E Micheler, 'Farewell Quasi-Negotiability? Legal Title and Transfer of Shares in a Paperless World' [2002] JBL 358

CW Mooney, 'Beyond Negotiability: A New Model for Transfer and Pledge of Interests in Securities Controlled by Intermediaries' (1990) 12 Cardozo L Rev 305

—. 'The (UNIDROIT) Geneva Securities Convention on Intermediated Securities' [2009] JIBFL 596

CW Mooney, SM Rocks and RS Schwartz, 'An Introduction to the Revised UCC Article 8 and Review of Other Recent Developments with Investment Securities' (1994) 49 Bus Law 1891

R Nolan, 'Property in a Fund' (2004) 120 LQR 108

D O'Sullivan, 'Distributing the Risk of Contract Fraud' (2001) 117 LQR 381

—. 'The Rule in Phillips v Phillips' (2002) 118 LQR 296

P Paech and K Löber, 'Post Trading of Securities: Shaping the European Response to Legal Barriers' [2009] JIBFL 211

M Pawlowski and J Brown, 'Mere Equities and Third Parties in Leasehold Law' [2010] L& T R 100

CR Reitz, 'Reflections on the Drafting of the 1994 Revision of Article 8 of the US Uniform Commercial Code' [2005] Rev dr unif 357

JS Rogers, 'Negotiability, Property and Identity' (1990) 12 Cardozo L Rev 471

—. 'Policy Perspectives on Revised UCC Article 8' (1996) 43 UCLA L Rev 1431

I Samet, 'Guarding the Fiduciary's Conscience—A Justification of a Stringent Profit-stripping Rule' (2008) 28 OJLS 763

R Scavone, 'Stronger Than Fictions: Canada Rethinks the Law of Securities Transfers in the Indirect Holding System' (2007) 45 Can Bus LJ 67

P Scherer and R Gallei, 'UNIDROIT Draft Convention and German Securities Law: Friend or Foe?' [2009] JIBLR 470

SL Schwarcz, 'Indirectly Held Securities and Intermediary Risk' [2001] Rev dr unif 283

S Shivji, 'Financial Collateral: Trust Issues in the Administration of

Lehman Brothers' [2010] JIBFL 11
E Sjostrand, 'Cash Matters: Unsecured Creditor or Proprietary Interest? Analysis of the Recent Lehman Brothers Case' [2010] CRI 9
JH Sommer, 'A Law of Financial Accounts: Modern Payment and Securities Transfer Law' (1998) 53 Bus Law 1181
ET Spink and MA Paré, 'The Uniform Securities Transfer Act: Globalized Commercial Law for Canada' (2004) 19 BFLR 321
L Thévenoz, 'New Legal Concepts regarding the Holding of Investment Securities for a Civil Law Jurisdiction – The Swiss Draft Act' [2005] Rev dr unif 301
V Tyrell, 'Client Monies: The CASS Rules under Scrutiny' [2010] JIBFL 520
UNIDROIT Secretariat, 'Explanatory Notes to the Preliminary Draft UNIDROIT Convention on Harmonised Substantive Rules regarding Securities Held with an Intermediary' [2005] Rev dr unif 36
Lv Vliet, 'The Transfer of Moveables in Scotland and England' (2008) 12 Edin LR 173
D Waters, 'The Trust in a Changed and Yet Changing World' [2008] JTCP 205
S Worthington, 'Pitfalls with Property Claims: Lehman Bros Again' [2009] JIBFL 321

Organisation Reports

Bank of England, 'The Future of Money Market Instruments: A Consultation (November 1999)'
—. 'The Future of Money Market Instruments: Next Steps (March 2000)'
—. 'The Future of Money Market Instruments: Progress towards Dematerialisation and Settlement in CREST, An Interim Report (January 2001)'
Euroclear, 'The Domestic Legal Framework (March 2002)'
—. 'CREST Rules (April 2012)'
—. 'CREST Terms and Conditions (September 2009)'
—. 'CREST Reference Manual (November 2012)'
European Commission, 'Second Advice of the Legal Certainty Group: Solutions to Legal Barriers related to Post-Trading within the EU (August 2008)'
European Financial Markets Lawyers Group, 'Harmonisation of the Legal Framework for Rights Evidenced by Book-entries in respect of Certain

Financial Instruments in the European Union (June 2003)'
Financial Markets Law Committee, 'Response of 1 June 2009 to European Commission Consultation Paper: Legislation on Legal Certainty of Securities Holding and Dispositions (G2/PP D (2009))'
—. 'Response of 21 January 2011 to the European Commission Consultation Paper: Legislation on Legal Certainty for Securities Holding and Dispositions, 5 November 2010 (G2 MET/OT/acg D(2010) 768690)'
FSA, 'Client Asset Sourcebook'
Giovannini Group, 'Second Report on EU Clearing and Settlement (April 2003)'
—. 'Cross-Border Clearing and Settlement Arrangements in the European Union (November 2001)'
Group of Thirty, 'Global Clearing and Settlement-A Plan of Action (2003)'
RD Guynn and others, 'Modernizing Securities Ownership, Transfer and Pledging Laws (International Bar Association 1996)'
IOSCO/BIS, 'Recommendations for Securities Settlement Systems (November 2001)'
HM Treasury, 'Developing Effective Resolution Arrangements for Investment Banks (May 2009)'
—. 'Establishing Resolution Arrangements for Investment Banks (December 2009)'
Law Commission, *Trustee Exemption Clauses* (Law Com No 301 Cm 6874, 2006)
—. 'Law Commission Project on Intermediated Investment Securities First Seminar: Objectives for a Common Legal Framework (22 March 2006)'
—. 'Law Commission Project on Intermediated Investment Securities Second Seminar: Issues affecting Account holders and Intermediaries (23 June 2006)'
—. 'Interim Advice in Relation to the EU Legal Certainty Group Advice and the UNIDROIT Convention on Substantive Rules regarding Intermediated Securities (October 2006)'
—. 'Law Commission Project on Intermediated Investment Securities Third Seminar: Issues affecting Transferees of Intermediated Securities (27 July 2006)'
—. 'The UNIDROIT Convention on Substantive Rules regarding Intermediated Securities Updated Advice to HM Treasury (May 2007)'
—. 'The UNIDROIT Convention on Substantive Rules regarding Intermediated Securities: Further Updated Advice to HM Treasury

(May 2008)'
Trusts Law Committee Working Party, 'Equitable Problems in the Securities Markets (1998)'
UNIDROIT, 'Draft Official Commentary on the Draft Convention on Substantive Rules regarding Intermediated Securities (UNIDROIT 2009 CONF 11/2-Doc 5)'
—. 'The UNIDROIT Study Group on Harmonised Substantive Rules Regarding Indirectly Held Securities: Position Paper (August 2003) (UNIDROIT 2003-Study LXXVIII-Doc 8)'
—. 'Study Group for the Preparation of Harmonised Substantive Rules on Transactions on Transnational and Connected Capital Markets. Restricted Study Group on Item 1 of the Project: Harmonised Substantive Rules regarding Securities Held with an Intermediary. Summary Report 3rd Session (13-16 November 2003) (UNIDROIT 2003-Study LXXVIII-Doc 11)'
—. 'Working Paper regarding So Called 'Transparent Systems'' (UNIDROIT 2006 Study LXXVIII-Doc 44)'
—. 'Supplementary Working Paper regarding So Called 'Transparent Systems' (UNIDROIT 2007 Study LXXVIII-Doc 44 Add)'
—. 'UNIDROIT Committee of Governmental Experts for the Preparation of a draft Convention on Substantive Rules regarding Intermediated Securities. Informal Working Group on Article 14 of the draft Convention. PRELIMINARY NOTE-November 2007 (UNIDROIT 2007-Study LXXVIII-Doc 96)'
—. 'Informal Working Group on Article 14 of the draft Convention-Comments on the questionnaire concerning 'good faith acquisition' (submitted by the German delegation) (UNIDROIT 2007-Study LXXVIII-Doc 98)'
—. 'UNIDROIT Committee of Governmental Experts for the Preparation of a draft Convention on Substantive Rules regarding Intermediated Securities. Informal Working Group on Article 14 of the draft Convention-Response to the Questionnaire Concerning Acquisition by an Innocent Person (submitted by the delegation of France)-January 2008 (UNIDROIT 2008-Study LXXVIII-Doc 107 Rev)'
—. 'UNIDROIT Seminar on Intermediated Securities-Bern, Switzerland, 15-17 September 2005-Rome 2005 (UNIDROIT 2005-Study LXXVIII-SEM 1)'
—. 'UNIDROIT Seminar on Intermediated Securities-Paris, France, 31 January-1st February 2006 (UNIDROIT 2006-Study LXXVIII-SEM 3)'

INDEX